JACK SULLIVAN

THE CUSTODY OF TRUTH

VANCE SAWYER

LIFE PUBLISHING HOUSE

The Custody of Truth
A Jack Sullivan Novel
by Vance Sawyer

Published by Life Publishing House

Cover design by Living Word Press

Printed in the United States of America

First Edition

*"Truth does not belong to the loudest voice.
When a child speaks, the first duty of adults is not
to shape the words. It is to listen."*

1

The rain had settled over Boston before midnight and showed no sign of letting up. From the seventeenth floor of Mercer, Hale & Dalton, the city was little more than a blur of lights shimmering through sheets of water. Most of the offices were dark, their doors closed until morning, but one light still burned near the end of the corridor. Richard Mercer had been telling himself for the last hour that he was about to go home, yet every time he reached for his briefcase, he found himself opening the same file again.

He had spent forty-seven years practicing law and nearly all of them in estate planning. Young attorneys often imagined the profession as dramatic courtroom arguments and surprise witnesses. Mercer knew better. The greatest legal battles rarely began in a courtroom. They began with signatures, amendments, handwritten notes tucked inside safe-deposit boxes, and families who believed love could survive the reading of a will. Over the years he had watched fortunes pull brothers apart, turn devoted children into suspicious adversaries, and expose resentments that had been hidden for decades. Wealth did not create greed nearly as often as it uncovered it.

The leather-bound file resting on his desk belonged to Victor Hale, a man whose name appeared regularly on magazine covers and financial news programs. Reporters described him as a visionary entrepreneur. Business rivals called him ruthless. Politicians praised his generosity whenever his donations found their way into campaign accounts or charitable foundations. Mercer had known a different man, one who was thoughtful, disciplined, and almost impossible to surprise. Victor rarely spoke more than necessary, but when he did, every sentence carried the weight of careful consideration.

Something about him had changed.

Mercer had noticed it gradually during the past several months. Victor had become distracted during meetings, pausing in midsentence whenever footsteps passed outside the conference room. He had begun asking unusual questions about document security, access logs, and who, besides Mercer himself, could view the original estate documents. At first Mercer dismissed the questions as the ordinary caution of a man whose fortune invited constant attention. Eventually the questions became so specific that they no longer sounded theoretical.

A soft knock interrupted his thoughts.

Margaret Ellis stepped inside carrying two mugs of coffee. She had worked with Mercer for almost three decades and had earned the rare privilege of walking into his office without waiting for permission.

"I was beginning to think you planned on spending the night here," she said, placing one mug beside his elbow. "The cleaning crew has already gone home, and the security guard downstairs asked if you intended to start paying rent."

Mercer smiled without looking up. "If I paid rent on this office, I'd have to bill even more hours."

"You already bill enough to make the younger associates nervous."

"They should be nervous. It keeps them from making careless mistakes."

Margaret settled into the chair across from his desk and looked at the open file. "Victor Hale again?"

"I'm trying to decide whether I've become overly cautious or not cautious enough."

"That sounds more serious than a punctuation dispute."

"It is."

She studied him for a moment. "You don't usually second-guess your work."

"I don't."

"So why tonight?"

Mercer closed the file and rested both hands on the cover. "Because Victor spent an hour asking questions that had almost nothing to do with estate law."

"What kind of questions?"

"He wanted to know who had access to the original documents. He wanted to know whether someone could replace a will without the drafting attorney discovering it. He asked whether electronic access logs could be altered and whether anyone outside this firm had ever requested copies of his estate plan."

Margaret raised an eyebrow. "Did he tell you why?"

"He said he wanted to understand his options."

"That isn't an answer."

"No."

She leaned back in her chair. "I've met Mr. Hale enough times to know he doesn't waste words. If he was asking questions like that, he already had a reason."

Mercer nodded slowly. "That's exactly what worries me."

Silence settled over the office for a moment. Rain tapped steadily against the windows while the heating system hummed through the ceiling vents. Margaret had learned over the years that Mercer rarely spoke about his instincts unless they had become impossible to ignore. He was not the sort of attorney who believed in conspiracy theories or dramatic conclusions. His confidence came from evidence, and his caution came from experience.

"What do you think is happening?" she finally asked.

"I honestly don't know. Victor has spent his entire life anticipating risk. He doesn't become frightened without a reason, and yesterday he looked like a man who expected something terrible to happen."

"You think someone threatened him?"

"He never said that."

"But you think it anyway."

Mercer hesitated before answering. "I think he believed someone was trying to gain control of his estate before he died."

Margaret let out a slow breath. "Twenty-four billion dollars gives people a great deal to fight over."

"More than that."

She looked at him with surprise.

"That's your estimate?"

"It's my educated guess."

Margaret shook her head. "I'll never understand that kind of wealth."

"I've represented enough wealthy clients to know that after a certain point, the numbers stop changing the person's life. What changes is the number of people who begin planning theirs around your death."

The words lingered in the room longer than either of them expected. Margaret had seen families disintegrate over estates worth a few hundred thousand dollars. She could only imagine what twenty-four billion might do.

She stood and walked toward the windows overlooking the city. "You know what bothers me?"

"What?"

"Victor Hale never struck me as someone who scared easily."

"He wasn't."

"So whatever frightened him must have been convincing."

Mercer joined her at the window. Far below, headlights crawled through the rain, their reflections stretching across wet pavement like ribbons of light. The city looked peaceful from that height, almost detached from the ordinary concerns of the people living in it.

"Yesterday," Mercer said quietly, "Victor asked me something I've never been asked before."

Margaret turned toward him.

"He asked whether I trusted my own security systems."

"What did you tell him?"

"I told him they were among the best in the country."

"And?"

"He asked if I trusted the people who maintained them."

Margaret frowned.

"How did you answer that?"

"I didn't."

She looked back at the file on his desk. "Maybe we should move it."

Mercer smiled faintly. "To where?"

"A bank."

"We already have better security than most banks."

"Then maybe your house."

"My house has one deadbolt and a Labrador that's been dead for six years."

"I was trying to be helpful."

"You usually are."

Margaret walked back to the desk and tapped the file with one finger. "Whatever you decide, don't leave this sitting here overnight."

"I wasn't planning to."

Mercer placed the file inside a black archival case and secured the brass latches. Together they walked down the quiet hallway toward the firm's secure records room. The portraits of retired partners watched from the walls with expressions that seemed permanently unimpressed, as though every generation believed it had inherited the profession from lesser lawyers.

Margaret glanced at one portrait and smiled. "Do you remember Harold Simmons?"

"The man who believed every legal problem could be solved with a stronger cup of coffee?"

"He also believed computers were a passing fad."

"He retired before anyone could prove him wrong."

"I still miss him."

"So do I."

The records room stood behind a reinforced steel door protected by a keypad, biometric scanner, and electronic access log. Mercer entered his code, pressed his thumb against the scanner, and waited while the locking bolts withdrew with a heavy mechanical sound.

Inside, rows of climate-controlled cabinets stretched across the room.

Margaret rubbed her arms against the cool air. "Every time I come in here, I feel like we've entered Fort Knox."

"Considering what's stored here, that's not far from the truth."

Mercer unlocked Cabinet Seven and carefully placed Victor Hale's file inside. Before closing the drawer, he paused.

"What is it?" Margaret asked.

Mercer studied the contents without answering. Nothing appeared disturbed. Every folder sat exactly where it belonged, and the electronic log showed no unauthorized access. Yet he couldn't shake the feeling that something was different.

"You've got that look," Margaret said.

"What look?"

"The one you get when your instincts are arguing with your evidence."

Mercer looked at the access log again.

"The system says no one has been in this cabinet since I opened it three weeks ago."

"And you believe it?"

"I believe the log."

"But?"

"But I don't completely trust the conclusion."

Margaret stepped closer.

"Richard, are we talking about facts or feelings?"

"I honestly can't tell."

She looked at the cabinet, then back at Mercer. "If Victor Hale has taught us anything, it's that ignoring an uneasy feeling rarely ends well."

Mercer slowly closed the drawer and locked it.

"I'll review the security footage tomorrow morning."

"Promise me you actually will."

"I promise."

They returned to his office together, gathered their coats, and rode the elevator to the lobby. The security guard looked up from his desk and wished them good night before returning to the baseball game playing quietly on a small television behind him.

Outside, Margaret unlocked her car and looked back toward Mercer.

"Call me when you get home."

"I'm seventy-two years old, Margaret, not seventeen."

"I know exactly how old you are. That's why I'm telling you to call."

Mercer laughed softly.

"Yes, ma'am."

She waited until he acknowledged her with a wave before pulling away from the curb.

Mercer crossed the street toward the parking garage, enjoying the cool rain more than he cared to admit. Long days at the office often left him feeling older than he was, and the crisp night air usually cleared his thoughts. As he reached his car, he happened to glance back toward the firm's entrance. A black SUV remained parked beneath a streetlamp across the street, its engine idling while rain collected on the windshield. There was nothing inherently suspicious about the vehicle, yet he found himself wondering why the driver seemed more interested in the law firm's front doors than in the traffic moving past.

Mercer slipped behind the wheel without immediately starting the engine. He watched the SUV through the opening of the garage, telling himself he was allowing his imagination to wander after an unusually long day. Nearly half a minute passed before the vehicle finally eased away from the curb and merged into traffic. Satisfied that he had probably assigned too much significance to an ordinary coincidence, he started his own car and pulled onto the street.

The sense of relief lasted only a few minutes. As he made his way toward Commonwealth Avenue, he noticed the same SUV several vehicles behind him. It maintained a comfortable distance through two intersections and followed when he made a turn he rarely used at that hour. Mercer resisted the temptation to overreact. Boston's streets offered only so many practical routes after midnight, and it was entirely possible that another driver simply happened to be traveling in the same direction. Even so, he found himself checking the rearview mirror more often than usual until the SUV continued straight through an intersection where Mercer turned toward his condominium.

By the time he parked in the underground garage beneath his building, he had almost convinced himself that the evening's uneasiness belonged more to Victor Hale than to him. He rode the elevator to the twelfth floor, unlocked his apartment, and stepped inside the familiar quiet that had become both companion and burden since his wife's death nine years earlier. He had just removed his coat when his phone rang.

The caller identification displayed Victor Hale's private number.

Mercer answered immediately.

"Victor?"

Only silence greeted him.

He listened for several seconds before a faint breath came across the line.

"Victor, can you hear me?"

The connection ended.

Mercer stared at the phone for a moment before dialing the number back. Instead of Victor's voice, an unfamiliar recording informed him that the subscriber was unavailable.

He had barely lowered the phone when another call arrived.

This time it was Margaret.

"I hope I'm not interrupting," she said.

"Actually, you may have perfect timing."

"What happened?"

"I just received a call from Victor Hale."

"I thought you said he never called this late."

"He doesn't."

"What did he want?"

"I don't know. No one spoke."

Margaret hesitated.

"Richard... call him again in the morning."

"I intend to."

Neither of them realized that before the sun rose, Victor Hale would be dead, Richard Mercer would vanish without explanation, and the estate file they had locked away only an hour earlier would become the center of the most complicated legal battle either of them had ever imagined.

2

JACK SULLIVAN DISLIKED COURTHOUSES before nine in the morning. They were crowded with anxious defendants, impatient attorneys, overworked clerks, and prosecutors who had already convinced themselves they were right before the first file was opened. By midmorning, the hallways settled into a rhythm that made sense to him. Lawyers stopped pretending to enjoy small talk, judges became less interested in speeches than solutions, and clients slowly realized that the law moved at its own pace regardless of how urgently they wanted an answer.

Jack had just finished a suppression hearing in Suffolk County Superior Court when his phone vibrated for the third time. The number was unfamiliar, but whoever was calling had been persistent enough to deserve a return call. He stepped away from the courtroom doors and found a quiet corner near the courthouse library before pressing the call button.

"This is Jack Sullivan."

"Mr. Sullivan, my name is Margaret Ellis. I'm calling from Mercer, Hale & Dalton."

Jack recognized the firm's name immediately. Richard Mercer had built one of the most respected estate practices in New England, and even attorneys who competed against him admitted there were few lawyers better at protecting complicated fortunes. Jack had met Mercer only a handful of times over the years, but each encounter had left the same impression. Mercer listened more than he spoke, and when he finally asked a question, it was usually the one everyone else had overlooked.

"What can I do for you, Ms. Ellis?"

"I hope I'm not interrupting your day."

"You probably are, but that isn't necessarily a bad thing."

She managed a brief laugh, though it carried none of the ease usually found in polite conversation.

"I don't know how to explain this without sounding dramatic."

"Try explaining it the way you would explain it to Richard Mercer."

There was a brief silence before she answered.

"Richard is missing."

Jack straightened almost imperceptibly.

"How long?"

"He went home after leaving the office last night. He called me when he arrived because I insisted he let me know he made it safely. That was the last conversation anyone has had with him."

"And the police?"

"They're at his condominium now."

Jack glanced through the courthouse window toward the gray Boston skyline.

"What makes you believe something happened instead of Richard simply deciding to disappear for a few hours?"

"Because Richard Mercer has spent forty-seven years doing exactly what he said he was going to do. He doesn't miss appointments. He doesn't forget meetings. He doesn't vanish without telling anyone."

Jack couldn't argue with that logic.

"What did the police find?"

"His car is still in the garage. His wallet is on the kitchen counter. His watch is beside it. His apartment isn't ransacked, and there are no obvious signs of violence."

"But Richard isn't there."

"No."

Jack leaned against the wall, allowing the facts to settle before asking another question.

"Why are you calling me?"

"Because Richard told me to."

Those five words carried more weight than Margaret probably realized.

"When?"

"Years ago."

"What exactly did he say?"

Margaret took a slow breath.

"He told me that if anything ever happened to him involving a client file, I was to call you before I trusted anyone else."

Jack frowned.

"He actually used my name?"

"He did."

"Did he tell you why?"

"He said you had an irritating habit of questioning facts everyone else accepted."

Jack smiled despite himself.

"That sounds like Richard."

"I always thought he was exaggerating."

"He probably wasn't."

Margaret hesitated before continuing.

"The client file is Victor Hale's."

The name changed everything.

Victor Hale's business empire touched industries on nearly every continent. His companies employed tens of thousands of people. Financial news covered his investments the way sports networks covered championships. Men like Victor Hale rarely became connected to missing-person investigations.

"What happened to Hale?"

"He died this morning."

Jack closed his eyes for a moment.

"Natural causes?"

"That's what everyone is saying."

"But you don't believe it."

"I don't know what I believe."

Jack appreciated the honesty. Too many frightened people filled uncertainty with certainty.

"Tell me what happened yesterday."

Margaret described Richard's concern over the estate documents, Victor's unusual questions about security, the late-night trip to the archive, and the black SUV Richard believed had followed him home. She repeated the conversation as accurately as she could remember it, never embellishing details she didn't know. Jack listened without interrupting, occasionally making a note in the margin of the legal pad he carried almost everywhere.

When she finished, he looked down at the page. Most of his notes weren't facts. They were questions.

Why ask about replacing a will?

Why call Mercer after midnight?

Why disappear before anyone knew Hale was dead?

Questions, Jack had learned, were usually more valuable than answers during the first twenty-four hours of an investigation.

"Has anyone opened the archive since last night?" he asked.

"No."

"How do you know?"

"The electronic log doesn't show anyone entering."

Jack considered that for a moment.

"Electronic logs only tell you what the system believes happened."

Richard Mercer had once said almost those exact words during a conference on legal ethics. Jack remembered because most attorneys placed enormous faith in technology while Mercer insisted that every system was designed by imperfect people.

"I'd like to come by the office," Jack said.

"I was hoping you'd say that."

"It'll take me about an hour."

"We'll be here."

Jack ended the call and remained standing in the hallway for another minute. His afternoon schedule disappeared from his thoughts as he replayed the conversation. Richard Mercer wasn't impulsive enough to invent danger, and Margaret Ellis sounded too composed to exaggerate it. Something had happened between the law firm's archive and Richard's apartment. Whether it was connected to Victor Hale's death remained to be seen, but Jack had no intention of dismissing the possibility simply because it sounded improbable.

Boston traffic offered plenty of time to think. As he crossed the Charles River, Jack found himself remembering the first time he had met Richard Mercer. It had been almost twelve years earlier during a civil fraud case involving a family trust. Jack had represented a trustee accused of diverting millions of dollars. Mercer represented another branch of the family and spent two weeks methodically dismantling everyone's assumptions before quietly proving that the missing money had never disappeared at all. It had been transferred legally under an agreement no one thought to read because everyone assumed someone else already had.

After the trial, Jack asked Mercer why he hadn't exposed the mistake earlier.

Mercer smiled and replied, "People rarely discover the truth until they're forced to question the story they liked better."

Jack had never forgotten the sentence.

Mercer, Hale & Dalton occupied several floors of one of Boston's oldest commercial buildings. The lobby reflected decades of understated wealth. Marble floors stretched beneath polished brass fixtures, and the receptionist greeted visitors by name rather than asking whom they wished to see. Firms that represented ordinary clients advertised success. Firms like Mercer, Hale & Dalton assumed success required no introduction.

Margaret met him before he reached the reception desk.

"Mr. Sullivan?"

"Jack."

"Thank you for coming."

"You sounded like you needed someone who wasn't already inside the circle."

She nodded without pretending to misunderstand him.

"The managing partners are in a meeting with the police. They believe Richard simply encountered the wrong person at the wrong time."

"And you don't."

"I've worked beside Richard for twenty-nine years. He trusted evidence more than emotion, but he also respected instinct. Last night, he had both."

She led him through the quiet hallways toward Richard's office. Associates glanced up as they passed, lowering their voices until the two of them disappeared around the corner. No one asked questions. Law firms had their own etiquette during a crisis, and speculation was usually reserved for closed doors.

Richard's office remained exactly as he had left it.

His legal pad sat open beside an empty coffee mug. A fountain pen rested across the top page. Bookshelves lined one wall, their volumes arranged more by subject than appearance. Family photographs occupied a corner of the credenza, though Jack noticed there were only a few. Richard had always kept his private life private.

Margaret stopped beside the desk.

"I haven't touched anything."

Jack appreciated that immediately.

"Walk me through last night again."

She did, beginning with Victor Hale's meeting earlier in the day and ending with Richard's phone call after he reached home. This time she remembered smaller details. Richard had sounded distracted. He mentioned the SUV almost as an afterthought, then apologized for worrying her. He laughed once during the conversation, but Margaret realized afterward that the laugh had been forced.

"I asked him to call building security," she said quietly.

"Did he?"

"I don't know."

Jack walked slowly around the office without touching anything. Good investigators, he believed, spent as much time observing the people connected to a room as they did examining the room itself. Margaret wasn't trying to convince him of a theory. She was trying to understand something that refused to make sense.

He stopped in front of the office window overlooking the rain-soaked city.

"What kind of man was Richard when no one else was around?"

Margaret seemed surprised by the question.

"He was patient."

"That's a nice thing to say after someone disappears."

"It's also true."

"What else?"

"He listened more than he talked. He remembered birthdays but forgot lunch. He believed there was almost always another fact waiting to be discovered if people would stop interrupting each other long enough to look for it."

Jack nodded.

"Did he trust people?"

"He trusted character. Not charm."

The answer sounded exactly like Richard Mercer.

Jack turned back toward the desk.

"I'd like to see the archive."

Margaret looked toward the office door before answering.

"I was hoping you would ask."

She picked up her access card from the desk and led him into the hallway, unaware that two floors below, detectives had just informed the managing partners of Mercer, Hale & Dalton that the medical examiner had requested a formal review of Victor Hale's death after inconsistencies were discovered during the preliminary examination. No one outside the conference room knew precisely what those inconsistencies were, but the assumption that Hale had died quietly in his sleep was already beginning to unravel.

Jack and Margaret continued toward the records room, still believing they were investigating a missing lawyer.

Neither of them yet realized they were walking toward the first piece of evidence in what would become the most significant criminal investigation of their careers.

3

MORNING LIGHT FILTERED THROUGH the frosted windows of the records room, softening the harsh fluorescent glow that usually gave the space the feel of a vault rather than a working archive. Jack Sullivan remained standing in front of Cabinet Seven while Margaret Ellis waited a few steps behind him. Neither of them had spoken for almost a minute. The drawer remained open, exposing rows of carefully organized documents that represented decades of legal planning, tax strategies, trust amendments, and corporate succession agreements. Everything appeared orderly, yet the one document that mattered most was nowhere to be found. It was an absence that carried more weight than any piece of paper Jack had seen in years.

Margaret finally broke the silence. "Richard always said people think stolen property leaves a mess behind. He believed the most dangerous thefts were the ones no one noticed until the right person reached for the wrong file."

Jack looked at the empty space inside the archival case before turning toward her. "Did he ever tell you why he became so meticulous about security?"

She nodded slowly. "Early in his career he represented an elderly woman whose nephew replaced the final page of her will without anyone realizing it. The forgery wasn't discovered until years after she died. Richard won the case, but he used to say that justice came too late because a family had already been destroyed while the lawyers argued over what should have been obvious."

"That sounds like something he'd remember."

"He remembered every mistake he ever saw, even when it belonged to someone else."

Jack stepped away from the cabinet and studied the room itself. Cameras overlooked every aisle, climate-control vents whispered overhead, and the electronic access terminal continued displaying the last recorded entry. If someone had removed the original will without leaving evidence, they had done so with remarkable confidence. Criminals often believed they were smarter than investigators. Professionals preferred to make investigators believe there had never been a crime at all.

The records room door opened quietly behind them, and Charles Dalton entered carrying a slim folder beneath one arm. His expression remained composed, but the confidence he had displayed earlier had given way to something more cautious. He closed the door before speaking, making certain they were alone.

"I've just finished with the detectives," Dalton said. "For the moment, Richard's disappearance is still being treated as a missing-person investigation. They aren't calling it an abduction, and they have no evidence connecting it to Victor Hale."

Jack folded his arms. "Do they know the original will is missing?"

"Not yet."

Margaret looked sharply toward him. "You didn't tell them?"

Dalton met her gaze without raising his voice. "Not until I understand exactly what we're dealing with."

"That isn't your decision."

"It most certainly is. I have a responsibility to protect this firm and every client whose confidential information is stored inside these walls."

Jack watched the exchange carefully before speaking. "You also have a legal obligation to preserve evidence. If the missing will is connected to Richard's disappearance, withholding that information from investigators won't protect the firm. It will make the firm part of the investigation."

Dalton's jaw tightened slightly. "I'm aware of my obligations, Mr. Sullivan."

"Then you already know the police are going to learn about the missing document. The only question is whether they hear it from you or discover it on their own."

For several seconds no one spoke. Dalton walked to the open cabinet and examined the remaining contents himself, though it was obvious he had already done so before returning. He checked the inventory sheet, compared it against the files in the drawer, and closed the archival case with deliberate care.

"Richard once told me," Dalton said quietly, "that a missing document is often more dangerous than a forged one because everyone immediately begins imagining what it might have said. Perhaps that's where we are now."

Margaret shook her head. "No. We know exactly what the document was. We just don't know who wanted it badly enough to take it."

Jack's attention shifted toward the access terminal mounted beside the cabinet. "I'd like to review the electronic logs from the past month, not just the cabinet access. I also want every maintenance record for this security system and the names of every employee or contractor who has serviced it during the last year."

Dalton looked surprised. "You think this began before last night?"

"I don't know when it began. I only know that people capable of removing a document from a secure archive rarely decide to improvise. Planning leaves a longer trail than execution."

Margaret reached into a nearby file drawer and removed a maintenance binder. "Richard insisted on keeping printed copies in addition to the digital records. He said computers were wonderful until they stopped cooperating."

Jack accepted the binder and smiled faintly. "That's exactly what I would have expected him to say."

He opened the first section and began reading. Most entries involved routine inspections, software updates, and annual equipment certifications. Nothing immediately stood out, but one notation near the back caught his attention. Three weeks earlier, the biometric scanner serving Cabinet Seven had been recalibrated after an unexplained authentication error. The technician's report described the issue as minor and indicated that the system had resumed normal operation after a firmware update.

Jack tapped the page with one finger.

"Did Richard mention this?"

Margaret stepped beside him and read the report. "No. If he had concerns, he kept them to himself."

Jack closed the binder.

"Then I'd like to speak with the technician who signed this report."

Dalton looked toward the maintenance entry. "He's an outside contractor. We use the same company that services several banks downtown."

"Good."

Dalton raised an eyebrow. "Why is that good?"

"Because if someone compromised this system, they either understood it exceptionally well or they had help from someone who did. Either possibility deserves attention."

Before anyone could respond, a knock sounded at the outer records room door. One of the firm's younger associates stepped inside, his face noticeably pale.

"Mr. Dalton, the detectives are asking for you."

Dalton nodded. "Tell them I'll be there in a moment."

The associate hesitated before leaving.

"They've also received another call."

Dalton frowned. "From whom?"

"The medical examiner."

The room grew noticeably quieter.

"What did they say?" Dalton asked.

"I only overheard part of the conversation, but Detective Ramirez told one of the officers that Victor Hale's death is no longer being classified as routine."

Jack exchanged a glance with Margaret.

The missing attorney and the missing will had suddenly acquired a third element neither of them had wanted to hear.

Someone now believed the billionaire's death deserved a homicide investigation.

4

JACK SULLIVAN HAD LEARNED early in his career that people rarely lied about the important things. They lied about the details surrounding them, hoping the truth would become buried beneath enough unnecessary information to discourage anyone from digging deeper. It was one reason he preferred speaking with ordinary people before interviewing executives or politicians. Secretaries remembered habits. Custodians noticed routines. Receptionists recognized unfamiliar faces. The people who considered themselves unimportant often carried the pieces everyone else overlooked.

An hour after leaving Mercer, Hale & Dalton, Jack pulled his car into the parking lot of Sentinel Integrated Security, a company occupying an unremarkable brick building on the edge of Boston's industrial district. The business specialized in commercial access systems, surveillance equipment, and biometric security. Their client list included financial institutions, pharmaceutical companies, private museums, and several law firms whose archives contained documents worth far more than the buildings that housed them.

The receptionist greeted him politely before asking whether he had an appointment.

"I don't," Jack replied, placing one of his business cards on the counter. "I'm hoping someone can spare a few minutes. I'm looking for the technician who serviced Mercer, Hale & Dalton about three weeks ago."

She glanced at the card before looking back at him.

"Was there a problem with the system?"

"I'm trying to determine that."

"Do you have a work order number?"

Jack smiled politely.

"If I had that, I probably wouldn't need to bother your technician."

The receptionist considered him for a moment before picking up the phone. She spoke quietly with someone in the back office, listened for several seconds, then nodded.

"Mr. Donovan can see you for a few minutes."

Jack thanked her and followed a hallway lined with framed photographs of completed installations. Most of the pictures showed bank vaults, server rooms, and data centers. The message was obvious. Sentinel sold confidence more than hardware.

Patrick Donovan stood as Jack entered the office. He appeared to be in his late fifties, broad shouldered, with the weathered face of someone who had spent more years on job sites than behind a desk. His handshake was firm without becoming a contest.

"I'm told you're asking about Mercer, Hale & Dalton."

"I am."

"We've serviced their building for almost fifteen years."

"Have they ever had security issues?"

Donovan gave a slight shrug.

"Every building has security issues. The question is whether anyone notices them before they become problems."

Jack appreciated the answer.

"I found a maintenance report indicating a biometric scanner malfunction about three weeks ago."

Donovan leaned back in his chair.

"I figured this was about that."

"You remember it?"

"I remember every unexplained failure. Electronics don't usually develop a conscience overnight."

"What happened?"

"The scanner rejected valid credentials twice in one afternoon. Our technician recalibrated the sensor, updated the firmware, tested it against multiple authorized users, and everything returned to normal."

"Was the hardware defective?"

"We couldn't prove it."

"Could someone have tampered with it?"

Donovan hesitated.

"There are only a handful of ways biometric systems fail unexpectedly. Hardware failure is one. Software corruption is another. Deliberate interference is a third."

"Which one seemed most likely?"

"My technician couldn't determine that."

Jack noticed the careful wording.

"But you formed an opinion."

Donovan looked toward the office window before answering.

"I've been doing this for thirty-two years. Equipment leaves fingerprints when it breaks. Something wears out. Something overheats. Something cracks. This system didn't behave like broken equipment."

"What did it behave like?"

"Like someone had briefly convinced it to believe the wrong person belonged there."

Jack remained silent, allowing Donovan to continue without interruption.

"The logs showed nothing unusual, which bothered my technician more than the malfunction itself. Systems usually leave clues when they fail. This one corrected itself almost too perfectly."

"Did you tell Mercer?"

"I wasn't there."

"Who was?"

"A technician named Daniel Reeves."

"Can I speak with him?"

Donovan's expression changed almost imperceptibly.

"I wish you could."

"What does that mean?"

"He resigned last week."

Jack studied him carefully.

"Without notice?"

"Effective immediately."

"That unusual?"

"For Danny? Very."

"What reason did he give?"

"He said he'd accepted another opportunity."

"Where?"

"He didn't say."

"You didn't ask?"

"I did."

"And?"

"He told me it was better if no one knew."

The room fell quiet.

Jack had conducted enough interviews to recognize the difference between coincidence and accumulation. A respected estate attorney had vanished. A billionaire had died. An original will had disappeared from one of the most secure legal archives in Boston. Now the technician who serviced the archive's biometric scanner had abruptly resigned under circumstances his own employer found unusual.

He removed a small notebook from his coat pocket.

"Would you happen to have his personnel file?"

Donovan smiled faintly.

"You're a defense lawyer, aren't you?"

"I am."

"I thought private investigators asked for personnel files."

"They do. Lawyers usually ask after they've learned enough to know what questions matter."

Donovan opened a filing cabinet beside his desk and removed a folder.

"I can't give you confidential employment records."

"I wasn't asking for those."

"But I can tell you Danny worked here twelve years, never missed a certification, never had a customer complaint, and never once hinted he was looking for another job."

"Family?"

"Divorced."

"Children?"

"One daughter in college."

"Financial problems?"

"Not that I know of."

"Would you recognize his handwriting?"

Donovan looked puzzled.

"I suppose so."

Jack reached into his briefcase and removed a photocopy Detective Ramirez had reluctantly agreed to share after Jack explained his relationship with Richard Mercer. It was the typed message that had been slipped beneath Mercer's apartment door.

You should have listened to Victor.

There was no handwriting, only the envelope.

Donovan examined it carefully.

"This isn't Danny's printing."

"I didn't think it would be."

"Why show it to me?"

"I wanted to see whether you expected it to be."

For the first time since the meeting began, Donovan laughed.

"Richard Mercer used to ask questions like that."

"You knew him well?"

"He insisted on meeting every technician personally before we worked on the archive. Said trust wasn't something you outsourced."

"What did you think of him?"

"I thought he was the kind of lawyer who paid attention."

Donovan handed the envelope back.

"If Richard Mercer believed something was wrong with that archive, I'd be inclined to believe him."

Jack slipped the copy back into his briefcase.

"So would I."

As he stood to leave, Donovan stopped him.

"Mr. Sullivan."

Jack turned.

"If you find Danny Reeves..."

"Yes?"

"Ask him why he emptied his company locker before anyone knew he'd resigned."

Jack frowned.

"I thought you said he resigned last week."

"He did."

"When did he clean out the locker?"

Donovan's voice grew quieter.

"The Friday before the scanner malfunction."

Jack walked out of Sentinel with more questions than answers. The afternoon sun had finally broken through the clouds, but the warmth did little to ease the growing sense that the investigation had begun long before Richard Mercer disappeared. Someone had been making preparations weeks in advance, and every answer seemed to uncover another layer rather than resolve the last.

As he reached his car, his phone rang.

The caller identification displayed Margaret Ellis.

He answered immediately.

"Margaret."

Her breathing was controlled, but he could hear strain beneath it.

"The police have finished searching Richard's apartment."

"Did they find anything?"

"Yes."

She paused, as though choosing her next words carefully.

"They found blood."

Jack stopped with one hand resting on the car door.

"How much?"

"Not enough for anyone to notice without forensic testing."

"Where?"

"On the leg of the dining room table."

Jack looked across the parking lot without really seeing it.

"Anything else?"

"They also recovered something from beneath the table."

"What was it?"

"The plastic evidence bag Richard used to preserve the envelope."

Jack felt the pieces begin to shift.

"The envelope wasn't inside?"

"No."

"The bag was empty."

Margaret's voice became almost a whisper.

"Whoever took Richard knew enough to remove the mes sage... but they never realized he'd already preserved the evidence."

Jack closed his notebook slowly.

For the first time since taking the case, he felt certain of one thing. Richard Mercer had not simply become the victim of opportunity. Someone had entered that apartment with a specific purpose, believing the missing will was the only document that mattered.

They had overlooked something far more dangerous. Richard Mercer had already begun leaving a trail.

5

Detective Elena Ramirez disliked walking into a room after uniformed officers had finished with it. Patrol officers were trained to secure scenes, protect lives, and establish order. Detectives, on the other hand, were trained to notice disorder. The difference mattered. By the time Ramirez entered Richard Mercer's condominium, the apartment had already been photographed, dusted for prints, and searched once from top to bottom. The evidence technicians had worked carefully, but experience had taught her that a room often revealed more on the second examination than it did during the first.

She stood just inside the doorway for several moments without speaking. The apartment reflected the habits of a disciplined man. Shoes were aligned neatly beneath a bench. The books on the shelves had been arranged by subject rather than height. A legal journal rested open beside an armchair with a pair of reading glasses folded carefully across the page. Nothing suggested panic, and yet nothing about the apartment felt complete. It was as though its owner had stepped away expecting to return within minutes.

One of the crime scene technicians approached carrying a tablet.

"We finished the luminol sweep," he said. "The trace blood came back exactly where we expected."

"The table leg?"

He nodded.

"And nowhere else."

Ramirez looked toward the dining room. The walnut table occupied the center of the space, large enough to seat eight people but more often used by one man reviewing legal documents over a quiet dinner. The technician pointed toward the corner nearest the kitchen.

"The blood transfer is small. If we hadn't tested, we probably wouldn't have seen it."

Ramirez crouched beside the table and examined the area without touching it.

"Impact?"

"Possibly."

"Or?"

"He could have struck his head while falling. There isn't enough to tell us much more than that."

She stood and slowly walked through the remainder of the apartment. The bedroom had not been disturbed. The closets were orderly. The bathroom cabinet contained prescription bottles arranged alphabetically inside a plastic organizer. Mercer had lived the way many attorneys did after decades of routine. Predictability simplified life.

"What about forced entry?"

The technician shook his head.

"No damage to the locks."

"So either Mercer opened the door voluntarily..."

"...or whoever entered had a way inside."

Ramirez stopped in front of the kitchen counter where Mercer's wallet, keys, and watch had been found.

"Most people don't leave home without these."

"No."

"Most kidnappers don't politely leave them behind either."

The technician smiled faintly.

"You think this wasn't a random abduction."

"I don't think anything yet."

She did, of course. Detectives formed theories almost immediately. The discipline lay in refusing to become loyal to them.

Another investigator stepped into the apartment carrying a sealed evidence envelope.

"We got the phone records."

Ramirez accepted the report and flipped through the preliminary summary.

Richard Mercer had made only three calls after arriving home. One had been to Margaret Ellis. Another had been to building security. The third had been to a number registered to Victor Hale's private residence.

She looked up.

"He called Hale?"

"No."

The investigator pointed to the timestamp.

"Hale's number called Mercer first. Mercer returned the call about twenty seconds later."

"What happened?"

"No connection."

Ramirez reread the page.

"What time did Victor Hale die?"

"The medical examiner estimates sometime between one-thirty and three-thirty this morning."

She frowned.

"So Mercer receives a call from Hale's private line after arriving home, returns it almost immediately, and by sunrise Hale is dead."

"That's what the records show."

Ramirez folded the report.

"I want every call placed from Hale's residence during the last forty-eight hours."

"Already requested."

"And everyone who had physical access to that phone."

The investigator nodded before leaving the apartment.

Ramirez walked back toward the dining room where the empty evidence bag had been recovered beneath the table. She had already spoken with Margaret Ellis, who insisted Mercer had preserved the threatening note inside the bag before disappearing. The message itself remained missing.

That detail bothered Ramirez more than the blood.

People who acted impulsively overlooked evidence.

People who removed only the message understood exactly what investigators would value.

Her thoughts were interrupted by another knock at the open apartment door.

A uniformed officer stepped inside.

"Detective?"

"Yes?"

"You asked us to canvas the neighboring apartments again."

"I did."

"I think we found someone."

Ramirez followed him into the hallway where an elderly woman stood beside her door holding a small Yorkshire terrier. She appeared embarrassed by the attention.

"My name is Helen Whitaker," she said. "I'm afraid I wasn't much help earlier."

Ramirez smiled reassuringly.

"Sometimes people remember things after they've had time to think."

Mrs. Whitaker nodded.

"I couldn't sleep last night because of the storm. Around two o'clock I looked through my peephole after hearing voic-es."

"How many voices?"

"I'm not certain."

"Were they arguing?"

"No."

"What did you hear?"

The woman hesitated.

"I heard Mr. Mercer say, 'You're making a mistake.'"

Ramirez remained silent, allowing her to continue.

"Then another man answered."

"Can you remember what he said?"

Mrs. Whitaker closed her eyes for a moment.

"Not exactly."

"Take your time."

"He said something about... the original."

"The original?"

"I think so."

Ramirez's expression changed only slightly.

"Are you sure?"

"No."

"What makes you think that's what he said?"

"Because it sounded like they were discussing an object, not a person."

"What happened next?"

"I heard something fall."

"The table?"

"I couldn't know that."

"And after that?"

"There wasn't any shouting."

"No struggle?"

"Not that I heard."

Ramirez wrote several notes.

"Did you open your door?"

Mrs. Whitaker looked horrified.

"Oh, goodness no."

"Did you look again?"

"About five minutes later."

"What did you see?"

The elderly woman looked down at the dog in her arms before answering.

"The hallway was empty."

Ramirez thanked her and watched her disappear back into her apartment.

The statement raised as many questions as it answered. If Mercer had spoken calmly with whoever entered, then he had probably known—or at least recognized—the visitor. There had been no sounds of a prolonged fight. No neighbors reported screams. The trace amount of blood suggested a brief act of violence rather than an extended assault.

Someone had entered the apartment with purpose.

Someone Mercer believed he could reason with.

As Ramirez returned inside, her phone vibrated.

The caller identified himself as Dr. Samuel Klein from the medical examiner's office.

"I have the preliminary toxicology on Victor Hale," he said.

Ramirez closed the apartment door behind her.

"That was quick."

"We expedited it after this morning."

"What did you find?"

"There were no obvious signs of natural cardiac failure."

"So what killed him?"

"We're not ready to say."

"Klein."

The medical examiner hesitated.

"There are elevated levels of a paralytic agent."

Ramirez stopped walking.

"Are you telling me he was poisoned?"

"I'm telling you the substance shouldn't have been in his bloodstream."

"Could it have been administered medically?"

"Not in that concentration."

She looked back toward Mercer's dining room table.

"What about timing?"

"If someone administered the drug intentionally, Hale would have remained conscious for several minutes before losing voluntary muscle control."

"And after that?"

"He would have appeared to die of natural causes unless someone looked very carefully."

Ramirez thanked him and ended the call.

She remained standing in the center of Richard Mercer's apartment, slowly fitting the new information beside everything else she had learned.

A billionaire had died under circumstances that no longer appeared natural.

His estate attorney had disappeared only hours later.

The original will had vanished from one of the most secure legal archives in Boston.

None of those events proved they were connected.

But for the first time since receiving the case, Detective Elena Ramirez no longer believed she was investigating a missing person.

She believed she was standing at the beginning of a murder investigation whose first victim might not have been Victor Hale.

6

Victor Hale's family gathered inside the private conference room on the thirty-second floor of Hale Global Holdings as if they had been summoned for a board meeting rather than the first legal step after a death. The room overlooked Boston Harbor, where the water moved beneath a pale afternoon sky and cargo ships drifted with the slow confidence of things too large to hurry. Everything inside the room had been selected to communicate control: the polished walnut table, the leather chairs, the abstract paintings that looked expensive without being memorable, and the wall of glass that made the city appear smaller than it was. Jack Sullivan stood near the windows and watched the family enter one at a time, each carrying grief in a different costume.

Eleanor Voss arrived first. She was Victor's eldest daughter, a woman in her early fifties whose posture suggested she had inherited her father's discipline along with his impatience. She wore a dark suit, minimal jewelry, and the expression of someone who believed emotion was useful only after all practical matters had been addressed. Her husband, Martin, followed behind her with the careful smile of a man who had spent years surviving wealthy rooms by agreeing slightly slower than everyone else. Eleanor did not sit at the head of the table, though Jack noticed she looked at the chair before choosing another. That told him something. People did not always reveal ambition by reaching for power; sometimes they revealed it by pretending not to.

The second to arrive was Grant Hale, Victor's only son. He came in without a tie, his jacket open, his eyes red in a way that might have been grief or lack of sleep. Jack knew his type from years of representing men who had mistaken inheritance for achievement. Grant had the expensive looseness of someone who had never carried consequences for long. He dropped into a chair, checked his phone, and looked around the room as if every person present had already disappointed him.

"This is ridiculous," Grant said, not to anyone in particular. "The man has been dead less than a day, and we're already sitting in a conference room with lawyers."

Eleanor looked at him. "We are sitting in a conference room because Father built a company that cannot run on your emotional schedule."

Grant laughed once, quietly and without humor. "There she is. I wondered how long it would take before you started sounding like him."

"I learned from him. You spent most of your life borrowing from him."

Martin Voss placed a hand lightly on the table, not quite touching his wife's arm. "Maybe this is not the time."

"It never is," Grant said. "That's the family motto. Not now, Grant. Not here, Grant. Not while the cameras are outside, Grant."

Jack observed the exchange without interrupting. He had not been invited as family counsel, and he was not there to mediate old resentments. Margaret Ellis had asked him to attend because Charles Dalton had suddenly become more interested in controlling access to information than finding Richard Mercer. Jack had agreed for one reason. If Victor Hale's will was missing, the first people to watch were the people who expected to benefit from whatever replaced it.

The third family member entered almost unnoticed. Lydia Hale was Victor's youngest child, though she was nearly forty and carried none of Grant's recklessness or Eleanor's command. She moved quietly, wearing a gray dress and a black coat she did not remove after sitting down. There was something withdrawn about her, not fragile exactly, but guarded in the way of people who had learned that speaking too soon in a powerful family invited punishment disguised as correction. She nodded politely to the others and placed her hands in her lap.

Behind Lydia came a woman Jack recognized from photographs but had never seen in person. Camille Durant Hale had been married to Victor for seven years, long enough to be called his wife but not long enough to escape being described as his second wife. She was elegant, younger than Eleanor by several years, and composed in a way that seemed neither cold nor warm. Her attorney, a compact man with silver hair and a severe navy suit, walked beside her and carried a legal pad without visible notes. Jack recognized him as Andrew Vale, one of the most expensive probate litigators in New York.

Eleanor's eyes hardened when Camille entered.

Grant straightened slightly, as if remembering he was supposed to perform some version of loyalty.

Lydia looked down at the table.

Camille took the chair farthest from Eleanor. "I know none of us wants to be here," she said. "But Victor was very clear that business matters were not to be delayed after his death."

Eleanor's smile was controlled and unpleasant. "How comforting that you remember his wishes so clearly."

Camille looked at her calmly. "Someone should."

The door opened again before Eleanor could respond, and Charles Dalton entered with two associates from Mercer, Hale & Dalton. Margaret Ellis followed, holding a file folder against her chest. Jack noticed immediately that Dalton had recovered some of his polish since their confrontation in the records room, though not all of it. Men like Dalton understood public rooms better than private danger. In front of clients, he could still sound like authority even while the ground shifted beneath him.

"Thank you all for coming on such short notice," Dalton said as he moved to the head of the table. "I understand this is a difficult day for your family. Mr. Hale's passing is a profound loss not only personally, but institutionally, and the firm wishes to express its condolences."

Grant leaned back. "Spare us the plaque language, Charles. Why are we here?"

Dalton's expression did not change. "Because your father's estate plan requires certain preliminary matters to be addressed promptly. Normally Richard Mercer would preside over this meeting, but given his current absence, I will be handling the initial discussion."

Camille's attorney looked up. "Current absence is a careful phrase."

"It is an accurate one," Dalton replied.

"Is Mr. Mercer missing or unavailable?"

Dalton hesitated only slightly. "The police are attempting to determine his whereabouts."

Grant sat forward. "Wait. Mercer is missing?"

Eleanor turned toward Dalton. "Why were we not told this before?"

"Because until this morning, there was no reason to believe his absence had any connection to Mr. Hale's estate."

"And now?" Camille asked.

Dalton folded his hands on the table. "Now we are still gathering information."

Jack watched the room absorb the answer. In legal settings, vague language often produced more fear than direct facts. The family had entered expecting conflict over money, control, and succession. They had not expected a missing attorney.

Eleanor's attention shifted to Jack. "Who are you?"

"Jack Sullivan."

"That does not answer my question."

"I am a criminal defense attorney."

Grant gave a short laugh. "That makes this meeting feel better."

Eleanor ignored him. "Who retained you?"

"No one in this room."

"Then why are you here?"

Margaret answered before Jack could. "Richard asked me to call him if anything happened involving a client file."

Eleanor's eyes narrowed. "And did something happen involving a client file?"

The question found Dalton before it found anyone else. Jack could see the managing partner weighing confidentiality against the reality that the information could not remain hidden for long. The old rules of client control had ended the moment the original will disappeared. What remained was preservation of evidence and survival.

Dalton looked at the family. "There appears to be an issue with the original executed will."

Camille's attorney put down his pen. "What kind of issue?"

"We are still confirming the status of certain documents."

"Is the original missing?" Vale asked.

No one moved.

Dalton's silence answered him.

Grant stood so quickly his chair pushed back against the carpet. "You lost the will?"

"No one said lost," Dalton replied.

"What word would you like? Misplaced? Temporarily invisible? Stolen from the most expensive law firm in Boston?"

Eleanor's face had gone pale, though her voice remained steady. "Charles, I want a direct answer. Is my father's original will in your possession?"

Dalton looked at her, then at the others. "At this moment, we have not located the original will."

Lydia spoke for the first time. Her voice was soft but clear enough that everyone heard it. "Richard would not have lost it."

Margaret looked at her with gratitude she did not try to hide. "No, he would not have."

Camille folded her hands on the table. "Does a copy exist?"

"There are copies," Dalton said. "But as you all know, an original executed will carries evidentiary importance, especially in an estate of this size."

Vale leaned back slightly. "If the original cannot be produced, there will be a presumption under Massachusetts law that the testator revoked it, unless sufficient evidence proves otherwise."

Grant stared at him. "In English."

"It means," Eleanor said, still looking at Dalton, "that if the will is missing, people can argue Father destroyed it intentionally."

"Did he?" Grant asked.

Eleanor turned on him. "Don't be absurd."

"I'm asking a question. Everyone in this room acts like they know what he wanted. Maybe he changed his mind."

Camille's gaze moved toward Grant. "Did he tell you that?"

Grant opened his mouth, then closed it.

Jack noticed.

So did Eleanor.

"What did Father tell you?" Eleanor asked.

"Nothing."

"That was not nothing."

Grant looked around the room with a sudden defensiveness that seemed larger than the question required. "He called me last week. That's all."

Lydia looked up. "Dad called you?"

"Yes, Lydia. Phones work both ways."

"What did he say?" she asked.

Grant shifted in his chair. "He wanted to know if I had been contacted by anyone claiming to represent a foundation."

Dalton's head turned slowly. "What foundation?"

"I don't remember the name."

Jack spoke for the first time in several minutes. "Try."

Grant looked annoyed. "Who are you again?"

"The lawyer who wants to know why Victor Hale was asking his son about a foundation one week before his death."

Vale's pen moved across the legal pad. Camille watched Grant with an expression Jack could not yet read. Eleanor looked as though she wanted to shake the answer out of him but knew better than to do it with lawyers present.

Grant rubbed his forehead. "I think it was called the Northstar something. Northstar Trust, maybe. Or Northstar Initiative."

Camille's attorney stopped writing.

Jack saw it.

"You recognize the name?" Jack asked.

Vale looked at him. "I recognize many names."

"That sounds like a yes wearing a tie."

Camille turned toward her attorney. "Andrew?"

Vale removed his glasses and set them beside the pad. "A representative from an entity called the Northstar Charitable Initiative contacted my office two months ago regarding potential coordination with several Hale philanthropic commitments. I did not return the call because I could not verify the organization."

Eleanor stared at Camille. "Your office was contacted by a charity none of us have heard of, and you said nothing?"

Camille's voice remained calm, though the first trace of strain entered it. "I receive requests constantly. Victor's name attracted charities, universities, hospitals, museums, and opportunists pretending to be all four. Andrew screened them, as he was paid to do."

Dalton looked uneasy. "Did Victor know about this contact?"

"I told him," Camille said.

"When?"

"Several weeks ago."

"What did he say?"

"He became quiet."

"That was his specialty," Grant muttered.

Camille ignored him. "Later that night he asked whether I had signed anything on his behalf. I told him no. Then he asked if anyone had given me documents to review that mentioned legacy gifts or charitable transfers."

Margaret's face tightened.

Jack turned toward her. "What is it?"

She looked at Dalton, then answered anyway. "Victor asked Richard almost the same question yesterday morning."

The conference room changed after that. Not dramatically, not in the visible way people imagine when secrets are exposed, but in the subtle rearrangement of attention that happens when everyone realizes the conversation has crossed into more dangerous territory. The family had come prepared to distrust one another. Now they were being forced to consider that someone outside the family had been circling Victor's estate before his death.

Eleanor stood and walked toward the windows. "My father spent his life building safeguards against exactly this kind of situation. He had lawyers, accountants, auditors, security consultants, private investigators, and enough enemies to justify all of them. Are you telling me a mysterious charity contacted multiple people around him, his estate lawyer disappeared, the original will is missing, and no one has any idea what is happening?"

Dalton said nothing.

Grant looked at the table.

Lydia's hands tightened in her lap.

Camille's expression was unreadable.

Jack stepped away from the wall. "Ms. Voss, did your father mention Northstar to you?"

"No."

"Did he ask whether you had signed documents?"

"No."

"Did he recently discuss changing his estate plan?"

Eleanor turned from the window. "My father discussed control, not change. He wanted the company protected. He wanted Grant kept away from operating authority. He wanted Lydia provided for without pressure from anyone. He wanted Camille treated fairly, though not given voting control. He wanted the foundation funded. None of that was new."

Grant's face reddened. "Thank you for summarizing the family hierarchy."

"I did not create it."

"No, you just benefited from it."

Lydia finally looked at both of them. "Can we not do this today?"

Grant softened, but only slightly. "We've been doing it our whole lives."

Jack watched Lydia more closely. She had said the least, but her reactions were the least rehearsed. Eleanor responded like a strategist, Grant like a wounded heir, Camille like a woman accustomed to being suspected, and Vale like a lawyer who knew more than he intended to reveal. Lydia responded like someone afraid that if the truth came out, the damage would not stop with money.

Dalton gathered his papers. "For now, the firm will cooperate with law enforcement as appropriate. We will continue searching for the original document and reviewing all access records. Until we have clarity, I advise everyone in this room not to make public statements regarding the estate, Mr. Mercer, or any supposed charitable organization connected to Mr. Hale."

Vale stood. "I want written confirmation from the firm by five o'clock today regarding the status of every executed testamentary document in your possession."

"You will receive a formal response."

"Not formal," Vale said. "Complete."

Eleanor moved toward the door. "I want my father's private counsel contacted immediately. Not the firm. His personal counsel."

Dalton looked unsettled. "Richard Mercer was his personal estate counsel."

"He had more lawyers than some countries," Eleanor said. "Find the ones who still answer their phones."

Grant lingered at the table after the others began leaving. Jack noticed him slip his phone into his pocket and turn toward the window as if trying to decide whether to say something. When the room had nearly emptied, Grant walked over to him.

"You're a criminal lawyer."

"That's what people keep telling me."

"If someone took the will, what happens?"

"That depends on whether they took it to hide the truth or replace it."

Grant swallowed. "And if they already replaced it?"

Jack studied him. "Then the replacement becomes the crime scene."

Grant looked toward the doorway to make sure no one else was listening. "My father called me because he thought I signed something. I told him I didn't. He didn't believe me."

"What did he think you signed?"

"I don't know. Some consent form. A waiver. Something connected to Northstar."

"Did you sign anything?"

Grant's answer came too quickly. "No."

Jack waited.

Grant looked away first. "Not knowingly."

There it was. The detail beneath the denial.

"What does that mean?"

"It means I sign a lot of financial documents. Loan renewals, investment disclosures, tax forms, things my business manager puts in front of me. I don't read every page."

"You should start."

Grant's jaw tightened. "I'm not stupid."

"I didn't say you were. I said you should start reading."

Grant looked offended for a moment, then frightened. The fear made him seem younger than he was. "If I signed something connected to this, Eleanor will use it to destroy me."

"That may be the least of your problems."

Grant stared at him. "You think someone killed my father."

Jack did not answer directly. "I think your father was afraid before he died, and I think the people around him need to stop assuming this is only about inheritance."

Grant left without another word.

Jack remained in the conference room after the door closed, looking out over the harbor while the late afternoon light spread across the water. The case was widening quickly, but not randomly. Northstar had contacted Camille's attorney. Victor had questioned Grant about a document. Richard Mercer had locked away the original will hours before disappearing. Somewhere between those facts was a plan, and someone had already acted with enough confidence to steal from a law firm, enter Mercer's apartment, and possibly murder one of the wealthiest men in America without leaving obvious evidence.

Margaret stepped back into the room a minute later.

"You were right," she said.

"About what?"

"Convenient facts."

Jack turned toward her.

"What did you find?"

She held out a printed email. "Richard forwarded this to himself yesterday afternoon from Victor Hale's private account. It was buried in a folder marked miscellaneous correspondence."

Jack took the page and read the subject line first.

Confirmation of Final Distribution Instructions.

The sender was Northstar Charitable Initiative.

The message was brief, formal, and carefully worded. It thanked Victor Hale for his confidence, referenced his revised testamentary intent, and stated that Northstar was prepared to receive the controlling share of his estate upon execution of the final instrument.

Jack read it twice before looking at Margaret.

"Did Victor respond?"

Margaret nodded. "Richard printed the reply."

"What did it say?"

She handed him the second page.

Victor Hale's response contained only one sentence.

I never authorized this.

Jack folded the pages carefully and placed them inside his notebook. The room felt quieter now, though nothing had changed except the arrival of proof. Northstar was no longer a name half-remembered by frightened heirs and cautious lawyers. It was an entity claiming to possess revised instructions from a man who had denied giving them one day before his death.

Jack looked toward the empty chair where Victor Hale should have been seated if death had not reached him first.

"Now we know what Richard was protecting," he said.

Margaret looked at the printed email in his hand. "The will?"

Jack shook his head. "No. The fact that Victor knew it was being stolen."

7

DETECTIVE ELENA RAMIREZ ARRIVED at Hale House shortly after six in the evening, when the last of the day's light had begun to drain from the sky and the estate's long driveway glowed under a row of old iron lamps. The property sat on several acres outside Boston, hidden behind stone walls, security cameras, and a gatehouse large enough to embarrass most suburban homes. Victor Hale had not built the estate to impress strangers. He had built it to keep them at a distance, and Ramirez understood that kind of architecture. Wealth often called itself privacy when what it really wanted was control.

A uniformed security officer met her at the front entrance and asked for identification even though two police vehicles were already parked near the circular drive. Ramirez showed her badge without comment. The officer checked it carefully, spoke into a radio, and opened the door only after receiving permission from someone inside. She did not resent the procedure. If anything, she preferred people who followed protocols after a death. The careless ones usually created more problems than they solved.

The foyer looked more like a museum than a home. Marble floors stretched beneath a high ceiling, and a curved staircase rose toward the second floor with the kind of elegance found in buildings designed before restraint went out of fashion. A portrait of Victor Hale hung above a long console table, his expression severe enough to make the room feel occupied even in his absence. Ramirez paused beneath it for a moment, studying the painted version of a man who had spent his life making other people wait outside doors.

A woman in a dark dress approached from the hallway. Ramirez recognized her from photographs as Camille Durant Hale. She moved with controlled grace, but her eyes showed the fatigue of someone who had either not slept or had slept poorly under the weight of suspicion.

"Detective Ramirez," Camille said. "I was told you wished to see Victor's study."

"I do. I also need to speak with everyone who had access to him last night."

Camille nodded. "Of course."

"You understand this is no longer a routine death inquiry."

"I was told the medical examiner had questions."

"That is a careful way to say it."

Camille looked toward the portrait, then back at Ramirez. "Careful language is what people expect in this house. It was one of Victor's rules."

"Did you follow his rules?"

"When they made sense."

"And when they didn't?"

A faint, tired smile touched Camille's face. "Then I learned to ask whether I misunderstood the rule."

Ramirez appreciated the answer more than she wanted to. In homicide work, witnesses often made themselves less believable by trying too hard to appear innocent. Camille did not perform innocence. She performed composure, which was different and potentially more useful.

"Where were you when Mr. Hale died?" Ramirez asked.

"In my bedroom."

"Separate from his?"

"Yes."

"Was that usual?"

"For the last year, yes. Victor slept poorly, and his doctors preferred that he rest without interruption. We were still married, Detective. We were not newlyweds."

Ramirez let the answer sit without reacting. "Who found him?"

"His night nurse, Angela Reed. She checked on him at six and called for the house physician."

"Was Mr. Hale under continuous medical care?"

"He had a cardiologist, a neurologist, a private physician, and more consultants than any one person should need. Victor believed medicine worked better when doctors were too well-paid to ignore him."

"Was he terminal?"

Camille hesitated. "No one used that word."

"That wasn't my question."

"No," Camille said quietly. "He was ill, but he was not expected to die last night."

Ramirez wrote the answer in her notebook. People in wealthy homes often believed their phrasing could manage reality. "What illness?"

"A degenerative neuromuscular condition. The diagnosis was recent, and Victor had not made it public."

"Could it explain paralysis?"

Camille's expression sharpened. "What kind of paralysis?"

"I'm asking whether his condition affected voluntary muscle movement."

"It caused weakness, tremors, fatigue. Not sudden paralysis."

Ramirez saw the fear before Camille could hide it. That told her Camille had not known about the toxicology. Either that, or she was a much better actress than most people grieving under police questioning.

"Take me to the study," Ramirez said.

Camille led her through a hallway lined with photographs of Victor shaking hands with presidents, governors, foreign ministers, and CEOs whose names Ramirez recognized only because they appeared on buildings. The study stood behind double doors at the rear of the house. It was large, dark-paneled, and organized with almost military precision. A massive desk faced the room rather than the windows, allowing Victor to sit with his back protected and his visitors exposed. Ramirez had seen the same arrangement in the offices of prosecutors, executives, and criminals. Some instincts crossed professions.

"Has anything been moved?" Ramirez asked.

"The police sealed the room this morning after the first officers arrived. Before that, I cannot say."

"Who entered after Mr. Hale died?"

"The nurse, Dr. Wexler, two security officers, myself, Eleanor, Grant, Lydia, and eventually the funeral director."

"That is a long list."

"This was a large house with a dead man in it. People came when they heard."

"Or when they wanted to see what could be found."

Camille did not answer.

Ramirez walked behind the desk. A leather blotter sat in the center, flanked by a phone, a brass lamp, and two stacked folders. The drawers had already been photographed and opened by the crime scene team. Nothing obvious had been removed, though obvious was rarely the point. A man like Victor Hale would not leave his most important secrets where house staff, family, or curious visitors could find them.

"Did your husband use this phone often?" Ramirez asked.

Camille looked at the desk. "Yes. He disliked using his cell phone for sensitive matters."

"Why?"

"He said cell phones made careless people feel private."

"Did he call Richard Mercer from this phone last night?"

"I don't know."

"The records say someone did."

Camille looked at her. "Then someone did."

"That does not mean it was Victor."

For the first time, Camille seemed genuinely unsettled. She stepped closer to the desk but stopped before entering the area Ramirez had mentally marked as evidence space. "Victor was alive when I last saw him around eleven. He was tired, but alert."

"What did you discuss?"

"His children."

"Which one?"

"All of them, in different ways."

Ramirez looked up from the desk. "That sounds like a diplomatic answer."

"It is the only accurate one."

"Try being less diplomatic."

Camille drew in a breath and released it slowly. "Victor worried Eleanor would turn grief into governance by sunrise. He worried Grant had signed something foolish without reading it. He worried Lydia would be pressured into taking sides before she knew what the sides were. He did not say it gently, but that was the substance."

"And what did he worry about you?"

Camille's face tightened slightly. "That everyone would assume I married him for money and killed him to get it."

"Did he say that?"

"No. He did not have to."

Ramirez closed her notebook for a moment. "Did you love him?"

The question seemed to catch Camille off guard more than the legal and medical ones had. She looked toward the desk, where Victor's reading glasses sat folded beside a silver letter opener. "Yes," she said finally. "But not in the way people want widows to love dead husbands. Victor was difficult, controlling, brilliant, suspicious, generous when it suited him, and cruel when he believed cruelty would save time. I loved him with my eyes open. That may not sound romantic, but it is more honest than most marriages people praise in public."

Ramirez had interviewed enough spouses to know that the answer was either deeply true or carefully constructed. Sometimes the difference did not matter immediately. Truth could still be incomplete.

"Did Victor fear Northstar Charitable Initiative?" Ramirez asked.

Camille did not pretend ignorance. "He feared what the name suggested."

"What did it suggest?"

"That someone had created a legal vehicle to receive assets he never intended to give away."

"Who knew he was looking into it?"

"Richard Mercer. Possibly Andrew Vale. Perhaps Grant, though Grant rarely understands the full meaning of conversations he repeats."

Ramirez moved to the bookshelves. Several framed family photographs occupied one shelf, though the arrangement interested her. Eleanor appeared in photos from corporate events. Grant appeared in childhood sailing pictures and one uncomfortable adult portrait. Lydia appeared in only a few images, mostly informal, standing beside Victor at a charity hospital opening. Camille had one photograph on the shelf, a black-and-white image of her and Victor seated outside a small café, neither of them looking at the camera.

"Who was closest to him?" Ramirez asked.

"No one."

"That sounds lonely."

"It was efficient, which Victor often mistook for better."

A knock came at the study door, and a man in his sixties entered after Camille acknowledged him. He wore a dark suit and carried a physician's bag that looked too old-fashioned to be accidental. Camille introduced him as Dr. Nathan Wexler, Victor's private physician.

"Detective," Wexler said, "I understand there are questions about Mr. Hale's death."

"There are. I assume you pronounced him?"

"I did."

"What did you observe?"

Wexler looked briefly at Camille before answering. "Mr. Hale was unresponsive, pulseless, and not breathing. Given his medical history, age, and recent deterioration, cardiac failure appeared likely."

"Did you notice anything inconsistent with that conclusion?"

"At the time, no."

"But now?"

He removed his glasses and cleaned them with a cloth from his pocket. The gesture bought him several seconds. "I spoke with Dr. Klein at the medical examiner's office. He mentioned an unexpected pharmacological finding."

"A paralytic agent."

Camille turned toward him sharply. "You knew?"

"I was informed shortly before Detective Ramirez arrived."

Ramirez watched both of them. "Would Mr. Hale have had any legitimate medical reason for that drug to be in his system?"

"No."

"Would it be stored in this house?"

"No."

"Could one of his prescribed medications produce a false positive?"

"Not that I am aware of."

"Who administered his medications last night?"

"The night nurse prepared them under standing orders. Mr. Hale was capable of taking oral medication himself, though the nurse documented each dose."

"I need the medication logs."

"I have already provided copies to the first officers."

"I need the originals."

Wexler looked uncomfortable. "They are maintained electronically."

"Then I need the device, the login history, and the name of every person with access."

Camille looked from Ramirez to Wexler. "Is Angela a suspect?"

"Everyone with access is a person of interest until the evidence tells me otherwise."

"That is a cruel answer."

"It is an honest one."

Wexler cleared his throat. "Angela Reed has worked here six months. She was hired through a private medical staffing agency after Mr. Hale's condition worsened."

"Who selected the agency?"

"I recommended several. Mr. Hale's office handled the final contract."

"Which office?"

"His personal administrative office."

"Name."

"Diane Carver."

Ramirez wrote it down. "Was Ms. Carver here last night?"

"No."

Camille corrected him quietly. "She was here in the afternoon."

Wexler looked surprised. "I didn't see her."

"She came through the east entrance. Victor asked to meet with her privately."

Ramirez looked at Camille. "What time?"

"Around four-thirty."

"How long did she stay?"

"Less than an hour."

"Do you know what they discussed?"

"No."

"Did she appear upset when she left?"

Camille hesitated. "Yes."

That answer shifted Ramirez's attention. "Upset how?"

"She was pale. I asked if everything was all right, and she said Victor had asked her to retrieve records she did not know existed."

"What records?"

"She did not say."

Wexler looked increasingly uneasy. "Diane has worked for Victor nearly eighteen years. If he asked for records, she would know where to find them."

"Apparently not these," Camille said.

Ramirez closed her notebook again. The case was expanding inside the house the same way it had expanded outside it. A missing will, a mysterious charity, a dead billionaire, a vanished attorney, a private assistant asked to retrieve unknown records, and a paralytic agent no one admitted having access to. The problem was not a lack of suspects. The problem was that everyone near Victor Hale seemed to have been handed one corner of a larger map and told not to compare it with anyone else.

“I need to speak with Angela Reed and Diane Carver tonight,” Ramirez said.

“I can have security locate Angela,” Camille replied. “Diane may have gone home.”

“Then security can give me her address.”

Camille nodded, but Wexler remained still.

Ramirez noticed. “Doctor?”

“There is something else,” he said.

Camille looked at him with visible frustration. “Nathan, if there is something else, this is not the time to ration it.”

Wexler folded his glasses and held them in one hand. “Victor asked me yesterday whether a person could be chemically restrained without appearing sedated.”

Ramirez felt the question settle over the room.

“What did you tell him?”

“I asked why he wanted to know.”

“And he said?”

“He said someone had been watching him closely enough to know when he was weakest.”

Camille’s face changed. For the first time since Ramirez arrived, her composure failed completely. It was not dramatic. She did not cry or raise her voice. She simply looked toward Victor’s desk with the stunned expression of someone realizing that a conversation she had dismissed as suspicion may have been a warning.

Ramirez turned back to Wexler. “Why didn’t you report that this morning?”

“Because Victor had become increasingly suspicious over the past several weeks. I believed his fear was part of the psychological strain of illness.”

"And now?"

Wexler looked toward the desk where Victor Hale had conducted the last private battles of his life.

"Now," he said, "I believe I may have mistaken a dying man's fear for a symptom."

Ramirez remained in the study for several minutes after Wexler and Camille stepped into the hallway to locate the nurse. She looked again at the phone, the folders, the shelves, the desk, and the carefully arranged photographs. Victor Hale had believed someone was preparing to control his death before it happened. Richard Mercer had believed someone was preparing to control what came after. Between those fears stood Northstar, a name that sounded charitable enough to hide behind and empty enough to belong to anyone.

Her phone vibrated with a message from the station. The records unit had traced Northstar Charitable Initiative to a corporate filing registered in Delaware six months earlier. The listed address belonged to a mail drop. The registered agent handled thousands of companies and knew nothing about the people behind it. The only useful detail was a scanned formation document bearing the digital signature of an attorney named Ethan Brooks.

Ramirez read the name twice.

She did not know Ethan Brooks.

But when she forwarded the document to Jack Sullivan, his reply came less than a minute later.

I do.

8

Jack Sullivan read Elena Ramirez's message twice before setting the phone on the edge of his desk. The name Ethan Brooks brought back memories he would have preferred to leave undisturbed. In Boston legal circles, Brooks had once been considered one of the brightest young attorneys in corporate formations and charitable trust work. He had started at a major firm, left for boutique practice, and developed a reputation for creating complicated entities that wealthy clients used when they wanted their business discreet but not necessarily improper. Jack had crossed paths with him three years earlier in a federal investigation involving a nonprofit accused of laundering political donations through educational grants. Brooks had not been charged, but Jack remembered the look on his face during the interview. He had looked like a man who knew enough to be afraid and not enough to protect himself.

Jack was still looking at the phone when Margaret Ellis stepped into his temporary office at Mercer, Hale & Dalton. The firm had given him a conference room with glass walls, a polished table, and a view of the harbor that made it hard to forget how much money moved through the building. Margaret carried a legal pad, two file folders, and the expression of someone who had not yet allowed herself to be tired.

"Detective Ramirez found the attorney who formed Northstar," Jack said.

Margaret closed the door behind her. "Who?"

"Ethan Brooks."

She reacted immediately, though not dramatically. Her grip tightened around the folders, and she glanced toward the hallway as if the name might have carried beyond the room.

"You know him," Jack said.

"Richard did."

"How well?"

"Well enough to distrust him without hating him."

"That is a very specific category."

"Richard believed Ethan had talent and poor judgment. He said that combination made lawyers useful to the wrong people."

Jack leaned back in his chair. "When did Richard last mention him?"

Margaret placed the folders on the table and sat across from him. "About six months ago. Ethan called asking whether Richard would be willing to consult on a charitable estate structure for an unnamed client. Richard declined before the conversation was finished."

"Did he say why?"

"He told me the request sounded backward."

Jack waited because Margaret had Richard Mercer's habit of offering precise answers only after she trusted the listener enough to hear them.

"Richard said legitimate estate planning begins with a client's intent and builds the legal structure around it," Margaret continued. "Ethan was describing a structure first and looking for a client intent afterward. Richard did not like that."

"That sounds like Northstar."

"It may have been."

"Did Richard document the call?"

Margaret opened one of the folders. "He documented everything. I pulled his phone memorandum after your text. It is brief, but it confirms the conversation."

Jack took the memorandum and read it carefully. Mercer's notes were disciplined, almost judicial in tone. Brooks had asked general questions about testamentary gifts, controlling interests in private companies, and whether a charitable entity could receive voting shares through a pour-over provision triggered at death. Mercer had written one sentence at the bottom that interested Jack more than the rest: Caller appears to be seeking method to validate decision already made by someone other than testator.

Jack looked up. "Richard knew."

"He suspected."

"In my line of work, suspicion written by Richard Mercer is better than certainty from most people."

Margaret almost smiled. "He would have pretended not to enjoy that compliment."

Jack handed the memorandum back. "I need to speak with Brooks before the police do, assuming they have not already picked him up."

"Is that wise?"

"No. It is necessary."

"That sounds like something lawyers say before making a bad decision."

"Sometimes. But if Brooks formed Northstar six months ago and Richard declined to help him with the structure around the same time, Brooks may know who was really behind it. He also may not realize yet that his name is the first one connected to the entity on paper."

Margaret studied him. "And if he does realize it?"

"Then he is either running, hiding, or waiting for someone to tell him what story to use."

Jack reached for his coat. Before leaving, he asked Margaret to make two copies of Mercer's memorandum and place the original in a secure evidence envelope. He did not yet represent the firm, Brooks, the Hale family, or anyone else officially connected to the matter, but he understood the practical truth of the moment. Once a criminal investigation began, paper became testimony waiting to be sworn. If documents moved casually now, someone would later claim they had moved dishonestly.

Ethan Brooks kept an office in a converted brownstone near Beacon Hill, the kind of address that sounded more impressive than it functioned. His name appeared on a brass plaque beside the door with three other solo practitioners, though only one light was on when Jack arrived. A woman at the reception desk looked up from a paperback novel and told him Mr. Brooks was not available without asking whether he had an appointment.

Jack placed his card on the counter. "Tell him it is about Northstar."

Her expression changed just enough to confirm he had chosen the right word. She disappeared down the hallway and returned less than a minute later.

"He has ten minutes."

"People always say that before giving me longer."

The office at the rear of the building was smaller than Jack expected. Bookshelves lined one wall, but half the volumes looked untouched. Stacks of corporate binders occupied the floor beside a credenza. Ethan Brooks stood behind his desk in shirtsleeves, his tie loosened and his face drawn from lack of sleep. He was younger than Jack by nearly fifteen years, but fear had aged him quickly.

"Jack Sullivan," Brooks said. "I heard you were involved."

"That was fast."

"Lawyers talk."

"Frightened lawyers talk faster."

Brooks gestured toward a chair. "I assume this is about Victor Hale."

"It is about Northstar Charitable Initiative."

Brooks looked toward the closed door. "Then I assume it is also about Victor Hale."

Jack sat without being invited a second time. "You formed the entity six months ago."

"I form entities every week."

"Not all of them appear in emails claiming control of a billionaire's estate the day before he dies."

Brooks closed his eyes briefly. "I knew this was going to happen."

"That is a dangerous sentence."

"I did not mean I knew Hale was going to die. I meant I knew the entity would become a problem."

"Who hired you?"

Brooks sat down slowly. "I cannot disclose client information."

Jack gave him a look of genuine disappointment. "Ethan, if you are about to hide behind privilege without knowing whether privilege even applies, we are going to waste time you may not have."

"I know how privilege works."

"Then you know it does not protect communications made to further a crime or fraud. You also know that forming an entity for an unnamed principal who uses it to steal testamentary assets is not routine legal work."

Brooks rubbed both hands over his face. "You still talk like a prosecutor."

"I was one."

"Yes, and now you defend people who are guilty of almost everything except what they were charged with."

Jack did smile then. "That is occasionally true."

Brooks leaned back and stared at the ceiling. "A consultant brought me the formation work. He said the client wanted to remain confidential until the charitable structure was finalized."

"Name."

"Caleb Rusk."

Jack wrote it down. "Who is Rusk?"

"A private wealth consultant. Former banker. He refers clients who want charitable vehicles, donor-advised structures, legacy foundations, that sort of thing."

"Did you meet the actual client?"

"No."

"Did you ask to?"

"Of course."

"And?"

"Rusk said the client valued privacy and would disclose identity once the preliminary structure was complete."

Jack let the answer sit between them. "You formed a charitable entity without knowing who controlled it."

"That is not illegal."

"It is also not smart."

"I understand that now."

"You understood it then."

Brooks looked away first. "Yes."

Jack softened his tone slightly, not out of sympathy but strategy. "Why did you do it?"

Brooks did not answer right away. Outside the office, footsteps passed in the hallway and faded toward the front of the building. When he finally spoke, his voice had lost its defensive edge.

"My daughter was sick last year. Rare autoimmune condition. The insurance fight was a nightmare, and the treatments were expensive. I took on work I should have refused because I convinced myself I could manage the risk."

"Did Rusk know that?"

"He knew I needed money."

"How much did he pay you?"

"Fifty thousand for formation and preliminary drafting."

Jack kept his face neutral. "For work that normally costs five."

"Yes."

"Paid by whom?"

"Wire transfer from a consulting company."

"Name."

"Mariner Strategic Services."

Jack wrote that down as well. "Did you draft testamentary instruments?"

"No."

"Think carefully before answering again."

Brooks leaned forward. "I drafted sample language for a charitable transfer structure. I did not draft Victor Hale's will. I did not witness it. I did not notarize it. I did not send him anything."

"But someone used your entity to tell Hale that Northstar was prepared to receive controlling shares under revised final instructions."

Brooks looked genuinely confused. "What are you talking about?"

Jack removed a folded copy of the Northstar email from his inside pocket and slid it across the desk. Brooks read it once, then again, the color leaving his face as he reached the final line.

"I didn't send this."

"Did Rusk?"

"I don't know."

"Could he have?"

Brooks pointed toward the header. "This uses the administrative address created for Northstar, but I closed that account after the engagement ended."

"When did it end?"

"Two months ago."

"Why?"

"Because Rusk asked me to prepare execution documents for a testator I still had not met. That was when I said no."

"Execution documents for Victor Hale?"

"He still did not use the name. But by then I had suspicions."

"Based on what?"

Brooks opened a drawer and removed a folder. His hand trembled slightly as he placed it on the desk. "Rusk sent me a capitalization table for a private holding company. He said the charitable entity needed to be prepared to receive voting shares upon death. He forgot to remove the subsidiary names from one page. Three of them belonged to Hale Global."

Jack took the folder. "You kept this?"

"I kept everything after I became uncomfortable."

"That may be the first good decision in this story."

"It may also be the reason I am still alive."

Jack looked at him. "Someone threatened you?"

Brooks stared at the Northstar email. "A week after I declined, a man came to my office. He did not give a name. He said people who misunderstood client confidentiality often became examples in malpractice seminars."

"That is a lawyer's threat written by someone trying not to sound criminal."

"It did not feel like a malpractice threat."

"Did you report it?"

"No."

"Why not?"

"Because I had already taken the money, formed the entity, and ignored every instinct that told me something was wrong. I thought if I stayed quiet, it would go away."

Jack looked around the office, at the binders and expensive furniture and the lawyer who had wanted success badly enough to rent the appearance of it before he could afford the substance. He did not despise Brooks. He had seen too many versions of him. Fear and ambition often arrived wearing the same suit.

"Richard Mercer is missing," Jack said.

Brooks looked up sharply. "Missing?"

"Victor Hale is dead, and the medical examiner found signs he may have been poisoned."

Brooks stood so abruptly his chair struck the wall behind him. "No. I had nothing to do with that."

"I did not say you did."

"You came here because my name is on the entity."

"I came here because your name is the first signature on the paper trail. That makes you valuable, exposed, and possibly expendable."

Brooks paced once behind his desk before stopping near the window. "I need a lawyer."

"You do."

"Are you offering?"

"Not yet."

"Why not?"

"Because I do not know whether you are a witness, a target, or a defendant."

Brooks laughed bitterly. "That is comforting."

"It is accurate."

Jack gathered the documents Brooks had provided but did not place them in his briefcase. "I am not taking originals from your office. Make copies, preserve the originals, and do not destroy anything. Do not call Rusk. Do not speak to reporters. Do not speak to anyone connected to Northstar, Mariner, or Hale Global without counsel present."

"You just said you are not my lawyer."

"I am giving you free advice before you accidentally become your prosecutor's favorite witness."

Brooks moved toward the copier near the credenza, then stopped. "There is one more thing."

Jack waited.

"The sample language I drafted included a condition."

"What kind of condition?"

"The charitable transfer would activate only if the testator's immediate heirs were deemed legally compromised."

Jack frowned. "Compromised how?"

"Fraud, incapacity, undue influence, criminal exposure, anything that could make them unsuitable to receive or control the assets. Rusk said the client wanted a moral safeguard."

"That is not a safeguard. That is a weapon."

"I know that now."

Jack thought of Grant Hale admitting he may have signed something without reading it, Camille's attorney receiving contact from Northstar, Eleanor preparing for corporate control, and Lydia sitting silently while the family fought around her. If someone had designed a structure that depended on the heirs becoming legally compromised, then the missing will might not be the only target. The family itself might have been placed under pressure deliberately, one member at a time, until the estate had nowhere left to go except Northstar.

Brooks made copies with shaking hands and returned the originals to his folder. Jack took the copies and stood.

"Where can I find Caleb Rusk?"

Brooks wrote an address on the back of a business card. "He keeps an office in the Seaport. But if he knows Hale is dead, he may already be gone."

Jack slipped the card into his notebook. "Then we should hope he is arrogant enough to believe he does not need to run."

Brooks opened the office door but did not step into the hallway. "Mr. Sullivan, if Richard Mercer is alive, whoever took him will want to know what he told you."

"Richard did not tell me anything."

Brooks looked toward the Northstar email still lying on his desk. "That may not matter. People behind structures like this do not fear what you know. They fear what you might find next."

Jack left the brownstone and stepped onto the sidewalk, where the early evening air had turned cold enough to carry the smell of rain from the previous night. He called Ramirez from his car and gave her the essential pieces without overstating what Brooks had provided. She listened without interrupting, which Jack took as a sign that she was either impressed or already ahead of him.

When he finished, Ramirez said, "Do not go to Rusk's office alone."

"I wasn't planning to."

"That means you were."

"It means I was considering the advantages of speed."

"The advantage of staying alive is that you can continue being annoying tomorrow."

Jack looked at the address Brooks had written on the card. "Meet me there."

"I'll bring a warrant if I can get one fast enough."

"And if you cannot?"

"Then I'll bring probable cause and a bad mood."

Jack ended the call and sat for a moment before starting the engine. The case had shifted again. Northstar was not merely a mysterious charity. It was a legal mechanism built to receive assets if Victor Hale's heirs could be disqualified or neutralized. Someone had designed it with knowledge of estate law, corporate control, family weakness, and the timing of death. That kind of plan required patience, money, access, and a willingness to ruin people before anyone understood they were being arranged.

By the time Jack pulled into traffic, he no longer believed Victor Hale had been the only intended victim. The will was missing, Richard Mercer was gone, and the Hale family had been placed inside a structure built to collapse around them.

Somewhere, Caleb Rusk was either the architect of that collapse or the next man in line to disappear.

9

Caleb Rusk's office occupied the eighth floor of a glass building in the Seaport District, where Boston had replaced old warehouses with restaurants, investment firms, luxury apartments, and enough steel-and-window architecture to make every company inside appear more important than it was. Jack Sullivan arrived ten minutes before Detective Ramirez and waited in the lobby rather than going upstairs alone. He had considered doing exactly what Ramirez told him not to do, but the longer he sat beneath the soft lighting and watched people move through security with briefcases and visitor badges, the more he understood that speed was not always an advantage. Caleb Rusk was either careful enough to help build Northstar or careless enough to become useful to someone who had, and neither version should be approached like an ordinary witness.

Ramirez entered wearing a dark coat over a charcoal suit, her badge clipped at her belt and her expression set in the neutral professionalism that made receptionists nervous before she said a word. She looked at Jack as if she had expected to find him upstairs already and was mildly disappointed that he had behaved responsibly. "You waited," she said, stopping beside him near the security desk. Jack stood and adjusted his coat. "I am capable of following instructions when they are attached to a homicide investigation." Ramirez gave him a look. "That is not the same as reassuring me." Jack glanced toward the elevators. "Did you get a warrant?" She shook her head. "Not yet. I have an assistant district attorney working on it, but right now we have a corporate formation attorney who says Rusk referred business, a suspicious charitable entity, and a dead billionaire. That gives us questions, not a search warrant."

They approached the security desk together. The guard was young, polite, and immediately uncomfortable once Ramirez identified herself. He checked the tenant directory and confirmed that Caleb Rusk leased Suite 812 under the name Rusk Advisory Group. When Ramirez asked whether Rusk was in, the guard made a call upstairs, listened for several seconds, then looked back at them with the guarded expression of a man who had just realized his ordinary shift had become part of something official. "No answer," he said. Ramirez asked whether Rusk had used his access card that day. The guard hesitated, then looked toward the computer screen as if hoping it would provide permission along with information. "I'm not sure I can disclose that without building management," he said. Ramirez placed her business card on the counter and kept her voice even. "Then call building management."

The property manager arrived five minutes later, introducing herself as Nora Keene. She was in her forties, neatly dressed, and carried a tablet pressed against her ribs like a shield. Ramirez explained that they needed to speak with Caleb Rusk regarding an active investigation and asked whether he was currently in the building. Keene checked the access system and said Rusk's card had not been used since the previous afternoon. Jack watched her face as she read the entry. It was a small change, a tightening around the eyes, but enough to matter. "Something else?" he asked. Keene looked from him to Ramirez before answering. "His office contacted us yesterday to request after-hours freight elevator access." Ramirez's expression did not change. "For what purpose?" Keene glanced down at the tablet again. "Moving archival materials. That was the description provided."

Ramirez asked to see the freight elevator logs and any related camera footage. Keene did not refuse, but she did become more careful. "Detective, I want to cooperate, but I need to protect tenant privacy. Without a warrant or consent, I cannot simply give you access to private tenant areas or internal records beyond basic safety information." Jack respected the answer. It was exactly what a competent property manager should say when law enforcement arrived without paperwork. Ramirez seemed to respect it too. "I am not asking you to let us search his office. I am asking whether there is reason to believe evidence connected to a suspicious death may have been removed from this building after business hours." Keene swallowed, and for the first time she looked more concerned than cautious. "I can show you the common-area footage. The freight lobby and elevators are not inside the tenant suite."

They followed her through a side corridor to the building management office. The space was cramped compared to the polished lobby, with monitors mounted along one wall and maintenance schedules pinned beside a coffee machine. Keene pulled up the footage from the previous night and scrolled to the freight elevator access window. The camera showed the service corridor at 9:42 p.m., empty except for a janitor pushing a supply cart. At 10:16, Caleb Rusk appeared with two men wearing dark jackets and work gloves. Jack recognized Rusk from an online photograph Brooks had shown him: mid-fifties, silver hair, trim build, expensive coat, confident posture. The kind of man who looked like he had never carried anything heavier than a leather portfolio.

The two men rolled three sealed plastic storage crates onto the freight elevator. The crates were large, black, and unmarked. Rusk did not help lift them, but he watched closely, speaking once to the taller of the two men before checking his phone. Ramirez leaned closer to the monitor. "Can you enhance the license plate on whatever vehicle they used?" Keene switched to the loading dock camera. The footage showed a white cargo van backed against the dock, but the plate was partly obscured by glare from the overhead light. "I can export this for you if your warrant covers it," Keene said. Ramirez nodded. "Preserve the footage immediately. Do not allow automatic deletion, and do not give copies to anyone else, including Rusk or anyone claiming to represent him."

Jack studied the still image of the van. "Did Rusk say he was leaving the building permanently?" Keene shook her head. "No. His lease runs another eight months." Ramirez asked whether anyone had entered Suite 812 since the crates were removed. Keene checked the access log again. "No access card activity after the freight elevator request." Jack looked toward the monitor showing Rusk in the loading dock. "People who leave in a hurry usually forget something." Ramirez glanced at him. "And people who remember everything usually leave someone else to be blamed." Keene looked between them, unsettled by how calmly they spoke about possibilities she had probably never needed to consider in building management.

The warrant process moved faster after Ramirez called the assistant district attorney and described the freight footage. While they waited, she asked Keene to accompany them to the eighth floor so they could conduct a limited knock and talk without entering the office. Jack knew the line Ramirez was walking. They could knock. They could observe what was visible from a lawful vantage point. They could not cross the threshold, open drawers, move objects, or treat the space like a crime scene until a judge gave them authority. Legal thrillers loved shortcuts. Real evidence was built by resisting them.

Suite 812 sat at the end of a quiet hallway with frosted glass and brushed-metal lettering that read Rusk Advisory Group. No receptionist waited inside. No light burned in the front office. Ramirez knocked twice, announced herself, and waited. When no one answered, she tried the handle only enough to confirm that the door was locked. Through the narrow clear strip beside the frosted glass, Jack could see part of a reception area, two chairs, and a low table with outdated financial magazines arranged too neatly to have been read. Nothing appeared disturbed, but abandonment had its own silence. Offices were meant to produce small noises: phones, printers, keyboards, voices behind doors. This one seemed to be holding its breath.

Keene stood behind them with her tablet. "I should tell you something," she said. Ramirez turned slightly. "Now would be the right time." Keene looked embarrassed, as if the information had been nagging her but she had not known whether it mattered. "Mr. Rusk paid six months of rent in advance when he signed the lease. He said his clients valued discretion and he did not want billing issues. We have several tenants who pay that way, so it did not seem unusual." Jack asked how long Rusk had occupied the suite. "Six months," she said. "Almost exactly." Ramirez and Jack exchanged a look. Northstar had been formed six months earlier. Rusk's office had appeared six months earlier. Structures, Jack thought, did not emerge around crimes by coincidence. They were built like scaffolding before anyone standing at ground level understood what was under construction.

Ramirez's phone rang a few minutes later. She listened, thanked the caller, and ended the call with the first visible sign of progress Jack had seen from her all evening. "Warrant signed," she said. "Search team is on the way." Keene unlocked the suite only after Ramirez confirmed the warrant number and authority. They did not enter immediately. Ramirez waited for the first two officers and a crime scene technician to arrive before crossing the threshold. Jack remained behind until she looked back and said, "You can observe, but do not touch anything." He raised both hands slightly. "I know the rules." Ramirez gave him a dry look. "You know them well enough to argue about them later. That is not the same as following them now."

The reception area was immaculate. Too immaculate, Jack thought. The desk drawers were empty, the computer monitor gone, the wastebasket lined but unused. In the inner office, the bookshelves held generic volumes on philanthropy, tax planning, private wealth, and family governance, none marked by notes or wear. The credenza had been cleared except for a small stone sculpture of a compass. Rusk had left behind the appearance of an office, not the working contents of one. Ramirez moved through the space slowly, narrating observations for the recording officer, while the technician photographed each room before anything was opened.

Jack stood near the doorway and studied what Rusk had chosen not to take. There were no personal photographs. No awards. No diplomas. No framed licenses. Even the coffee mug beside the sink in the small kitchenette looked unused. Men who built businesses around trust usually displayed credentials aggressively. Rusk had displayed atmosphere instead. That suggested he was less interested in proving who he was than in creating the impression clients needed long enough to accept him.

A young officer opened a supply closet after photographing it. Inside were two empty shelves, a vacuum, printer paper, and a narrow cardboard box containing old mailing labels. Ramirez stepped closer, reviewed the labels, and held one up with gloved fingers. "Mariner Strategic Services," she read. Jack looked at the label from where he stood. "That is the company that paid Brooks." Ramirez placed the label into an evidence bag. "At least Rusk was kind enough to leave us a bridge." Jack shook his head. "Or someone wanted the bridge found." Ramirez did not disagree. Good detectives disliked gifts almost as much as defense lawyers did.

In the desk drawer, the technician found a single key taped beneath the back panel. It was small, brass, and marked with a number etched into the head. Ramirez photographed it in place before allowing it to be removed. Keene looked at the number and frowned. "That looks like a private mailbox key," she said. Ramirez asked whether the building had mailboxes for tenants. Keene confirmed they were located in a secured mailroom on the lobby level. The group returned downstairs, where Keene opened the mailroom under Ramirez's direction. Box 812 contained several envelopes, most of them ordinary solicitations, but one padded mailer had no return address and had been postmarked the previous morning.

Ramirez had the mailer photographed before opening it. Inside was a burner phone wrapped in a sheet of printer paper. The phone had been powered off, and the paper contained a printed address in South Boston with no name, note, or explanation. Jack looked at the address and felt the case take another deliberate step sideways. Ramirez bagged the phone separately and held the paper by the edges. "Do you know this location?" she asked. Jack did, though not because he had ever been there. "It is a storage facility near the old industrial waterfront," he said. "Private units, month-to-month rentals, mostly contractors and small import businesses. I had a client store records there during a federal tax case." Ramirez looked at him. "Of course you did."

They remained in the building another hour while the search team finished documenting the suite. The result was both useful and unsatisfying. Rusk had removed the working files, the computers, and anything likely to identify clients directly. What remained suggested planning, but not authorship. Northstar, Mariner, Brooks, Victor Hale, Richard Mercer, and Caleb Rusk were now connected by fragments, each one legally significant but incomplete by itself. Jack had tried enough cases to know how dangerous that could be. Prosecutors loved patterns until jurors asked whether anyone had proved the line between them.

Outside the building, the city had grown dark and the Seaport's restaurant windows glowed with people who had no idea that a dead billionaire and a missing lawyer were beginning to pull half of Boston's legal world into a widening investigation. Ramirez stood beside her unmarked sedan while an evidence technician secured the burner phone in a transport case. "I am going to get a warrant for the storage facility," she said. Jack looked toward the harbor, where the water reflected broken pieces of city light. "By the time we get there, whatever was in those crates may be gone." Ramirez nodded. "Maybe. But if we go without a warrant and find something important, it becomes a suppression hearing instead of evidence." Jack appreciated the sentence more than he expected. "That is the most beautiful thing a detective has ever said to me."

Ramirez almost smiled, then looked at him with the tired seriousness that had become the mood of the case. "Ethan Brooks needs counsel before someone decides he is easier to charge than protect." Jack understood what she was really saying. Brooks was exposed, frightened, and useful. That combination made him vulnerable to both prosecutors and the people behind Northstar. "I have not agreed to represent him," Jack said. Ramirez opened her car door. "You will." Jack did not answer because he suspected she was right. Some clients hired lawyers. Others became clients the moment the truth left them nowhere else to stand.

As Jack walked back to his own car, his phone vibrated with a message from Margaret Ellis. She had found another memorandum in Richard Mercer's files, this one labeled only with a date from two weeks earlier and the initials C.R. The note was brief, but it was written in Mercer's precise hand.

Caleb Rusk requested meeting through intermediary. Refused to identify principal. Asked whether moral-disqualification clauses survive challenge when heirs are under active criminal investigation. Advised no discussion without named client. Caller ended abruptly.

Jack read the message twice under the white glow of the parking garage lights. The implication was no longer hidden inside structure or theory. Rusk had been asking how to move Victor Hale's estate away from his heirs before any of them had been charged with anything. That meant the plan had never been limited to stealing a will. Someone intended to create the legal conditions that would make the theft appear justified when the time came.

He forwarded the memorandum to Ramirez and sat behind the wheel without starting the engine. For the first time, the shape of the case began to show itself in negative space. Victor Hale had been killed, Richard Mercer had been taken, Ethan Brooks had been used, Caleb Rusk had vanished, and the Hale heirs had been positioned as future defendants before they even understood they were targets. The law was not being avoided in this case. It was being used as the weapon, sharpened by someone who knew exactly how courts, wills, charities, and public suspicion could be made to work together.

By the time Jack pulled out of the garage, he was thinking less about who murdered Victor Hale and more about who intended to inherit the damage.

10

The storage facility in South Boston sat between a plumbing supply warehouse and a fenced lot filled with delivery trucks that had not moved in years. At night, the building looked less like a business than a place the city had forgotten to finish. A row of security lights washed the loading bays in a pale glare, and the wind coming off the water carried the smell of salt, diesel, and wet pavement. Jack Sullivan arrived behind Detective Ramirez and parked near the front office, leaving enough distance from the entrance to stay out of the way when the crime scene unit arrived.

Ramirez stepped out of her car with a folded warrant in one hand and the tired resolve of someone who had spent the entire day asking judges for permission to chase evidence that might already be gone. Two uniformed officers waited near the door with a building manager who looked as though he had been pulled from dinner and had not yet decided whether to be annoyed or afraid. Jack recognized that expression from dozens of investigations. People liked rules until rules arrived with badges, paperwork, and the possibility that their ordinary business had become part of a homicide inquiry.

The manager introduced himself as Kevin Larkin and unlocked the front office after Ramirez showed him the warrant. He was in his early sixties, broad across the middle, and wore a navy jacket with the company logo stitched over the pocket. His hands shook slightly as he took the warrant and adjusted his glasses to read it. Ramirez did not rush him. A search conducted cleanly mattered more than a search conducted quickly, especially when a defense lawyer was standing close enough to later remember every shortcut.

"You understand what this authorizes?" Ramirez asked. Larkin nodded, though his eyes remained on the paper. "Unit 417, access logs, payment records, surveillance from the loading dock, and any records identifying the renter," he said. "I'll cooperate, Detective. I just want it understood that we don't open customers' units unless rent is overdue or there's a court order." Ramirez took the warrant back and slid it into a folder. "That is why I brought the court order."

Jack stood near the doorway while Ramirez and the officers entered the office. He had no official role in the search, and he knew better than to create confusion by acting as if he did. He was there because Ramirez understood that his connection to Richard Mercer and Ethan Brooks might help interpret whatever they found, but presence did not become participation. If the case ever reached trial, the distinction would matter. Evidence collected by police under a warrant entered court differently than evidence discovered by a private lawyer wandering through a storage unit.

Larkin logged into the facility's computer and pulled up the rental records. Unit 417 had been leased four months earlier under Mariner Strategic Services, paid six months in advance with a business credit card issued through a Delaware bank. The listed contact person was Caleb Rusk, but the mailing address belonged to the same Seaport office they had searched earlier. Ramirez asked for the access history, and Larkin printed it without argument. The unit had been accessed five times in four months, twice in the last week, and once the previous night at 11:08 p.m., less than an hour after Rusk's crates left the Seaport building.

"Do the logs identify who entered?" Ramirez asked. Larkin pointed to the printed page. "Only by access code. The code is assigned to the renter, but we don't have biometric identification or anything like that." Ramirez looked toward Jack, then back at the manager. "How many people could have used that code?" Larkin shrugged with discomfort. "Anyone who knew it. We tell customers not to share codes, but people share everything." Jack made a mental note. Access without identity created opportunity, but it also created reasonable doubt.

The surveillance footage from the previous night confirmed what the access log suggested. At 11:06, a white cargo van entered through the rear gate and pulled to the loading area. Two men unloaded three black storage crates that matched the ones removed from Rusk's office. Caleb Rusk did not appear on the recording. The men wore hats low over their faces and moved with practiced efficiency, neither rushing nor hesitating. They entered the code, rolled the crates through a service door, and returned to the van eighteen minutes later without the crates.

Ramirez asked Larkin to preserve and export the footage, then led the group toward the storage units. The hallway beyond the office was long, concrete-floored, and lit by fluorescent strips that hummed overhead. Doors with painted numbers lined both sides, each one secured by a rolling metal gate and a customer-provided lock. Unit 417 sat near the rear of the building, far enough from the office to avoid casual attention but close enough to the loading dock to move heavy items without difficulty. A crime scene technician photographed the door, the lock, the surrounding floor, and the numbered placard before anyone touched anything.

Ramirez looked at Jack before the bolt cutters came out. "You stay outside unless I tell you otherwise," she said. Jack nodded. "I know. I observe, I do not search, I do not touch, and I do not later pretend I was surprised by the Fourth Amendment." One of the uniformed officers glanced at him, unsure whether to smile. Ramirez did not. "Good. Keep impressing me."

The lock snapped under the bolt cutters with a sharp metallic sound that echoed down the hallway. Ramirez lifted the rolling door with gloved hands while the technician recorded the opening on video. The unit smelled of cardboard, plastic, and something faintly medicinal that Jack noticed before anyone named it. Inside, the three black crates sat in the center of the concrete floor. Against the rear wall stood two filing boxes, a folded moving blanket, and a metal shelving unit that held nothing except a small cardboard container sealed with packing tape.

Nothing about the unit looked abandoned.

Nothing about it looked accidental either.

Ramirez waited while the technician photographed the entire unit from several angles. The first crate contained binders labeled with the names of Victor Hale's children. Eleanor Voss had two binders. Grant Hale had three. Lydia Hale had one thick binder and a smaller envelope sealed with red tape. Camille Durant Hale had a separate file marked marital rights, prenuptial exposure, and election strategy. Jack read the labels from the hallway and felt the purpose of the room settle into place. These were not ordinary financial records. They were dossiers.

Ramirez opened Grant's first binder and flipped through it with gloved hands. It contained loan documents, private investment agreements, emails from lenders, and copies of signature pages attached to transactions he may or may not have understood. Several pages were marked with colored tabs. One tab identified an offshore loan guarantee. Another marked a personal certification stating that Grant had no undisclosed debts or pending claims. Jack knew enough about estate litigation to see the design. If Grant could be accused of fraud, insolvency, or concealment, someone could challenge his suitability to manage inherited assets or corporate voting rights.

Eleanor's binders were different. They contained board minutes, internal Hale Global memoranda, and printed emails suggesting she had discussed post-death corporate succession before Victor died. Some of the language looked incriminating at first glance, but Jack had spent too many years reading selected excerpts to trust anything presented without context. A sentence taken from a longer email could become a weapon in the hands of someone who knew where to cut it. Ramirez seemed to understand that as well. She did not react to the highlighted sections except to have them photographed and bagged according to the warrant protocol.

Lydia's file made Ramirez pause. Jack saw it in her posture more than her face. She opened the envelope carefully and removed medical records, psychiatric notes, and private correspondence that should never have been in a storage unit rented by a wealth consultant. Ramirez closed the folder almost immediately and instructed the technician to seal it separately. "This may include privileged medical information," she said, speaking for the recording as much as for the officers present. "We preserve it, but we do not review further without guidance from the court or a taint team." Jack respected the restraint. It was the kind of procedural discipline that kept evidence alive after judges began asking uncomfortable questions.

Camille's file contained copies of the prenuptial agreement, drafts of spousal election analyses, correspondence between her attorney and charitable foundations, and several photographs of meetings that appeared to show her with men Jack did not recognize. The photographs were shot from a distance, most likely through a long lens. In one, Camille left a restaurant beside Andrew Vale, her attorney. In another, she entered a medical building with Dr. Wexler. Alone, the images proved almost nothing. Arranged inside a binder labeled motive and leverage, they became something more deliberate.

"This is not evidence collected for litigation," Jack said from the hallway. Ramirez looked back at him. "Explain." He kept his hands in his pockets and his feet outside the threshold. "Litigation files are messy because real disputes are messy. These are curated. Someone built an argument before there was a lawsuit, and every argument points in the same direction: the heirs are compromised, the widow is conflicted, and someone else should receive or control the estate."

Ramirez nodded slowly. "Northstar."

"Or whoever stands behind it."

The second crate contained corporate documents. Some were public filings. Others were internal materials that likely came from Hale Global or one of its subsidiaries. There were organizational charts showing the ownership structure of Victor Hale's private companies, trust diagrams showing how assets moved at death, and handwritten notes that appeared to map several routes by which voting shares could be transferred away from the family if the original estate plan failed. Jack watched Ramirez remove one page and hold it under the light. A phrase had been underlined twice: moral disqualification event.

"That phrase appeared in Brooks's sample language," Jack said. Ramirez placed the page into an evidence sleeve. "Then Brooks is going to need that lawyer you keep pretending you are not becoming." Jack did not answer, partly because she was right and partly because silence was the only response that did not create a commitment.

The small cardboard container on the shelf changed the mood of the search. Inside were medical supply invoices, disposable syringes, sealed sterile pads, and a printed pharmacology article concerning neuromuscular blocking agents. There was no vial of poison, no convenient label, no confession hidden beneath the supplies. The absence was almost irritating. Whoever assembled the box had included enough material to suggest knowledge, but not enough to prove use. Ramirez had every item photographed, sealed, and documented, her face giving away nothing.

The final crate contained documents related to Richard Mercer. That discovery slowed the entire room. The first folder held copies of his professional biography, bar records, speaking engagements, and articles he had written about estate integrity and testamentary fraud. The second contained photographs of him entering and leaving Mercer, Hale & Dalton, including several taken from across the street in the weeks before he disappeared. The third contained a floor plan of his condominium building, marked with elevator locations, security desk sight lines, and camera placements. Ramirez stood over the open crate for a long moment before instructing the technician to photograph everything twice.

Jack felt the anger arrive quietly. He had known Richard Mercer only professionally, but there was something deeply personal about seeing a man reduced to surveillance angles and access points. The file proved preparation. It proved Mercer had not been taken because he happened to notice something at the wrong moment. Someone had studied him, measured his routines, and decided his life was an obstacle to be managed.

Ramirez opened the last folder in the Mercer crate and found a printed sheet containing three columns. The first listed dates. The second listed locations. The third contained short notes. One date matched the night Mercer vanished. Beside it, someone had typed: confirm original before removal. Jack stepped forward without entering the unit. "Detective," he said carefully, "you need to look at the entry above that." Ramirez shifted the page under the light. The prior entry was dated two days earlier and read: pressure test through E.B.; if unstable, isolate.

Ramirez looked at him. "E.B. is Ethan Brooks."

"That would be my concern."

"Pressure test how?"

Jack thought of Brooks receiving threats, taking money, forming Northstar, and keeping documents because fear had finally overcome ambition. "Maybe they wanted to see whether he would talk. Maybe they already knew he was weak enough to be blamed." Ramirez sealed the page and handed it to the technician. "Then we find him before they decide which one he is."

The search continued for another hour. Each discovery pointed toward planning, but none solved the central question of who directed it. Caleb Rusk appeared throughout the documents as intermediary, organizer, and possible architect, yet Jack saw too many gaps to accept him as the final answer. Men like Rusk built schemes for money, influence, or access. This felt larger than a consultant's private hustle. It had legal sophistication, medical knowledge, corporate intelligence, family surveillance, and enough resources to compromise a secure law firm.

Outside the unit, Larkin watched from the hallway, his earlier irritation completely gone. "I had no idea any of this was in there," he said. Ramirez looked at him without accusation. "Most storage facilities do not." He nodded uneasily. "People rent units for furniture, business records, tools, Christmas decorations. Sometimes they hide things from ex-spouses or creditors. I never thought someone would store something like this." Jack looked back at the crates. "People hide what they are not ready to destroy."

Ramirez arranged for the entire contents of Unit 417 to be transported to the evidence warehouse under seal. She also requested immediate patrol checks on Ethan Brooks's office and residence. Jack called Brooks three times while the officers packed the crates, but the calls went to voicemail. He then called Margaret and asked whether Brooks had contacted the firm, but she had heard nothing. By the time Jack stepped outside, the cold air felt sharper than before, and the lights over the loading dock buzzed above the white van's empty space on the surveillance still.

Ramirez joined him near the front of the facility after the evidence van pulled away. "Brooks is not answering," she said. Jack slipped his phone into his coat pocket. "That may mean he is frightened, asleep, avoiding calls, or already gone." Ramirez looked toward the road. "You are not as comforting as you think." He glanced at her. "I rarely aim for comforting." She folded her arms against the wind. "I am sending units to his home and office. If he is there, we bring him in as a witness before someone makes him unavailable."

Jack did not argue. The storage unit had turned Ethan Brooks from a careless lawyer into a man placed on a board by players he might not understand. Whether he had helped willingly at first mattered less urgently than whether he could survive long enough to explain what he knew. The phrase pressure test through E.B. remained in Jack's mind with the cold precision of a diagnosis. Someone had tested Brooks, and tests usually led to decisions.

His phone finally rang as Ramirez began walking toward her car. Jack recognized Brooks's number and answered on the first ring. The line crackled with wind and movement, and Brooks's voice came through low and strained. "I did not know where else to call," he said. Jack signaled Ramirez, who turned immediately. "Where are you, Ethan?" he asked, keeping his voice calm. Brooks breathed hard before answering. "I found something in my apartment that was not mine, and I think whoever put it there wanted the police to find it before I did."

Jack pressed the phone tighter against his ear while Ramirez moved closer to listen. He asked Brooks what he had found, expecting documents, cash, perhaps a weapon planted clumsily enough to frighten him into running. Brooks did not answer for several seconds. When he did, his voice had flattened into shock. "It is a vial," he said. "It has Victor Hale's name on a prescription label, and I have never seen it before in my life."

Jack looked at Ramirez, and neither of them needed to say what the discovery meant. The storage unit had shown them the plan. Brooks's apartment, if he was telling the truth, had just become the place where someone intended the plan to become a prosecution.

11

THE NEXT MORNING BEGAN with a court order and a mistake. The order arrived first, entered at 7:18 a.m., granting the limited carrier subpoena and confirming that all responsive records would be produced to Robert Chen for sealed handling before counsel received anything. Judge Harrow's language was precise, giving Chen authority to obtain subscriber identity, activation records, billing information, call and text metadata, and account notes for the relevant period. Content remained excluded absent further order, and the court repeated that Lily Cole was not to be questioned about the device by either parent. Jack read the order twice, then forwarded it to Caleb with a single instruction to serve it cleanly and document every step.

The mistake arrived seven minutes later from Marissa Cole. It came as a text message to Ethan, and Ethan did exactly what Jack had ordered him to do with any questionable communication. He did not answer. He took a screenshot and sent it to Jack. The message was short and sounded ordinary until read against the order. Lily says she left something in your living room. Please do not make her feel worse about the phone.

Jack stared at the last five words. They were not enough to prove Marissa had discussed the phone with Lily. They were enough to create a problem. The court had forbidden both parents from discussing the device with the child, and the timing made the message impossible to ignore. He sent Ethan a reply telling him not to respond, not to mention the text to Lily if she contacted him, and not to call Marissa. Then he walked into the conference room, where Nora was already placing fresh coffee beside his chair.

"You have the look," Nora said.

"What look?"

"The one that means someone did something avoidable before breakfast."

Jack handed her the phone. Nora read the screenshot and frowned with the weary disapproval of a woman who had seen smart people create unnecessary work for decades. She sent the screenshot to the secure case folder, printed a copy, and placed it in the communications log. Jack appreciated the efficiency because it kept him from saying what he wanted to say. Anger did not make evidence stronger. It only made lawyers easier to bait.

Caleb arrived while Jack was drafting a short email to Claire. He read the text and sat without speaking, which showed he was learning. Mara came in a few minutes later, took the printed screenshot from Nora, and added it to the board under Parent Communications. Amelia arrived last, saw the new line on the board, and stopped long enough for her expression to sharpen. No one asked her opinion. Everyone knew it.

Jack's email to Claire was restrained. He attached the screenshot, cited Judge Harrow's no-discussion order, and asked whether Marissa had discussed the phone with Lily after the court's ruling. He requested confirmation by noon and reminded counsel that Ethan would not respond directly to the message. He copied Angela Morrissey because the issue involved Lily's emotional state and the court's protective order. He did not accuse Marissa of violation. He did not need to, because the question was clear.

Caleb reviewed the email before it went out. "This is cleaner than a motion."

"It may prevent one."

"Do you think she answers honestly?"

"I think Claire understands that silence will read badly."

Mara looked at the board. "Marissa may have slipped. Or Lily mentioned it first."

"Both possibilities stay open," Jack said.

Amelia set her bag on the table. "And if Marissa was warned by someone else to shape Lily's reaction?"

Jack looked at her. "That possibility stays open too."

The answer did not satisfy Amelia, but it did not need to. Jack wanted the record to remain large enough for truth and small enough for court. If Marissa had violated the order, they would raise it. If Lily had raised the phone herself, the court needed to know that too. The point was not to punish Marissa before understanding the facts. The point was to stop adults from making Lily responsible for what the adults had created.

At nine, Caleb served the carrier subpoena with the court order attached. He used the carrier's legal compliance portal, sent a courtesy copy by certified mail, and logged the service confirmation. Jack made him print everything, including the portal receipt, because electronic systems had a way of becoming unreliable at the exact moment a lawyer needed proof. Caleb did it without complaint. He had stopped treating Jack's paper habits as superstition. Some superstitions, once tested in litigation, became procedure.

Mara spent the morning tracing the device model and SIM activation patterns from public sources. She found nothing dispositive, but enough to suggest the phone had likely been purchased retail rather than through a school or clinic program. The model was inexpensive, prepaid-friendly, and common enough to avoid standing out. That made it less helpful than a device tied to an institution. It also made the account records more important, because the phone had been chosen for ordinary anonymity.

Nora appeared at the conference room door with another printed email. "Claire responded."

Jack took it and read it where he stood. Claire stated that Marissa denied discussing the phone with Lily and said Lily herself had appeared upset after Angela's office addressed the device. Marissa's text, Claire wrote, was meant only to discourage Ethan from making Lily feel responsible if the topic came up during future exchanges. Claire acknowledged the message was poorly worded and stated that Marissa would not communicate directly with Ethan about the phone again. She also requested that neither side turn routine co-parenting communications into accusations.

Jack handed the email to Caleb, then to Mara. "Reasonable answer."

Amelia made a sound from the end of the table. "Convenient answer."

"Those overlap sometimes."

"Do you believe it?"

"I believe it is a position Claire can defend."

"That was not my question."

"It was the one that matters right now."

Ethan called five minutes later, and Jack took the call in his office with the door partly closed. Ethan wanted to know whether Marissa had broken the order. Jack told him the answer was not clear and that the safest course was still no response. Ethan did not explode, which Jack marked as another useful development. Anger was still there, and so was the father's instinct to protect Lily by force of will. He was learning that in court, restraint could become a form of protection if it was chosen early enough.

"She keeps getting to say things," Ethan said. "I keep getting told not to."

"You are both under the same order."

"It doesn't feel like it."

"Feeling unequal and being unequal are different issues. Today we document and preserve. If the pattern continues, we ask the court to intervene."

Ethan was quiet. "Lily asked if she can bring her drawings next time."

"What did you say?"

"I told her she can bring whatever she wants as long as her mom and Angela say it's okay."

"That was good."

"I wanted to say she doesn't need permission to draw."

"I know."

"She shouldn't."

"No, she shouldn't."

The conversation ended without resolution, which was the natural shape of most custody calls. Jack returned to the conference room and found Amelia studying the Ramirez article again. Mara had placed a new document beside it, a printout from an old conference website showing Dana Keene listed as a panelist for Family Futures Coalition. The panel title was Supporting Youth Through High-Conflict Resistance. Beneath Dana's name was another name Jack recognized from the previous night's records: Tessa Laird.

"Tessa Laird again," Jack said.

Mara nodded. "She appears in Julia's notes and in the old coalition article. She later consults for Civic Bridge. Public bio says she specializes in narrative strategy for youth-centered litigation reform."

Caleb looked up from his laptop. "Narrative strategy?"

Amelia answered before Jack could. "Message discipline. Media framing. Getting everyone to use the same terms so the public hears a clean story before the facts get messy."

Jack studied the printout. Tessa Laird was not a lawyer, at least not according to the bio, and not a clinician. She occupied a more flexible space. Communications consultant. Advocate. Strategist. People like that could be harmless, even useful, in public policy work. In litigation involving a child, the same skills could become dangerous if they reached witnesses, parents, or professionals before the court had the full record.

"Any link to Lily?" Jack asked.

"Not yet," Mara said. "Only to Dana, Civic Bridge, Family Futures, and the old Ramirez case."

"Then she stays in the outside communications request."

Amelia leaned forward. "Julia said Tessa was around Ramirez."

"Julia has notes that say that."

"Fine. Julia has notes that say that."

"We need more."

"You always need more."

"Yes."

Caleb's email chimed before Amelia could answer. He opened it, read silently, and then straightened. "Carrier acknowledged service. Estimated response by tomorrow afternoon unless expedited review clears sooner."

Jack nodded. "Good."

"There is also a billing-contact field noted in their acknowledgement."

Mara looked over. "Meaning they already see account structure."

"Maybe," Caleb said, then glanced at Jack as if catching himself. "Sorry. Maybe."

Jack gave him a faint nod. "That one was appropriate."

The office settled into work again. Jack reviewed Dr. Warren's prior testimony and marked the exact places where the undisclosed note would matter. She had testified that Lily's distress increased when Ethan resisted recommended care. She had testified that delay could intensify harm. She had not testified that Lily had written a note saying adults were finishing her sentences or that Dr. Warren had received a photo of it weeks earlier. The omission did not automatically make her testimony false. It did make it incomplete in a way a judge would understand.

Mara built a side-by-side chart of Dr. Warren's testimony, the text from Dana, and the petition language Claire had filed. Caleb pulled the transcript excerpts and checked line numbers against the court reporter's rough draft. Amelia worked separately at the far end of the table, tracking Tessa Laird through old nonprofit pages, archived event programs, and public posts. Jack allowed her in the room because she was not viewing sealed child records. He still had Nora place a blank divider folder over protected exhibits every time Amelia stood near them, which annoyed Amelia and pleased Nora.

At noon, Angela Morrissey called. Jack put her on speaker after confirming that only the legal team was in earshot and Amelia had stepped into the hallway. Angela had received Claire's explanation regarding Marissa's text and did not believe immediate court intervention was necessary. She planned to remind both parents in writing that Lily was not to be asked about the phone, the note, her statements, or court consequences. Jack agreed and offered to review proposed language only if Angela wanted input. Angela declined politely, which Jack respected.

Before ending the call, Angela added one more detail. Lily had asked whether both parents would get in trouble if she said the wrong thing. Angela had not asked what wrong thing meant. She told Lily that the court wanted her safe and that adults were responsible for adult decisions. Jack thanked her and wrote the words in his notebook. They were not evidence for a filing yet. They were a warning about the emotional architecture being built around the child.

When Amelia returned, she saw the room's mood and stopped. "What happened?"

Jack closed his notebook. "Angela is reminding both parents about the order."

"That is all?"

"For public purposes, yes."

She held his gaze, understood she was not getting the rest, and returned to her seat. Jack appreciated that more than he said. Amelia could push hard, and she often did, but she knew when sealed material was sealed. She wanted the story. She did not want to become the reason a judge stopped trusting Jack's side of the room.

At two, Sonia Patel produced the district's first set of records. The email arrived with a password-protected download link, a privilege log, and a cover letter that sounded defensive before it reached the second paragraph. The production included attendance records, counseling referral forms, emails between Dana Keene and Dr. Warren, and staff meeting notes. It did not include the original blue folder. Patel stated that the district had not yet located it and had placed Dana's office materials in administrative custody. Jack read that sentence aloud.

Mara's face went flat. "Administrative custody needs a custodian."

Caleb wrote it down. "Request identity of custodian and inventory."

Jack nodded. "And the date the office was secured."

Amelia spoke from the end of the table. "If the folder is missing, Dana had time."

Jack looked at her. "Maybe."

She raised a hand. "I know. Maybe."

They divided the production. Caleb took referral forms. Mara took emails. Jack took staff notes. Nora printed a second copy for physical review and began labeling binders without being asked. The office took on the quiet intensity of document review, the kind of work outsiders imagined as tedious because they did not understand that most cases turned on a sentence someone forgot to hide properly. Jack had built trials from footnotes, timestamps, and bad summaries. A single unguarded phrase could open an entire room.

The first important email came from Mara's stack. Dana had written to Dr. Warren four weeks before the petition: Parent resistance is increasing. Mother is aligned but worried about legal exposure. Child presents mixed language depending on setting. Recommend staged approach and documentation before father re-engagement. Dr. Warren replied the next morning: Agree. Need consistency across support team. Avoid creating space for reversal before stabilization.

Jack read the exchange and felt the case narrow. The language was clinical enough to sound responsible and strategic enough to sound like litigation preparation. Child presents mixed language depending on setting. That sentence should have made every adult slow down. Instead, according to the response, they treated mixed language as something to manage before father re-engagement. Jack did not need to exaggerate it. The words were damaging because they were careful.

Caleb found the next piece. The referral form listed the reason for Horizon referral as acute distress connected to paternal nonaffirmation and resistance. The section for other possible stressors was left blank. School performance decline was noted. Peer conflict was not noted. Online influence was not noted. Family litigation history was not noted. The form did not mention Lily's note to Mrs. Palmer, even though the referral date came after the note had been sent to Dr. Warren.

Nora brought in another printed page from the download. "This one was flagged by the district as possibly privileged, then produced."

Jack took it. It was a staff meeting agenda with handwritten notes in the margin, apparently scanned from a copy found in Mercer's administrative file. One line read: DK: avoid father contact until EW guides language. Another read: MP concerned re note. DK says do not elevate. The initials were not explained, but the surrounding emails made their meaning obvious enough for discovery. Dana Keene. Elise Warren. Margaret Palmer.

Jack placed the page on the table and looked at the others. "We need Mercer."

Mara nodded. "Declaration?"

"First. Deposition if necessary."

Caleb looked at the agenda. "This puts Palmer's concern in a staff meeting."

"Yes."

"And Dana says do not elevate."

"Allegedly," Jack said. "We authenticate before we argue."

Amelia leaned back in her chair. "You are going to make me admire procedure against my will."

"That sounds painful."

"It is."

By four, the conference table was covered in organized stacks. The board now showed a sequence that no longer relied on speculation. Lily writes note. Palmer copies. Dana receives original. Dana sends photo to Warren. Warren responds that ambivalence is expected and father involvement should wait. Referral form omits other stressors. Petition later relies on professional urgency. Court receives none of Lily's qualifying language until Mercer brings the copy.

Jack stood before the board and did not add a conclusion. He did not need to. The sequence spoke in the restrained voice judges trusted. It showed that Lily's full statement had not traveled cleanly. It showed that the adults who claimed to be interpreting her distress had seen material that complicated their interpretation. It showed that father involvement was not delayed merely because Lily feared Ethan. It may have been delayed because adults had already decided how her fear should be understood.

Claire called at four-fifteen. Jack took the call in the conference room with Caleb present. Claire's tone was controlled, but thinner than usual. She had received the district production too. She said she would not oppose Dr. Warren's limited recall and would make Marissa available for a supplemental declaration if necessary. She also said she intended to withdraw any reliance on broad statements in Dr. Warren's first declaration that were not based on direct knowledge.

"That is a significant concession," Jack said.

"It is a clarification."

"Call it what you like."

"I am trying to keep this case from becoming a public execution of everyone who tried to help Lily."

Jack paused before answering. "Then help me find out who edited her before she reached the court."

Claire was silent for a moment. "You think I knew."

"I think you filed what you were given."

"That is not an answer."

"It is the only fair one I have right now."

Her voice softened just enough to sound human. "Marissa is scared too."

"I believe that."

"Do you?"

"Yes. Scared parents can still make bad decisions."

"So can fathers."

"Yes."

The call ended with Claire agreeing to a joint stipulation narrowing the next hearing around three issues: Lily's complete statements, the handling of the note, and the separate phone. She did not agree to discovery into Fairchild beyond what the court had ordered. Jack did not expect her to. It was enough that she had stopped defending the petition as if it were complete. A careful retreat was still a retreat.

At five, Ethan came to the office for a short meeting. Jack had warned him that the documents were under seal and that he would not get every detail. Ethan accepted that with visible effort. He looked older than he had two days before, as if the case had taken a year from him and replaced it with a language he never wanted. Jack gave him the permitted summary: the court had received records showing Lily's note was known before the petition, the note had not been included, and Dr. Warren would likely be questioned again. Ethan listened with his hands folded tightly on the table.

"So they knew she was confused," Ethan said.

"They knew her statements were mixed."

"And they used the part that helped them."

"That is what we are investigating."

Ethan looked at Jack. "Please don't say maybe right now."

Jack let the request stand. "They did not give the court the full picture."

Ethan looked down, and the anger that came over his face was quieter than before. That worried Jack more than yelling would have. Quiet anger often lasted longer and made better plans. Jack reminded him again that he could not contact Dana, Dr. Warren, Marissa, the school, or anyone connected to the case. Ethan nodded. Then Jack made him say it back.

"I won't contact them," Ethan said. "I won't post. I won't talk to reporters. I won't ask Lily about the note or the phone."

Jack studied him. "Good."

"I can still be her father."

"Yes."

"How?"

"Be ordinary. Ask about food, homework, shows, sleep, pencils. Let the court carry the case when she is with you."

Ethan swallowed. "That feels too small."

"It is not small to her."

Ethan nodded slowly. He seemed to receive that in a way he had not received the legal warnings. Jack had seen parents mistake dramatic advocacy for love because it felt more powerful than making dinner. Lily did not need more adults proving points around her. She needed someone who could sit in the same room without turning her pain into testimony.

After Ethan left, Jack stayed at the table with the district production spread before him. Nora dimmed the outer office lights. Caleb packed his laptop, and Mara began photographing the whiteboard for the secure file. Amelia stood near the doorway with her coat over one arm. No one had said much for several minutes. The case had moved, and everyone understood the movement had cost Lily more exposure.

Amelia looked back at the board. "The story is there now."

Jack gathered the staff notes into a sealed folder. "The record is there."

"That's what I meant."

"No, it isn't."

She accepted the correction without argument. Jack appreciated that too. A story could reveal truth, and a record could protect it, but they were not the same instrument. Lily needed the second before anyone earned the right to tell the first.

Jack locked the sealed folder in the cabinet and turned off the conference room light. The whiteboard remained visible through the glass wall, its lines and dates softened by the darkness. They had found the path of Lily's note from a classroom desk to a counselor, from a counselor to a clinician, and from there into a petition that had left her own words behind. The next hearing would not fix that by itself. It would require the adults to answer, on the record, why a child's whole sentence had been treated as less useful than the parts that served the case.

12

THE HEARING CALENDAR ON Friday morning was crowded with the ordinary grief of family court. Parents sat on opposite sides of the hallway, lawyers carried thin files that represented years of conflict, and children were mostly absent because the building had learned that childhood did not belong in those chairs unless there was no other choice. Jack Sullivan arrived early enough to watch the room form around the day's anxieties. Claire Whitcomb stood near the clerk's counter with Marissa Cole beside her, speaking quietly and without visible strain. Ethan sat in the conference room Jack had reserved downstairs, away from cameras, away from hallway contact, and away from the temptation to read Marissa's face as evidence.

Caleb sat beside Jack in the courtroom with two binders, a laptop, and the transcript excerpts organized by witness. Mara remained in the hallway to coordinate with Mrs. Palmer and Daniel Mercer, both of whom had arrived under subpoena and both of whom looked as if they would rather be anywhere else. Amelia was not in the courtroom, by Jack's instruction and her reluctant agreement. She had taken a seat in the public overflow area downstairs, where she could observe the public portions of the proceeding without placing herself near sealed material or witnesses. Jack had not needed to say that her presence at counsel table would create the wrong record, because by now she understood the line even when she disliked it.

Judge Harrow took the bench at nine-thirty exactly. The room rose, settled, and grew quiet in the way courtrooms do when everyone remembers that procedure has a sound. The judge looked through the file before speaking, her face giving away very little. On her desk sat the sealed supplemental filing, the district production index, Horizon's limited production, and the forensic preservation receipt from Robert Chen. The case had become heavier in paper since the first hearing, and Jack could see that the judge felt the added weight.

"We are here on the continued emergency request and the court's limited inquiry into supplemental matters," Judge Harrow said. "The court will not revisit every issue from the prior hearing this morning. We will address three areas: the minor child's written note and its handling, the separate mobile device, and whether the court received a complete picture when the emergency petition was filed."

Claire stood first. "Your Honor, petitioner is prepared to proceed within that scope. We continue to object to any insinuation that petitioner or counsel intentionally withheld material information."

Jack stood. "Respondent is prepared to proceed. We are not asking the court to make final credibility findings today. We are asking that temporary orders be based on the complete record, including the portions of Lily's statements that were not presented initially."

Judge Harrow nodded. "That is the proper frame. Call your witness, Mr. Sullivan."

Jack called Margaret Palmer first because the case needed to begin where Lily's own words had begun. Mrs. Palmer entered the courtroom with a careful expression and a canvas tote bag held against her side. She took the oath, sat in the witness chair, and placed both hands on her lap. She looked like a teacher who had spent a career in rooms full of children and now found herself in a room full of adults who had made childhood complicated. Jack gave her a moment to settle before approaching the lectern.

He began with background. Mrs. Palmer had taught art for thirty-two years, twenty-six of them in public schools, and had known Lily Cole as a student in an elective art class. She was not Lily's therapist, not a family member, and not aligned with either parent. She had noticed changes in Lily's classroom work during the semester: fewer colors, fewer faces, then fewer figures altogether. Jack moved slowly through the details, not because he wanted sentiment, but because the judge needed to understand why a note left on a teacher's desk mattered.

"Did Lily Cole leave you a handwritten note?" Jack asked.

"Yes."

"When?"

"Three weeks before the emergency petition, near the end of the school day."

"What did you do with it?"

"I read it after class. I became concerned and made a copy before giving the original to Ms. Keene, the school counselor."

Claire stood. "Objection to any testimony about the contents unless the note is received under seal and subject to the court's privacy order."

Judge Harrow looked at Jack. "Mr. Sullivan?"

"We agree the contents should remain under seal. I intend to ask limited questions about handling and general subject matter unless the court wants to review specific language in camera."

"The objection is sustained as to public recitation of the note's contents. You may ask about handling and the witness's understanding in general terms."

Jack nodded. That ruling was expected and useful. He did not need Mrs. Palmer to read Lily's private words into a public courtroom. The judge already had the note. What mattered now was whether the adults who received it treated it as important, inconvenient, or both. Jack adjusted his notes and continued.

"Why did you make a copy before giving the original to Ms. Keene?"

Mrs. Palmer looked at the judge before answering. "Because I was concerned the note might not be described accurately later."

"Why did you have that concern?"

Claire stood again. "Objection. Relevance and improper reference to unrelated prior matters."

Jack kept his eyes on the judge. "Goes to the witness's reason for preserving a copy and to record handling."

Judge Harrow considered it. "Limited answer. Do not identify unrelated minors or disclose confidential details."

Mrs. Palmer nodded. "Several years ago, I was involved in another school situation where a child wrote something important, and the child's exact words were not given the weight I believed they deserved. I learned from that experience that summaries can change meaning."

Jack let the answer breathe without making it dramatic. "After you gave the original note to Ms. Keene, did you discuss it with her?"

"Yes."

"What did Ms. Keene say?"

Claire objected on hearsay, and Jack responded that Dana's statements were not offered for the truth but to show handling, notice, and the basis for later actions. Judge Harrow allowed limited testimony. The rhythm of objections was normal, and Jack did not resent it. Claire was preserving her record. Jack was building his.

Mrs. Palmer said Dana described Lily's note as ambivalence. She said Dana believed ambivalence was expected when a child was receiving inconsistent support at home. She said Dana did not believe the note should be elevated because it could intensify what Dana called resistance dynamics. Mrs. Palmer's voice stayed even, though her hands tightened slightly. She was careful not to exaggerate what she remembered, which made Jack trust her more.

"Did you believe the note was a custody preference?" Jack asked.

"No."

"What did you believe it was?"

"A child trying to be heard without hurting either parent."

Claire did not object. The answer was too human to attack safely, and too general to strike cleanly. Judge Harrow wrote something on her pad. Marissa looked down at the table. Jack noticed, then moved on.

Mrs. Palmer testified that she later raised concern during a staff meeting. Her handwritten notes, already lodged under seal, reflected discussion of father involvement, the child's mixed language, and whether the note should be treated as a complicating factor. Jack asked about the margin note that read, MP concerned re note. DK says do not elevate. Mrs. Palmer confirmed that MP referred to her, DK referred to Dana Keene, and the phrase reflected her understanding of what Dana said in the meeting. Claire objected to foundation and completeness, and the judge allowed the answer subject to later authentication by other witnesses.

On cross-examination, Claire was careful. She did not attack Mrs. Palmer personally. She asked whether teachers are trained to assess clinical risk, whether Mrs. Palmer knew all facts considered by Horizon, whether she understood Lily's full therapeutic context, and whether the note could reasonably be viewed as part of a broader pattern of distress. Mrs. Palmer answered each question plainly. She was not a clinician. She did not know everything. She still believed Lily's actual words should have been preserved and disclosed to the professionals and the court with care.

Claire's final question was quiet. "Mrs. Palmer, is it possible that everyone involved was trying to help Lily?"

Mrs. Palmer looked at Marissa, then back to Claire. "Yes. It is possible."

"Thank you."

Jack stood for brief redirect. "Mrs. Palmer, when people are trying to help a child, can they still misunderstand what the child is saying?"

"Yes."

"And if the child's own words are not fully carried forward, does that increase that risk?"

"Yes."

Jack sat down. He had what he needed. Mrs. Palmer had not become an advocate. She had become a witness, and that was far better. Judge Harrow thanked her and told her she remained subject to recall. Mrs. Palmer stepped down with visible relief, and Mara guided her out of the courtroom through the side door.

Jack called Daniel Mercer next. The principal entered with a district lawyer seated behind him, though Sonia Patel remained at counsel table as district counsel for the record. Mercer looked less composed than Mrs. Palmer, and Jack adjusted his examination accordingly. A frightened administrator could become defensive if pushed too hard, and defensive witnesses often buried useful facts beneath institutional language. Jack began with job duties, record policies, and the usual path for student concern documents.

Mercer confirmed that Dana Keene maintained student concern folders in her office, including blue folders used for ongoing support issues. He confirmed that Lily's note was not found in the central student file and that the original had not yet been located. He also confirmed that Dana's office materials were placed in administrative custody after the court ordered preservation. When Jack asked who secured the office, Mercer glanced toward Sonia Patel before answering. An assistant superintendent and a district compliance officer had done it after Dana was placed on leave.

"Why was Ms. Keene placed on administrative leave?" Jack asked.

Sonia Patel stood. "The district objects to personnel details beyond the scope of this hearing."

Judge Harrow looked at Jack. "Narrow it."

"Was Ms. Keene placed on leave in connection with record-handling issues involving Lily Cole?"

Patel objected again, and Judge Harrow allowed the question. Mercer answered yes.

Jack did not press further. He did not need the district's internal reasoning yet. The judge now knew that the counselor at the center of the referral was on leave because of record-handling issues connected to the child whose note had gone missing. That was enough for the present hearing. More detail could come through written discovery, where district counsel would be less able to claim surprise.

Mercer testified that Dana had told him early father involvement could escalate Lily's distress. He testified that Dr. Warren had participated in one staff support call, and that he understood Horizon wanted a staged approach before involving Ethan. He admitted that Ethan was not contacted about the note, the referral, or the staff concerns before the emergency petition. Claire objected that Mercer could not testify to clinical judgments. Jack agreed and clarified that he was asking only what Mercer was told and what the school did in response. Judge Harrow allowed the testimony with that limitation.

On cross, Claire emphasized Mercer's lack of clinical training and the school's duty to protect students who report distress. Mercer agreed with both. Claire asked whether school officials sometimes limit parent contact temporarily when they fear escalation. Mercer said that can occur, though usually under clear procedures and documentation. Claire asked whether he personally intended to conceal information from the court. Mercer said no, and Jack believed him.

When Mercer stepped down, Judge Harrow called a ten-minute recess. Jack returned to the conference room downstairs, where Ethan waited with Nora beside him like a guard assigned by common sense. Ethan stood as soon as Jack entered. Jack motioned for him to sit, then closed the door behind Caleb. He gave Ethan a limited summary because witnesses were still under examination and the court had not ruled. Ethan listened, tense and silent.

"Mrs. Palmer did well," Jack said. "Mercer confirmed the note was not in the central file and the original has not been found."

Ethan rubbed both hands over his face. "They just lost it."

"That is what we are examining."

"They lost the one thing where Lily tried to say what she meant."

Jack sat across from him. "Mrs. Palmer made a copy."

"Thank God she did."

"Yes."

Ethan looked toward the covered window. "Does the judge understand?"

"She understands the record is incomplete."

"That's not the same."

"It is the court version of beginning to understand."

Nora gave Ethan a bottle of water. He took it without drinking. Jack watched him work through the anger again, watched him press it down because the room, the case, and his daughter required it. Ethan was becoming better at restraint. Jack hated that he had to become better so quickly. Family court often punished parents who could not regulate their fear, then asked why the child felt unsafe around them.

The next witness was Dr. Elise Warren. She entered the courtroom with Martin Cho beside her and took the oath with professional composure. Her suit was conservative, her posture controlled, and her expression suggested she understood the stakes had changed since her first testimony. Jack did not dislike her on sight. He rarely found that useful. Most damaging witnesses believed they were helping, and belief could make a person more dangerous than malice.

Jack began with her role at Horizon, her treatment relationship with Lily, and her prior declaration. Dr. Warren confirmed she had submitted the declaration supporting temporary medical decision-making authority for Marissa. She confirmed the declaration did not include Lily's handwritten note to Mrs. Palmer. She confirmed that before signing the declaration, she had received a photograph of the note from Dana Keene. The courtroom remained still as each answer entered the record.

"Why did you not include the note in your declaration?" Jack asked.

Dr. Warren folded her hands. "I did not consider it a clinical record in the formal sense, and I viewed it as consistent with the ambivalence we were already observing."

Jack did not move from the lectern. "You considered the note consistent with ambivalence."

"Yes."

"And your declaration told the court Lily was experiencing distress related to her father's resistance."

"Yes, based on my clinical observations and information available to me."

"Did the note also suggest Lily was distressed by adults interpreting her statements?"

Claire objected, and Cho joined. Judge Harrow looked at the sealed note, then allowed the question in general form without requiring the witness to recite contents. Dr. Warren answered carefully. "The note reflected confusion and distress. In my view, that confusion existed in the context of inconsistent parental responses."

Jack took a breath and slowed the pace. "Did you consider the possibility that adults involved in the process were contributing to the confusion?"

Dr. Warren hesitated. "I considered multiple stressors."

"Where is that reflected in your declaration?"

She looked toward the document in front of her. "It may not be stated in that language."

"Is it stated at all?"

Claire objected that the document spoke for itself. Judge Harrow allowed the answer. Dr. Warren said, "Not specifically."

Jack moved to the text message from Dana. He established that Dr. Warren received a photo of the note three weeks before the petition. He established that Dr. Warren replied, Ambivalence expected. Need to support stabilization before father involvement. The message was displayed only to the court and counsel under seal, not read into the public record beyond the quoted language already authorized. Dr. Warren acknowledged the message. Her voice remained steady, though the room had shifted.

"What did you mean by father involvement?" Jack asked.

"I meant direct involvement in the therapeutic process."

"Not contact with Lily generally?"

"No."

"Your message does not say therapeutic process."

"That was the context."

"Was Ethan Cole told that Lily had written a note expressing mixed or complicated feelings?"

"I did not tell him."

"Did anyone from Horizon tell him?"

"I do not know."

"Did you recommend that he be told?"

"No."

Jack paused, letting the answer rest without ornament. "Why not?"

Dr. Warren looked briefly toward the judge. "Because I believed premature involvement could increase Lily's distress if not handled carefully."

"Premature because he was her father, or premature because he disagreed with the treatment direction?"

Claire objected immediately, and the judge sustained as argumentative. Jack accepted the ruling. The question had done some work even without an answer, and he did not need to fight for it. He rephrased in the proper shape.

"What factors made you believe Ethan Cole should not be informed of the note at that time?"

Dr. Warren listed Lily's reported fear, Marissa's concerns, the counselor's observations, and the need for stabilization. Jack wrote each down. Then he asked whether Dr. Warren had spoken with Ethan before forming that view. She had not. He asked whether she had reviewed prior counseling records. She had not. He asked whether she had spoken with Mrs. Palmer. She had not. He asked whether she had considered that Lily might speak differently depending on which adult was present. Dr. Warren said yes, but could not identify where that possibility had been addressed in her declaration.

Claire's cross-examination of Dr. Warren was more repair than attack. She brought out that clinicians often see ambivalence in distressed adolescents, that staged involvement can be clinically appropriate, and that Dr. Warren had not intended to mislead the court. Dr. Warren testified that her goal had been Lily's stability, not litigation advantage. She also testified that she would have provided the note had she understood the court expected all raw child statements rather than clinical summaries. Jack wrote that down. Judges often cared about intent, but they cared more about what they had not been given.

On brief redirect, Jack stood with only one page of notes. "Dr. Warren, if a child says adults are not hearing the full sentence, is a clinical summary enough?"

Claire objected. Judge Harrow overruled.

Dr. Warren looked at the judge before answering. "It depends on the context."

"In an emergency petition asking the court to limit one parent's authority, would the safer course be to disclose the child's actual words under seal?"

Dr. Warren was quiet for several seconds. "Yes."

Jack sat down. That was enough.

The phone issue came next, though no live testimony was taken. The parties stipulated to Chen's preservation receipt, the active SIM, the carrier order, and the fact that Lily had reported not knowing the passcode. Claire insisted that no inference be drawn regarding Marissa, and Jack agreed there was no evidence yet identifying who provided the phone. That agreement mattered. Jack would not let the court think he was overreaching when the stronger evidence remained on the note.

Judge Harrow took a longer recess before ruling. Jack spent it downstairs with Ethan, who had listened to none of the testimony directly because sealed child matters were being discussed. Jack gave him the permitted summary. Dr. Warren admitted she had seen the note and that the safer course would have been to disclose Lily's actual words under seal. Ethan stared at the table for a long time. He did not ask to see the note, and Jack respected the effort it took not to ask.

When court resumed, Judge Harrow spoke slowly. She found that the emergency record previously presented to the court was materially incomplete. She did not find bad faith by any party at that stage, and she declined to make final findings about Dr. Warren, Dana Keene, or Marissa. She ordered that the temporary medical decision-making request remain continued, that no new major treatment decisions occur without further court order or written agreement of both parents, and that Lily continue ordinary supportive counseling only with a neutral provider selected through Angela Morrissey. She further ordered production of the carrier records, continued preservation obligations, and a limited evidentiary hearing the following week.

Ethan lowered his head when Jack told him the ruling. He did not cry, though his face looked close to it. The order did not restore everything. It did not undo what had happened or answer who gave Lily the phone. It did something narrower and therefore more real. It stopped the case from moving forward on a partial version of Lily's voice.

Outside the courtroom, Claire approached Jack while Marissa stood several feet behind her. Her expression was controlled, but the confidence from the first hearing was gone. Jack did not enjoy that. Good lawyers did not need to enjoy an opponent's loss to recognize what had happened. Claire had been handed a record that could no longer support the urgency she had argued.

"I want to discuss a temporary framework before next week," Claire said.

"So do I."

"Neutral counseling, no treatment escalation, no parent discussion, and maybe a structured communication protocol."

"Put it in writing."

"I will."

Claire looked past him toward the hall where Marissa waited. "This is becoming harder on Lily."

"It was already hard on Lily."

Claire looked back at him. For a moment, there was no argument in her face. "I know."

Jack nodded once and walked away. In the hallway, Mara stood with Mrs. Palmer, who looked relieved and shaken. Caleb gathered the binders. Nora texted from the office to say reporters were calling again and she was ignoring them with professional excellence. Amelia stood near the elevators, not approaching until Jack signaled that sealed discussions were over. She read his face before asking anything.

"The judge slowed it down," Jack said.

Amelia let out a small breath. "That matters."

"Yes."

"Dr. Warren?"

"Admitted disclosure under seal would have been safer."

Amelia closed her notebook. "That matters too."

Jack looked toward Ethan, who was standing near the far wall with Caleb beside him. The man looked less like someone who had won and more like someone who had been allowed to keep standing. That was the truth of the morning. No one had won. Lily had been heard a little more completely, and the court had admitted that the first record had not been enough. In family court, that counted as progress because progress was often measured by how much harm could be stopped before anyone claimed victory.

By late afternoon, the written order was entered. Jack read it at his desk while the office moved around him, each person returning to the practical work the ruling had created. Carrier records still had to arrive. Dana Keene still had to be located through counsel. The blue folder was still missing. The next hearing would require a cleaner timeline and witnesses who could withstand cross-examination. Jack placed the order into the binder and labeled the tab Continued Emergency Hearing.

He looked through the glass wall at the whiteboard. Lily's note had traveled farther than anyone intended when she left it on a teacher's desk. It had been copied, minimized, photographed, summarized, omitted, and finally placed before a judge. Jack did not know yet whether the adults around Lily had acted from fear, ideology, ambition, or a confused mixture of all three. He only knew that her words had survived because one teacher made a copy before the system could turn them into something easier to use. That was not justice yet. It was the first piece of truth given legal custody long enough to breathe.

13

The carrier records arrived Monday morning through Robert Chen, sealed, indexed, and accompanied by a declaration that said less than everyone wanted and more than enough to move the case again. Jack Sullivan read the cover page before allowing anyone else near the packet. The subscriber name was not Marissa Cole, Ethan Cole, Horizon Youth Wellness, Civic Bridge, Fairchild, or the school district. The account had been opened thirty-four days before the emergency petition at a retail store in Riverside, paid for in cash, and activated with an email address that looked temporary. The billing contact was a name no one recognized: Karen Mills.

Mara Voss took the name without reacting and began building the first search tree. Caleb Price sat beside her, logging the carrier production into the sealed evidence index and separating subscriber information from metadata so the court's privacy order stayed intact. Amelia Grant was not in the room for the sealed review, which she had accepted with visible irritation and no argument. Nora Bell had placed her at the small table near the front window with coffee and a stack of public articles about Family Futures Coalition, which Amelia treated like a banishment and then began reading with professional focus. Jack let her stay there because her discipline on sealed material had earned some trust, and because sending her away entirely would have been less useful.

The call and text metadata was more important than the subscriber field. The phone had communicated with six numbers during the relevant period. Two belonged to Lily's classmates, which Jack immediately placed outside the first review unless the guardian determined otherwise. One belonged to Angela Morrissey's office because Angela's assistant had called the device during preservation to confirm it was powered down and documented. One belonged to Marissa, though the contact occurred only after Angela had taken custody and Claire had asked for logistical confirmation. The last two numbers mattered because they appeared repeatedly before the petition and clustered around the days Lily's note had been photographed, the Horizon referral was completed, and Dr. Warren's declaration was drafted.

Mara traced the first number to a prepaid account with no reliable subscriber. The second number produced a stronger hit through public records, old conference registrations, and one archived nonprofit page. It belonged to Tessa Laird, the communications consultant whose name had already surfaced in Ramirez, Family Futures, and Civic Bridge materials. Jack did not respond when Mara said the name. He looked back at the metadata and counted the contacts again. Twelve calls. Thirty-four text events. No content yet, and no need to pretend metadata was content.

Caleb looked up from the index. "Tessa Laird communicated with the phone before the petition."

"According to carrier records, this number associated with Tessa Laird communicated with the device," Jack said.

Caleb corrected his note. "Right."

Mara pointed to the date column. "The heaviest activity is the night before Lily's note was photographed and the night before Dr. Warren signed her declaration."

Jack leaned over the table. "Any calls after the court ordered preservation?"

"One attempted text after the phone was powered off."

"From Tessa?"

"From the prepaid number."

Jack wrote that down. The unknown prepaid number might be the real control point, or it might belong to a friend, adult, advocate, or someone entirely unrelated. The temptation to complete the pattern was strong, which meant he had to resist it harder. Tessa Laird's number was enough for a subpoena and a hearing question. The unknown number was enough for further process. Neither was enough to accuse someone of coaching a child in open court.

Nora opened the conference room door and stepped inside. "Dana Keene's attorney called."

Jack looked up. "Name?"

"Rebecca Sloane. Employment lawyer. She says Ms. Keene will not speak voluntarily and will respond only to subpoena or court order."

"Expected."

"She also says any suggestion that Ms. Keene destroyed records is defamatory."

"Did anyone suggest that to her?"

"No."

"Then she brought it herself."

Nora placed the message slip on the table. Jack read it and passed it to Caleb. The blue folder was still missing, and Dana now had counsel who was already defending against a destruction theory no one had formally raised. That did not prove anything either. Employment lawyers often arrived speaking defensively because their clients had already been frightened by administrative leave. Still, Jack had learned to pay attention when a lawyer denied the allegation before anyone made it.

"Set a call with Sloane," Jack said. "Attorney to attorney. Today if possible."

Nora nodded. "She offered eleven."

"Take it."

After Nora left, Jack turned back to the carrier records. He prepared a short sealed notice to Claire, Angela, Sonia Patel, and Horizon's counsel stating that the carrier production had been received and that respondent would seek limited discovery relating to numbers associated with Tessa Laird and an unidentified prepaid account. He attached nothing outside the sealed process and revealed no child content because there was none to reveal. The point was procedural notice, not surprise. Surprise was useful in television trials. In real court, surprise often created continuances.

Claire responded within twenty minutes. She objected to any discovery directed at Tessa Laird absent a showing that the communications involved Lily rather than public advocacy or unrelated matters. Jack found the objection predictable and partly fair. Metadata showed contact with the device, not the substance of the contact. The issue was that the device belonged to no known parent, had been found in Lily's backpack, and had been used during the exact period when her statements were being shaped for court. Judge Harrow would understand why that mattered.

At eleven, Jack took Rebecca Sloane's call with Caleb in the room. Sloane had the guarded tone of an employment lawyer who understood family court only enough to distrust it. She stated that Dana Keene was cooperating with the district's internal process, denied destroying or concealing any student record, and objected to any direct contact from counsel, investigators, journalists, or parties. Jack agreed to communicate through her. He did not agree to soften the subpoena.

"I need the original blue folder," Jack said.

"My client does not have it."

"Where is it?"

"She does not know."

"When did she last see it?"

"I am not providing testimony on an informal call."

"Then we will set it through court."

Sloane paused. "Mr. Sullivan, Ms. Keene is not a party to this custody fight. She is a school counselor who acted within district procedures."

"Then the records should show that."

"She is concerned she is being scapegoated."

"She may be. She may also have material information about an omitted child statement, a referral, and communications with third parties."

"That sounds like accusation dressed as neutrality."

"It is discovery dressed as discovery."

The call ended with Sloane agreeing to accept service of a subpoena for records and a limited deposition, subject to objections and a protective order. Jack had expected less, so he accepted the narrow opening. Dana would not speak freely. Her lawyer would try to confine the testimony to school procedures. That was fine. Procedures were exactly where the first failure had occurred.

By noon, the office had shifted from review to drafting. Caleb prepared a subpoena for Tessa Laird's communications with the device number, Dana Keene, Dr. Warren, Horizon, Civic Bridge, Family Futures, and any person acting on behalf of Marissa Cole concerning Lily or the Cole proceeding. Jack cut the first draft in half because it reached too broadly and gave Claire an easy target. The final version requested records tied to specific dates, names, and the device number, with production under seal. Legal realism required discipline, especially when suspicion wanted a larger net.

Amelia knocked once on the glass, then entered without waiting. "I have something public."

Jack covered the sealed carrier packet with a file before she reached the table. "Public means public."

"Yes, counsel. Public means public."

"What is it?"

She placed a printout on the table. "Tessa Laird spoke at a Family Futures panel seven years ago. The archived description says the panel taught advocates how to help professionals maintain consistent language across school, clinical, legal, and media settings in urgent child-protection disputes."

Mara looked at the printout. "That is almost a blueprint."

Jack read the page twice. The language was polished enough to pass as professional coordination and vague enough to avoid admitting improper influence. Consistent language across settings could mean reducing confusion. It could also mean making sure witnesses used the same frame before any judge heard the child's full words. The difference depended on how it had been applied. In Lily's case, the emerging record suggested the frame had arrived before the court had the facts.

"Source?" Jack asked.

"Archived nonprofit event page. I saved the capture data and sent it to Mara."

"Good."

Amelia sat across from him. "Julia says Ramirez had the same panel materials in the old file."

"Julia's lawyer needs to provide that through proper channels."

"She knows."

"Do you?"

Amelia gave him a look. "I am not going to ruin your sealed record."

"I am making sure."

"No, you are managing anxiety by insulting me."

Mara looked up from her laptop. "He does that to everyone."

Jack did not respond. The exchange was close enough to humor to release some of the pressure in the room, and he allowed it to pass. Then he took Amelia's printout and placed it in the public-source file, separate from sealed carrier records. That separation mattered. If the court later reviewed the file, it had to be clear what came from public research and what came from protected evidence. Blending the two would invite unnecessary challenges.

At one-thirty, Angela Morrissey called to report that Lily's neutral counseling intake had been scheduled for the next morning. The provider was Dr. Hannah Patel, no relation to Sonia Patel, a child psychologist with no disclosed connection to Horizon or either parent. Claire had agreed after initially requesting a list of alternatives. Ethan had agreed through Jack within minutes. Angela sounded relieved, though relief in her voice had become a temporary thing.

"She is still anxious," Angela said.

"About the phone?"

"About everything. She asked if the new counselor will tell everyone what she says."

Jack leaned back. "What did you tell her?"

"That there are privacy rules and safety rules, and I would explain them with Dr. Patel before anyone asks her to talk."

"Good."

"She also asked whether she could bring drawings instead of talking."

Jack looked toward the glass wall, where Amelia was pretending not to listen from the outer room. "That may be the healthiest request I have heard all week."

"I thought so too."

After the call, Jack sat quietly for a moment. Children often found safer ways to speak than adults allowed. A drawing did not force a child to choose a parent, accuse someone, adopt professional language, or answer a lawyer's question. It let fear become shape before it became words. The court might never see those drawings, and perhaps it should not. Their value might belong in healing, not evidence.

The peace lasted less than ten minutes. Nora entered with a FedEx envelope addressed to Jack and marked personal and confidential. There was no return name, only a downtown Los Angeles shipping label paid in cash. Nora had already photographed the envelope before bringing it in because she had become part office manager, part evidence technician, and part unwilling participant in a case that refused to behave. Jack put on gloves from Mara's kit before opening it. No one joked about that.

Inside was a thumb drive and a single sheet of paper. The paper contained one sentence printed in twelve-point font: Ask Tessa who wrote Lily's words before Lily said them. Jack placed the page flat on the table and did not touch the thumb drive. Caleb looked pale. Mara reached for an evidence sleeve. Amelia, seeing the room freeze through the glass, came to the door and stopped when Jack held up one hand.

"Do not come in," Jack said.

She stayed where she was. "What happened?"

"Unverified delivery."

Her eyes moved to the table, then to his face. She understood enough to step back.

Mara bagged the thumb drive without inserting it into any office device. "I'll send it to Chen."

"Not Chen," Jack said. "This is outside the court-ordered phone process. We need a separate forensic review and malware check."

"I know a lab."

"Use one with declarations suitable for court."

Mara nodded. "Chain of custody starts with Nora receiving it."

Nora stood at the doorway. "I photographed the courier label and the envelope before I touched it. I can write a declaration."

Jack looked at her. "Of course you can."

"I have worked here long enough to know when trouble needs paperwork."

The sentence on the page did not become truer because it was anonymous. Anonymous tips were often contaminated by motive. They could come from whistleblowers, cranks, rivals, manipulators, or people trying to steer a case toward bad evidence. Jack did not like thumb drives because they invited curiosity and punished it. Still, the wording landed too close to the record they already had. Tessa's number. Lily's mixed language. Adults finishing her sentences. The tip did not create the theory. It pressed on a bruise that was already there.

Caleb looked at Jack. "Do we notify Claire?"

"Not until we know whether it contains anything and can safely describe it."

"Do we notify the court?"

"Not today. We preserve and examine. If it is relevant, authenticated, or dangerous, we disclose appropriately."

Amelia spoke from the doorway, keeping her hands visible and her feet outside the room. "Could be a trap."

"Yes," Jack said.

"Could be someone inside trying to help."

"Yes."

"You hate both options."

"Yes."

That was all the dialogue the moment needed. Mara sealed the drive and paper separately, then created a fresh evidence log entry. Nora wrote a declaration of receipt while the details were still fresh. Caleb photographed the envelope, label, paper, and seal numbers under Mara's direction. Jack watched the process and felt the case shift again, not toward certainty, but toward a more complicated kind of pressure. Someone wanted him looking at Tessa. Someone also knew enough to understand he already was.

By midafternoon, the thumb drive was on its way by bonded courier to a forensic lab Mara trusted. Jack instructed everyone not to speculate about its contents in email, text, or any written communication outside the evidence log. Speculation had a way of becoming discoverable embarrassment. He also instructed Amelia not to write about the envelope, which she found offensive and then agreed to because she understood that publishing an anonymous tip could destroy its legal value. Her restraint looked painful. Jack respected it more for that.

The rest of the afternoon returned to less dramatic work. Caleb filed the subpoena request for Tessa Laird under seal. Mara prepared a declaration summarizing the carrier metadata without revealing content or exceeding the court's order. Jack drafted a proposed stipulation with Claire for neutral counseling and parent communication rules through Angela's office. Nora called Ethan and told him the counseling intake was set, then transferred him to Jack when his questions became less administrative and more father.

Ethan sounded tired again. "Lily asked if she has to start over with another doctor."

"What did you tell her?"

"That Dr. Patel is there to help her, and she can go slow."

"Good."

"She asked if she can bring her pencils."

"Say yes."

"Marissa says she wants copies of the drawings."

Jack closed his eyes briefly. "Do not agree to that. Tell her all questions about counseling materials go through Angela and Dr. Patel."

"She said the drawings might matter."

"They might. That does not mean parents get them."

"I don't want to fight over drawings."

"Then do not fight. Redirect to Angela."

Ethan was quiet long enough for Jack to hear traffic on his end. "Everything she touches becomes evidence."

"That is why you need to give her things that do not."

"I'm trying."

"I know."

The call ended with Ethan calmer than when it began. Jack placed the phone on the table and looked at the counseling stipulation again. It now included a sentence stating that Lily's therapeutic materials, including drawings, writings, and expressive work, would not be disclosed to either parent or counsel absent recommendation by the neutral therapist and court order. Claire would likely agree. Marissa might not. The court would.

At five-forty, Claire sent back proposed edits. She accepted the counseling language with one change: both parents could receive general progress updates, not content. Jack accepted immediately. The stipulation was filed by six. Judge Harrow signed it at six-thirty, which told Jack the court was watching the docket closely. By seven, Lily had a protected space that did not belong to Horizon, either parent, or the lawyers. It was not enough, but it was something.

Amelia left after seven, taking only public-source materials and leaving her notes for Mara to scan. Caleb left shortly after, carrying a sealed binder to be locked in his office safe overnight. Nora had already gone home after making Jack promise not to open unexpected mail without calling Mara, a promise he had no difficulty making. Mara remained long enough to confirm the forensic lab had received the thumb drive and would not connect it to any networked system. Then she finally left too, claiming she slept better when no one was mishandling evidence.

Jack stayed alone in the office and reread the anonymous sentence. Ask Tessa who wrote Lily's words before Lily said them. It was a clever sentence, and that made him distrust it. Real whistleblowers sometimes wrote badly because fear crowded their hands. Manipulators often wrote cleanly because they wanted the sentence to land. This one landed exactly where it was designed to land.

He placed the paper into the locked evidence cabinet and turned back to the whiteboard. The board now had three paths running toward Lily: school, clinic, and communications. Dana had handled the note. Dr. Warren had interpreted it. Tessa's number had reached the phone. Somewhere in that triangle, Lily's own words had been treated as raw material instead of testimony from a frightened child. Jack erased nothing this time. He only added one more careful line beneath Tessa Laird's name: Did communication precede language?

The question was awkward, legal, and less satisfying than the anonymous sentence. That made it better. Court did not need clever. Court needed something that could be asked under oath, answered without theatrics, and tested against records. Jack capped the marker and looked at the board until the office lights dimmed around him again. The case was moving closer to the adults who had taught Lily what her fear was supposed to mean, and the closer it moved, the more important it became not to let their methods become his.

14

Dr. Hannah Patel's office was in a converted craftsman house near the edge of downtown, far enough from the courthouse that Jack Sullivan took it as a good sign. The porch had potted lavender, a wooden bench, and a small sign by the door that gave no hint of the kinds of cases that found their way inside. Angela Morrissey had arranged the intake for Lily, and neither parent was allowed to attend beyond transportation and waiting-room logistics. That was the point. For the first time since the case began, Lily would be in a room that did not belong to lawyers, school officials, advocacy groups, or either parent's fear.

Jack did not go inside. He sat in his car across the street because Ethan had asked whether he should be nearby, and Jack had decided nearby was acceptable only if it remained invisible. Ethan had dropped Lily off through Angela's assistant, then left as instructed and parked two blocks away to wait for a call. Marissa had agreed not to come, though Claire had sent a long email confirming that her absence should not be construed as indifference. Jack had answered with one word: Agreed. Sometimes one word kept more peace than a paragraph.

Mara sat in the passenger seat with a tablet on her lap and a cup of coffee balanced in the holder. She had already checked the street twice, not because she expected danger, but because habit was cheaper than regret. Jack watched a mother push a stroller past the office and tried to separate ordinary life from the case that had occupied almost every waking hour. The office door opened once for a delivery driver and once for Angela Morrissey. Then it closed again, and the lavender moved in the breeze as if nothing inside the house mattered to anyone outside it.

"Do you think she'll talk?" Mara asked.

"That is not the goal."

"It is always a goal somewhere."

"Not today."

Mara glanced at him. "You sound certain."

"I'm choosing to be."

She accepted that and returned to her tablet. Jack had read enough child-therapy literature during custody cases to know that first sessions were often more about safety than disclosure. A lawyer wanted facts, sequence, dates, names, and admissions. A child wanted to know whether the next adult would punish honesty by making it useful. Lily had already learned that words could travel. Jack hoped Dr. Patel would teach her that some words could stay.

His phone buzzed with a message from Nora. The forensic lab had completed the initial safety review of the anonymous thumb drive. No malware detected on the forensic workstation. Contents copied to isolated image. Preliminary file index available. Jack read the message twice, then handed the phone to Mara. She read it and looked toward the therapist's office before speaking. Her discipline showed in the fact that she did not ask to leave immediately.

"Lab can send index?" she asked.

"To the secure portal."

"I'll review from the office."

"Not here."

"I know."

Jack texted Nora to hold the report unopened until he returned. Then he placed the phone facedown and looked back at the house. The thumb drive could wait because Lily could not be turned into a scheduling inconvenience. The case had already taught too many adults to prioritize the next document, the next filing, and the next tactical move. Jack refused to add himself to that list while the child sat inside a therapist's office trying to decide whether adults could be trusted with a pencil drawing.

The session lasted forty-eight minutes. Angela came out first and spoke briefly with Dr. Patel on the porch. They were too far away for Jack to hear, which was appropriate. Lily emerged a few minutes later holding a folder against her chest. She looked smaller in daylight than she had in the courtroom, dressed in jeans, a gray sweatshirt, and sneakers with untied laces. Angela's assistant walked with her to the curb, where Ethan pulled up exactly when called and stayed in the driver's seat as instructed. Lily got in, and the car pulled away without anyone waving, staging, or performing care for the benefit of observers.

Jack exhaled only after Ethan's car turned the corner.

Mara noticed. "You were holding that."

"No, I wasn't."

"You lie badly when sleep-deprived."

"Then I should sleep before trial."

"That would create confusion in the office."

Jack started the car and drove back toward Monterey Street. He did not call Ethan right away. If Lily spoke in the car, Ethan needed to hear her as a father, not as a client reporting to counsel. If she said nothing, silence needed room too. Jack gave them twenty minutes before sending a simple text: No need to call unless there is an issue. You did well with logistics. Ethan replied five minutes later: She asked for tacos. I'm taking her. No court talk. Jack read the message and felt a quiet measure of relief that did not change the work waiting at the office.

Nora had the forensic lab report printed and sealed when Jack arrived. Amelia sat at the front table, watching the conference room door as if she could will it transparent. Caleb had already returned from filing a proof of service on Tessa Laird's subpoena request. Mara went straight to the secure laptop and signed into the lab portal. Jack closed the conference room door before opening the report. Amelia remained outside, and this time she did not knock.

The thumb drive contained nine files. Four were PDFs of training materials from Family Futures Coalition, dated across a three-year span. Two were screenshots of text-message threads with numbers partially redacted. One was an audio file labeled StaffPrep_LC.m4a. One was a spreadsheet titled Language Map. The last was a readme file with a note: I copied what I could before access was removed. I am not the one who hurt her.

Caleb read the index and looked at Jack. "That sounds like an insider."

"It sounds like someone wants us to think insider."

Mara nodded. "The metadata may help."

"Maybe. We do not rely on metadata from an anonymous drive without forensic context."

Caleb wrote that down. He had started doing that whenever Jack said something in the tone of a future mistake prevented. Jack noticed and approved. Young lawyers learned as much from what not to trust as from what to believe.

They began with the PDFs. The training materials were polished, branded, and broad enough to look like public-policy education. The slides discussed high-conflict families, youth stabilization, resistance dynamics, and messaging consistency. One slide read: Establish shared language across school, clinical, legal, and caregiver systems to reduce contradictory inputs. Another read: Avoid premature amplification of ambivalence where safety framing has not stabilized. Jack did not speak for a long moment after reading that one.

Mara photographed the screen for the evidence log. "That phrase again."

"Not exact," Jack said.

"Close enough to search."

"Search, not argue."

Caleb pulled up the district production and ran terms through the searchable set: shared language, contradictory inputs, premature amplification, safety framing, stabilization. Hits appeared in emails from Dana Keene, one note from Dr. Warren, and an agenda attachment from a training Dana had attended. None of that authenticated the anonymous drive, but it showed the language existed in independent productions. That mattered. The thumb drive was no longer a lone voice. It was a map pointing to records already in the case.

The spreadsheet came next. It was more troubling because it was specific. Rows listed phrases under three columns: child language, support-team interpretation, court-safe description. Some entries were generic training examples. Others looked uncomfortably close to Lily's situation. I feel trapped became child experiences pressure from resistant parent system. I don't want to hurt either parent became child displays loyalty conflict. I am confused became ambivalence expected during stabilization. Jack did not need anyone to explain the problem.

Caleb sat back from the screen. "This is bad."

"Yes."

"If authentic."

"Yes."

Mara enlarged the file properties. "Created six weeks before the petition. Modified two days before the petition. Author field says TLaird."

"That field can be manipulated," Jack said.

"Of course. It also matches our subpoena target."

Jack nodded. "Document it. Do not conclude."

The audio file remained. Jack disliked audio more than documents because tone seduced listeners into certainty before context arrived. He had seen jurors decide what a speaker meant from one sigh, one pause, one tired inflection. Still, if the file contained what its label suggested, they needed to know. He called Amelia into the room only after covering the sealed carrier records and confirming the anonymous drive materials were not under a court seal yet, though he warned her they were unverified and not for publication.

Amelia stepped in, saw the screen, and became still. "What is that?"

"Anonymous thumb drive index."

"You opened it?"

"Forensic lab did. Isolated review."

She sat down without being invited. "Play the audio."

Jack looked at her. "You are here to listen as a source-development consultant, not as press."

"That is not a real title."

"It is today."

"I understand."

Mara started the audio. The sound quality was uneven, with voices in a room, papers moving, and someone tapping near a microphone. No one identified themselves at first. A woman's voice said Lily was using inconsistent language and that the team needed to avoid giving the father an opening to destabilize progress. Another voice, male, asked whether the note to the art teacher created disclosure issues. A third voice, calmer and more polished, said the note could be framed as ambivalence if handled with proper clinical context.

Jack paused the file after twenty seconds. "We need voice identification before any use."

Amelia looked at him. "That sounded like Tessa."

"You know her voice?"

"I've heard panels."

"That is not identification."

"I know."

He resumed the audio. The polished voice continued, explaining that the court did not need raw uncertainty, only clinically relevant risk language. Another voice asked whether

Marissa was comfortable with that. Someone replied that Marissa wanted Lily safe and would follow guidance if the professionals stayed consistent. Then the recording caught a sentence that made Caleb look up sharply. The polished voice said, "The child's words are not the message. The message is what the words mean when placed in the right frame."

Jack stopped the audio again. The room stayed quiet.

Mara spoke first. "That sentence was not accidental."

"No," Jack said.

Amelia's face had gone hard. "That is the whole case."

"It is a file from an anonymous drive."

"It is still the whole case."

"It is a lead until authenticated."

She leaned back, frustrated enough to be silent. Jack appreciated the restraint. The file, if real, could change the case dramatically. It could show that Lily's statements had been discussed in terms of framing before the petition reached the court. It could identify adults who believed raw uncertainty should be translated into risk language. It could also be edited, incomplete, illegally recorded, or seeded by someone with motives that would make it unusable.

Caleb looked at the audio timeline. "California consent issue."

"Yes," Jack said. "If recorded without consent, admissibility gets complicated. Criminal exposure too."

Mara nodded. "There are exceptions, but we should assume problems until counsel reviews."

"Do not distribute the file. Do not quote it in any email. Memo only says anonymous drive contains audio purporting to capture meeting regarding LC, requiring forensic authentication and legal review."

Caleb wrote the instruction in his notebook. "Got it."

Amelia looked at Jack. "Can we use it to find the meeting?"

"Yes. That is the safer route."

"How?"

"Calendar entries. Emails. Conference links. Phone records. People present. Room noises if needed. The recording points to records that may be admissible even if the recording is not."

Mara added, "And if someone on the call saved meeting notes, those are discoverable."

Jack turned to Caleb. "Subpoena language for Tessa now includes meeting notes, agendas, recordings, drafts, language maps, and communications concerning Lily's note or any description of Lily's statements."

"Under seal?"

"Yes."

Amelia stood and walked to the whiteboard. She did not touch it. Jack watched her read the sequence from Lily's note to Dana's text to Dr. Warren's omission to Tessa's number to the anonymous drive. The board no longer looked like a theory. It looked like a system that had forgotten a child was not a document to be edited.

Nora entered with a message from Claire. She had signed the neutral counseling stipulation addendum and wanted confirmation that Lily's drawings would not be requested by either side. Jack answered immediately and agreed. Then, after a moment, he asked Nora to call Ethan and remind him of the same rule. It was not that he distrusted Ethan. It was that good rules protected everyone better when repeated before anyone broke them.

By two-thirty, the lab sent a supplemental note. The audio file appeared to be unedited at a basic waveform level, though deeper forensic analysis would take longer. File metadata suggested it had been recorded on a common smartphone application and exported two days later. The creation date matched the day before Dr. Warren signed her declaration. The device identifier was not available from the file alone. The lab could not determine who recorded it.

Mara read the note aloud. Jack listened without moving. Preliminary authenticity was not admissibility. Lack of visible edits did not answer consent. Matching dates did not prove speakers. Still, the file had not immediately collapsed under technical review. That meant it needed to be handled as potentially significant, which was always more work than finding out something was useless.

At three, Jack called Claire. He did not mention the audio's contents. He told her his office had received anonymous electronic materials purporting to relate to communications concerning Lily's statements and that the materials were being forensically reviewed. He said he would not disclose unverified material publicly or use it in court without proper foundation. He also said the existence of the materials required immediate preservation of any meetings, recordings, drafts, language summaries, or communications involving Tessa Laird, Dana Keene, Dr. Warren, Marissa, Horizon, Civic Bridge, or any consultant discussing Lily. Claire listened without interrupting.

When she finally spoke, her voice was careful. "Are you accusing my client of participating in a recorded strategy meeting?"

"No. I am telling you what must be preserved."

"Do you have a recording?"

"I have anonymous electronic material under review."

"That is not an answer."

"It is the answer I can give responsibly."

Claire was quiet. "Send the preservation demand in writing. Copy all counsel. Do not send the material."

"I do not intend to."

"Good."

The call ended with professional restraint and no trust. Jack sent the preservation demand within ten minutes, narrow enough to be defensible and broad enough to prevent anyone from claiming they did not understand the categories. He copied Claire, Martin Cho, Sonia Patel, Rebecca Sloane, Angela Morrissey, and Victor Hale for Fairchild. He did not copy Amelia. She saw the email later only after Jack printed a redacted version for the public-source file, which made her glare at him and then return to work.

Ethan arrived at four-thirty for a scheduled meeting. Jack did not tell him about the audio because it was unverified and potentially inadmissible. He told him the investigation had produced additional leads involving how Lily's words may have been interpreted before court. Ethan wanted more, and Jack refused without sounding apologetic. Clients did not need every dangerous fact the moment a lawyer learned it. They needed enough to comply with orders and make informed decisions.

"Is Lily in more danger than yesterday?" Ethan asked.

Jack considered the question before answering. "No immediate safety information suggests that."

"That sounds lawyerly."

"It is."

"Can you say it like a person?"

Jack folded his hands. "We found information that may help explain what happened. It does not mean you should act differently tonight."

Ethan nodded slowly. "So I do nothing."

"You parent. That is not nothing."

Ethan looked down at his hands. "She texted me a picture of tacos."

Jack almost smiled. "That is good."

"She put the pencils next to the plate so I would see them."

"Did you respond?"

"I said those tacos look serious."

"That was safe."

"It was also true."

For a few minutes, the case stepped back and allowed something ordinary to stand in the room. Jack did not force it into meaning. He did not tell Ethan the picture mattered legally. He did not turn pencils into symbolism or tacos into progress. He let a father keep one small moment unclaimed by the file.

After Ethan left, Amelia found Jack in his office. She closed the door halfway, a courtesy he noticed. The late sun cut across the floor and left the room in uneven light. She held the public printout about Tessa Laird, not the anonymous-drive notes. That was another courtesy.

"You know the audio is bigger than the custody petition," she said.

"I know it may be."

"Fairchild, Civic Bridge, Family Futures, Horizon. If they are building language frameworks for litigation, this is not just one father."

"Maybe."

"You still won't say it."

"I will not say what I cannot prove."

Amelia sat in the chair across from him. "You're afraid of becoming like them."

Jack looked at her then. She had not said it sharply. That made the sentence harder to dismiss. He thought of the anonymous note, the spreadsheet, the recording, and the polished voice explaining that a child's words were not the message. He had spent the week fighting people who treated language as a tool for control. He would not answer that by treating language the same way.

"Yes," he said.

Amelia nodded, as if she had expected the answer and respected it more because he gave it plainly. She stood without pushing further. "Then prove it right."

After she left, Jack returned to the conference room and looked at the whiteboard. The anonymous sentence was not written there. Neither was the audio quote. He had chosen questions instead of slogans, because questions could be asked under oath and answered against records. The next hearing would not be won by outrage, no matter how justified outrage felt. It would be won, if it could be won, by showing the court how Lily's own words moved through adult hands until they became something more useful to everyone except Lily.

15

The next morning, Jack Sullivan made the office remove three arrows from the whiteboard. Mara did it with an expression that suggested the arrows had earned their place. Caleb looked relieved because he had never liked how crowded the board had become. Amelia Grant stood near the window with a cup of coffee, watching the erasures as if Jack were weakening the case in real time. Nora Bell watched from the doorway and said nothing, which usually meant she agreed with Jack and did not want to reward him by saying so.

The arrows connected Tessa Laird to Dana Keene, Dana Keene to Dr. Warren, and Dr. Warren to the emergency petition. Jack did not remove the names, the dates, or the documents. He removed only the lines that made the board look more certain than the record allowed. Tessa's number had contacted the separate phone, Dana had sent Lily's note to Dr. Warren, and Dr. Warren had omitted the note from her declaration. Those were facts. The lines between motives were still being built.

Amelia finally spoke. "You are making it look weaker."

"I am making it look accurate."

"Accurate can be weak."

"In court, inaccurate is weaker."

Mara capped the marker and stepped back from the board. "He's right."

Amelia looked at her. "You are becoming impossible."

"I was hired that way."

Jack ignored both of them and placed a new heading above the middle column: Admissible Path. Beneath it, he wrote note, transfer, interpretation, omission, device, third-party contact. It was plain language, almost dull, and exactly what he wanted. The next evidentiary hearing would not be about whether everyone in the room believed Lily had been manipulated. It would be about whether Jack could show the court how her words moved from a classroom desk into a legal request that nearly stripped Ethan of decision-making authority.

Caleb had already prepared a witness outline for Dana Keene's limited deposition. Rebecca Sloane had agreed to produce Dana for two hours under protective order, with objections preserved and no questions outside Lily's case unless tied to the court's discovery order. Sonia Patel would attend for the district. Claire had reserved the right to appear but had not confirmed. Jack expected her to appear, because good lawyers rarely let the center of a case talk without someone listening.

The deposition was scheduled for one o'clock in Jack's conference room. Jack had chosen his office rather than a court-reporting suite because the documents were already secure, the recording setup was reliable, and the atmosphere might keep Dana from feeling ambushed. He did not want her cornered. Cornered witnesses either collapse or perform. Jack wanted neither. He wanted her comfortable enough to explain herself and formal enough to remember she was under oath.

Before the deposition, Ethan called from his truck. He was parked outside work because he said he could not go in until he heard whether Lily's counseling intake had gone well. Jack had no more information than Angela had already provided. Lily had attended. She had brought pencils. Dr. Patel had reported only that the session occurred and that she would continue under the court's privacy terms. Ethan wanted more because every parent would want more.

"She's my daughter," Ethan said. "I'm not asking for secrets. I just want to know if she's okay."

"I understand."

"That doesn't answer me."

"No, it doesn't."

"So what am I supposed to do with that?"

"Go to work. Answer your phone if she calls. Do not make her responsible for making you feel better."

Ethan was quiet for a moment. "That hit harder than I liked."

"It was supposed to."

"I keep wanting her to tell me she's okay so I can breathe."

"That is natural. It is also too much weight for her."

Ethan exhaled slowly. "I hate how much of this I understand only after you say it."

"That is why you called."

Jack ended the call after making sure Ethan had no immediate issue. He sat with the phone in his hand for a few seconds before setting it down. Ethan was learning restraint in the most painful classroom available. That mattered because the case was moving toward adults who had failed to show it. If Ethan became the loudest adult in Lily's life, even for good reasons, he would give the other side a language the record no longer supported.

At noon, Nora ordered sandwiches no one had asked for and placed them in the conference room with the severity of a court order. Amelia tried to take one into the hallway, and Nora told her the wrappers stayed out of sealed review areas. Amelia obeyed, which Jack found remarkable. Mara reviewed the anonymous-drive forensic update while eating with one hand. Caleb reviewed the deposition notices and exhibits with the nervous care of someone who knew Jack would ask for a page and expect it to appear before the sentence ended.

The forensic lab had not identified the source of the thumb drive. It had confirmed that the audio file showed no obvious signs of splicing, though the report cautioned that absence of evidence was not proof of full authenticity. The spreadsheet metadata still listed TLaird as the author field, and portions of the spreadsheet language matched phrases in district emails independently produced by Sonia Patel. Jack marked those matches for potential impeachment only. He would not lead with the anonymous files. He would use the verified records to ask questions, then see whether Dana gave the anonymous materials a place to stand.

At twelve-fifty, Dana Keene arrived with Rebecca Sloane and Sonia Patel. Dana was younger than Jack expected, mid-thirties, with a navy blazer, simple earrings, and the guarded expression of someone who had spent the last week being told her career might become evidence. She did not look like a villain. Jack rarely trusted that category anyway.

Harm often came through people who believed their intentions should excuse their methods.

The court reporter swore Dana in at one. Jack placed the first exhibit in front of her: her job description. He began with background, education, licensure, prior employment, and her role at San Aurelio Unified. Dana answered clearly, though Sloane objected several times to scope and relevance for the record. Jack kept his tone calm. Depositions rewarded patience because the transcript remembered everything and forgave nothing.

Dana confirmed she had referred Lily to Horizon. She confirmed she had received the original note from Mrs. Palmer. She confirmed she had photographed the note and sent it to Dr. Warren. She confirmed the original was placed in a blue student concern folder in her office. When Jack asked where the folder was now, Dana looked at her lawyer before answering. Sloane objected to form and instructed her to answer only if she knew.

"I don't know where it is now," Dana said.

"When did you last see it?"

"The week before the petition."

"Where?"

"In my office."

"Was it in the blue student concern folder?"

"Yes."

"Did you remove it from that folder?"

"No."

"Did anyone ask you to remove it?"

"No."

Jack did not press harder. Not yet. Dana's answers were clean and rehearsed enough to be useful later if contradicted. He moved to the staff meeting agenda. Dana identified her own initials, Dr. Warren's initials, and Mrs. Palmer's initials. She agreed that Mrs. Palmer had raised concern about Lily's note. She disputed the margin note stating DK says do not elevate as incomplete.

"What is incomplete about it?" Jack asked.

Dana sat straighter. "I did not mean ignore it. I meant it should be handled through the appropriate support process rather than turned into a custody issue by people without clinical training."

Jack nodded as if the answer were entirely reasonable. "Who were the people without clinical training?"

"Mrs. Palmer is an art teacher."

"Anyone else?"

"The principal. School staff generally."

"Ethan Cole?"

Sloane objected. Dana paused. "I was concerned Mr. Cole would react strongly and increase Lily's distress."

"Had you spoken with Mr. Cole about the note?"

"No."

"Had you spoken with him about Lily's distress?"

"No."

"Then what was the basis for your concern about his reaction?"

Dana's answer came more slowly. "Lily had expressed fear about how he would respond. Marissa had expressed concern. Dr. Warren believed father involvement should be staged."

Jack let the answer sit. It was the same structure they had seen elsewhere. Lily's fear, Marissa's concern, Dr. Warren's interpretation, and Dana's process reinforcing all of it. No direct contact with Ethan. No broader evaluation. No place where Lily's mixed language stopped the train long enough for someone to ask whether the track had been laid correctly.

He moved to the text message: Parent resistance is increasing. Mother is aligned but worried about legal exposure. Child presents mixed language depending on setting. Dana confirmed she wrote it. She explained that mixed language meant Lily used different words depending on whether she was in a school setting, a clinical setting, or speaking informally. Jack asked whether that concerned her. Dana said yes. He asked whether mixed language could mean a child was being influenced by more than one adult. Dana said it could.

"Did you investigate that possibility?" Jack asked.

"I assessed it within my role."

"What did that involve?"

"Conversations with Lily, consultation with Dr. Warren, and coordination with Marissa."

"Any conversation with Ethan?"

"No."

"Any conversation with Lily's pediatrician?"

"No."

"Any conversation with Mrs. Palmer after she raised concerns?"

"One brief conversation."

"Any written assessment analyzing whether Lily's mixed language reflected pressure from adults other than Ethan?"

Dana hesitated. "Not in those words."

"In any words?"

Sloane objected. Dana answered anyway. "No formal written assessment."

Jack turned a page in his outline. "You attended a training titled Emergency Family Intervention: Legal Tools for Resistant Parents."

Dana glanced at Sloane. "Yes."

"Funded by Fairchild Family Foundation?"

"I believe Fairchild was one sponsor."

"Presented through Civic Bridge?"

"I don't remember the exact host."

Mara, sitting beside Caleb, quietly slid the event program to Jack. Jack placed it in front of Dana. She reviewed it and acknowledged the program listed Civic Bridge as host and Fairchild as sponsor. Her face remained controlled, but her voice tightened. Jack kept the pace steady. The transcript would show the documents better than a raised voice ever could.

"Was Tessa Laird a presenter at that training?" Jack asked.

"Yes."

"Did you have any communications with Ms. Laird regarding Lily Cole?"

Sloane objected sharply. "Scope, privacy, and assumes facts not established."

Jack looked at Dana, not Sloane. "You may answer unless instructed not to."

Sloane did not instruct her not to answer.

Dana said, "Not directly about Lily as a client or student."

Jack wrote down directly. "Did you communicate with Ms. Laird about the Cole matter?"

Dana's mouth tightened. "I may have discussed general process concerns."

"What does that mean?"

"I asked for guidance on managing communications around a sensitive school-family situation."

"Did you identify Lily by name?"

"No."

"Did you identify Ethan Cole?"

"No."

"Did you identify Marissa Cole?"

"No."

"Did you provide details specific enough for Ms. Laird to understand the family involved?"

Dana took a breath. "I don't believe so."

Jack marked the answer. I don't believe so was not no. He moved carefully because Sloane was watching for overreach. He asked Dana whether she had Tessa's phone number. She did. He asked whether she had ever used Tessa to coordinate language around school, clinical, and legal responses. Dana said Tessa provided communication tools from trainings, not case strategy. Jack placed the public training slide in front of her and asked whether the language looked familiar. Dana said yes.

Then Jack placed the spreadsheet excerpt from the anonymous drive in front of her without identifying the source. He had redacted anything not needed for the question and marked it as an unverified document for identification only. Sloane objected immediately, asking where it came from. Jack said he was not offering it as evidence and was asking only whether Dana recognized the language or format. Sonia Patel objected for the district as well. Jack agreed the objections could stand and asked a narrower question.

"Have you ever seen a document referred to as a language map?" Jack asked.

Dana's face changed. It was small, but everyone at the table saw it.

Sloane leaned toward her. "Take your time."

Dana took a sip of water. "I have heard the term."

"From whom?"

"I don't remember."

"At a training?"

"Possibly."

"From Tessa Laird?"

"Possibly."

"Did you use a language map in connection with Lily Cole?"

"No."

"Did anyone else use one in connection with Lily Cole?"

"I don't know."

Jack did not show the spreadsheet again. The answer had given him enough to subpoena the term directly and ask Tessa under oath. Dana recognized the concept, linked it possibly to Tessa, and denied using it for Lily. That denial was now locked into a transcript. If the thumb drive or future production showed otherwise, the denial would matter.

After a short break, Jack asked about the separate phone. Dana denied giving Lily a phone. She denied knowing who did. She denied communicating with Lily through any device other than school-approved systems. Jack showed the carrier metadata identifying calls between Tessa's number and the device, with numbers partially redacted as required. Dana said she did not know about those contacts. Her surprise appeared genuine, though Jack did not rely on appearances.

Sloane's tone sharpened near the end. "Mr. Sullivan, are you suggesting Ms. Keene conspired with outside advocates to coach a child?"

Jack looked at the court reporter, then at Sloane. "I am asking questions authorized by court order about communications involving Lily's statements, referral, and the emergency petition."

"That is not an answer."

"It is the only answer appropriate for a deposition."

Dana looked down at her hands. For the first time, she seemed less guarded than frightened. Jack noticed and adjusted. A frightened witness could become more truthful or more loyal to the people who frightened her. He did not know which direction Dana would go. He softened his voice without softening the question.

"Ms. Keene, did anyone tell you not to elevate Lily's note because it would complicate the emergency petition?"

Dana stared at the table. Sloane objected. Sonia Patel objected. No one instructed her not to answer.

Dana said, "Not in those words."

Jack waited a moment. "What words?"

Dana swallowed. "Tessa said raw uncertainty could be weaponized by a resistant parent."

The room went still in the way deposition rooms do when a witness finally gives a sentence no one can unhear. Jack did not react. Caleb's pen moved carefully. Mara's eyes stayed on

Dana. Sloane leaned back, no longer objecting, perhaps because the answer had already landed.

"Was that before or after you sent the photograph of Lily's note to Dr. Warren?"

"Before."

"Was Dr. Warren aware of that discussion?"

"I don't know."

"Was Marissa Cole?"

"I don't know."

"Did that statement affect how you handled Lily's note?"

Dana's eyes reddened, though she did not cry. "I thought I was protecting Lily from having her confusion used against her."

Jack nodded once. "Did you also prevent the court from seeing her confusion?"

Sloane objected to form, argumentative. Dana did not answer immediately. Jack let the objection stand and rephrased.

"Did your handling of the note result in the court not receiving Lily's full written statement with the emergency petition?"

Dana looked at the transcript machine, then at the table, then at Jack. "Yes."

Jack stopped there. He did not need to punish her with the next question. The answer was enough, and pushing beyond it would make him look cruel rather than precise. He asked a few cleanup questions about documents, devices, communications, and preservation. Dana agreed to search for communications with Tessa and provide them through counsel. Sloane reserved objections but did not refuse.

The deposition ended after two hours and twelve minutes. Dana left with her lawyer through the rear hall, avoiding the front of the office where Amelia had been waiting with enough restraint to qualify as personal growth. Sonia Patel lingered long enough to tell Jack the district would continue searching for the blue folder and would supplement its production. Her face carried the expression of counsel who understood the district's problem had just become more serious. Jack thanked her and did not say anything that would turn cooperation into defensiveness.

When the door closed, Amelia entered the conference room. "Well?"

Jack removed the exhibit stickers from the table. "Dana admitted Tessa told her raw uncertainty could be weaponized by a resistant parent."

Amelia sat down slowly. "That's the language."

"Yes."

"She admitted it affected the note?"

"She said she thought she was protecting Lily from having confusion used against her."

"And the court never got the note."

"She admitted that result."

Amelia looked toward the whiteboard. "That is not maybe."

Jack did not answer immediately. The record had moved. It had not finished moving. Dana's testimony connected Tessa to the handling of Lily's uncertainty. It did not prove who gave the phone, who created the language map, or whether Dr. Warren and Marissa participated in a strategy meeting. It did show that a communications consultant's concept had influenced the school counselor's handling of the child's written statement. For the next hearing, that was enough to matter.

Caleb looked drained in the satisfied way young lawyers get after witnessing a transcript become useful. Mara was already updating the timeline, adding Dana's deposition quote beneath Tessa Laird's name with the date and page placeholder. Nora entered to collect empty cups and saw the room's expression. She looked at Jack, then at the board, then back at Jack.

"I assume this means no one is going home early," she said.

"No," Jack said.

"Then I am ordering dinner."

Amelia looked at Nora. "Do I get a vote?"

"No," Nora said.

The smallest laugh moved through the room, and Jack allowed it because they needed it. The case had spent the afternoon showing how a child's uncertainty had been treated as a liability by adults who claimed to protect her. It was hard to sit with that for too long without either anger or humor giving the room a way to breathe. Jack preferred humor when he could get it. Anger would be needed later, and he did not want to waste it on dinner.

By early evening, Caleb had ordered the rough transcript expedited. Mara had prepared a declaration summarizing only the testimony needed for the upcoming hearing. Jack drafted a supplemental notice to the court, attaching the deposition excerpts under seal once available and stating that Dana Keene had testified that Tessa Laird advised her that raw uncertainty could be weaponized by a resistant parent. He kept the filing short. Judges trusted short filings when the facts were strong.

Ethan called at seven. Jack took the call alone in his office and gave him the permitted summary. Dana had admitted the note should have reached the court and that outside language influenced how she handled Lily's uncertainty. Ethan did not speak for several seconds. Jack could hear him breathing, controlled but heavy.

"She called Lily's feelings raw uncertainty?" Ethan asked.

"That was the phrase attributed to Tessa."

"She was thirteen and scared."

"Yes."

"They made her sound like a problem to manage."

Jack looked through the glass wall at the whiteboard. "That is what we are showing."

Ethan's voice lowered. "I want to hate them."

"I know."

"Tell me not to."

"Do not let hate make decisions for you."

"That's not the same."

"It is better advice."

Ethan gave a tired, broken laugh. "You are impossible."

"Professionally."

The call ended after Jack reminded him again to keep Lily out of all case discussions. When he returned to the conference room, Amelia was standing at the board with her arms folded. She had not touched the marker. The restraint was becoming a pattern. Jack wondered how much it cost her.

"She deserves a headline," Amelia said.

"Lily deserves a childhood."

Amelia turned. "Those things are not always enemies."

"No. They are not always friends either."

She nodded after a moment. "I know."

Jack believed she did. That was why she was still in the office instead of outside building the story into something the court would punish. Amelia wanted exposure. Jack wanted admissibility. Lily needed protection from both when either one became too hungry.

At nine, the rough transcript arrived. The quote was there exactly as Caleb had written it. Tessa said raw uncertainty could be weaponized by a resistant parent. Jack read the line, then the question before it, then the question after it. The transcript was clean. No one had stepped on the answer. Sloane's objection preserved form but did not weaken the substance. Jack attached the excerpt to the sealed supplemental notice and sent it through the court system.

The office emptied slowly after that. Caleb left with another stack of assignments. Nora left after extracting a promise that Jack would at least go home before midnight. Mara left last among the staff, carrying copies of the subpoena drafts and muttering about people who made evidence harder than necessary. Amelia stayed a few minutes longer near the door. She looked tired, though the tiredness sharpened rather than softened her.

"You were careful with Dana," she said.

"She may be more useful scared than destroyed."

"That sounds cold."

"It is practical."

"It was also kind."

Jack looked at the deposition binder. "Maybe."

Amelia smiled faintly. "There it is."

After she left, Jack returned to the whiteboard and looked at the line he had added the night before: Did communication precede language? Dana's testimony had moved the answer from possible to supported. Not proven fully. Supported. That was how truth entered court most of the time, not as a thunderclap, but as a word placed carefully beside another word until denial had less room to stand. Jack turned off the light and left the board visible in the dark, because tomorrow the case would move closer to the person who had taught adults to treat a child's unfinished sentence as something to be managed before it could be heard.

16

Tessa Laird did not appear for the subpoena conference in person. Her lawyer appeared instead, a compact man named Grant Ellison who wore a gray suit, rimless glasses, and the professional expression of someone paid to turn every doorway into a wall. He arrived at Jack Sullivan's office at ten the next morning with a letter objecting to the subpoena, a privilege log that contained almost nothing useful, and a warning that his client was not part of the custody dispute. Jack accepted the letter, read the first page, and placed it neatly beside his legal pad. He had learned that lawyers who arrived angry usually hoped the volume would substitute for law.

Caleb sat to Jack's right with the Dana Keene deposition excerpt tabbed and ready. Mara sat near the end of the table with the carrier records in a sealed binder, opened only to the page the court had permitted them to discuss. Nora had made sure Amelia stayed in the front office with public documents, which Amelia accepted less gracefully than before. Jack did not blame her. Tessa was the kind of person Amelia had been chasing for months, and keeping a reporter outside the room while the person's lawyer tried to bury the trail was almost a personal insult.

Ellison opened with a prepared position. Tessa Laird was a communications consultant who provided public education to nonprofits and schools. She did not treat Lily Cole, did not represent either parent, did not make clinical recommendations, and did not participate in the filing of the emergency petition. Her work, according to the letter, involved generalized training about youth-centered communication in high-conflict environments. Jack listened without interrupting because the speech was useful. It told him where Ellison thought the weak places were.

When Ellison finished, Jack turned one page in his notebook. "Did Ms. Laird communicate with a mobile phone later found in Lily Cole's backpack?"

Ellison's expression did not change. "We dispute the characterization."

"I did not characterize. I asked whether she communicated with the device."

"I am not prepared to answer that outside a properly noticed deposition."

"You came to meet and confer regarding a subpoena for those records."

"I came to state our objections."

"Then state whether your client will produce communications with that device number under the court's protective order."

Ellison leaned back slightly. "Subject to objections, Ms. Laird may produce a limited set of communications if they exist, reviewed for privilege, privacy, and relevance."

Jack wrote may, if they exist, and reviewed. "By when?"

"Fourteen days."

"The hearing is next week."

"That is not my client's emergency."

Jack looked at him for the first time with real attention. "It became her problem when her number appeared in metadata from a phone found in a thirteen-year-old child's backpack during a court-supervised custody exchange."

Ellison's jaw tightened. "That assumes the phone was the child's."

"No. It assumes the phone was in her backpack. That is established."

Mara slid the sealed receipt toward Jack without speaking. He did not open it. He did not need to. Ellison already understood the receipt existed, and in a meet-and-confer, sometimes the unopened binder did as much work as the opened page. Jack kept his voice even. He wanted Ellison to leave worried, not cornered. Worried lawyers produced records to protect themselves. Cornered lawyers produced motions.

Ellison tried a different path. "Mr. Sullivan, you appear to be building a theory that communications professionals somehow controlled what a child said in a family matter. That is inflammatory and unsupported."

Jack placed the Dana deposition excerpt on the table. "Dana Keene testified under oath that your client told her raw uncertainty could be weaponized by a resistant parent. She testified that this statement occurred before the photograph of Lily's note was sent to Dr. Warren."

Ellison read the excerpt, and for the first time his face lost its prepared smoothness. The change was brief. It was enough.

He placed the page back on the table and adjusted his glasses. Jack waited, letting the transcript do what transcripts did best.

"My client disputes any suggestion that statement concerned Lily Cole specifically," Ellison said.

"Then her communications should clarify that."

"Or reveal confidential consulting work with nonparties."

"Produce a privilege log with enough detail for evaluation."

"We already provided one."

Jack lifted the single-page log. "This identifies twelve entries as consulting communications without dates, recipients, or subject matter. That is not a privilege log. That is a refusal with columns."

Caleb looked down at his notebook to hide his reaction. Mara did not bother hiding hers. Ellison stared at Jack, then took back the log and made a note. The room remained civil because everyone in it understood that incivility would only lengthen the record. Jack had no interest in making Ellison the story. He wanted Tessa's documents, her devices, her meeting notes, and any communication involving Lily's language before the petition.

After forty minutes, Ellison agreed to produce nonprivileged communications between Tessa and Dana Keene concerning Lily, Ethan, Marissa, the Cole matter, or any unidentified child scenario matching Lily's facts, for the period beginning sixty days before the petition. He also agreed to preserve communications with the unknown device number pending further court order. He refused to produce language maps, training drafts, or materials from Family Futures without a narrower order. Jack expected that refusal and thanked him for making the dispute clear.

When Ellison left, Amelia stepped into the conference room before Nora could stop her. "Well?"

Jack gathered the notes. "He gave us enough to ask the judge for the rest."

"That means he gave you nothing."

"It means he admitted there is something to fight over."

Amelia frowned. "You lawyers have a low threshold for optimism."

"We have to. Judges ration certainty."

Mara opened her laptop. "Ellison reacted to the Dana quote."

Caleb nodded. "He knew it was bad."

Jack held up a hand. "Careful. He understood it required response."

Amelia sat despite not being invited. "You are allergic to plain English."

"No. I am allergic to overstatement."

Nora entered with a stack of mail and looked at Amelia in the chair. "I see boundaries are going well."

Amelia stood halfway. "I can leave."

Nora placed the mail on the table. "Too late now."

The room shifted back into work. Caleb drafted a letter memorializing the meet-and-confer. Mara updated the discovery chart, separating what Tessa agreed to produce from what would require court intervention. Jack reviewed Judge Harrow's prior order and began drafting a motion to compel limited third-party production. He kept the tone restrained. Tessa's lawyer had been difficult, not lawless. Judges expected difficult lawyers. They intervened when difficulty blocked relevant evidence.

At noon, Angela Morrissey called with a brief update. Lily had completed her second session with Dr. Patel. No content would be disclosed, but Dr. Patel reported that Lily engaged through drawing and agreed to return. Angela wanted both parents reminded that progress updates would remain general. Jack said he would tell Ethan. Claire would tell Marissa. Angela sounded grateful that, at least for one hour, the adults had not created another dispute.

Jack called Ethan from his office. Ethan answered on the second ring and spoke in a low voice because Lily was in the kitchen making tea. The detail made Jack pause. Lily making tea was not evidence, not strategy, and not a ruling. It was a child doing something ordinary in a world adults had made too organized around her fear.

"Angela says the session happened and Lily agreed to go back," Jack said.

"That's good?"

"Yes."

"That's all I get?"

"That is all anyone gets."

Ethan let out a slow breath. "She seems calmer after drawing. Then she gets quiet again."

"Let quiet be quiet."

"I'm learning."

"You are."

"She asked if you are the man from court."

Jack leaned back. "What did you say?"

"I said yes, and that you are helping the adults talk to the judge."

"Good."

"She asked if you're mad at her."

Jack closed his eyes for a moment. "What did you say?"

"I said no one is mad at her."

"That was right."

After the call ended, Jack remained in his office for several minutes. Lily had seen him only as another adult in a courtroom, another man in a suit whose presence meant her life was being argued about. He had become part of the landscape of pressure even while trying to reduce it. That was one of the harder truths of child cases. Good intentions did not make a lawyer harmless. They only required the lawyer to notice the harm and limit it where he could.

By midafternoon, Robert Chen sent a short supplemental report through the sealed channel. The unknown prepaid number that had contacted Lily's device had been active for only nine days and had gone dark the evening the phone was taken into Angela's custody. The carrier records showed no subscriber name beyond the same kind of placeholder used for the device account. Payment had been cash. Activation occurred at a retail kiosk inside a shopping mall less than two miles from Civic Bridge's regional office.

Mara read the report twice. "That is not coincidence."

Jack looked at the page. "It may be geography."

"A prepaid phone near their office goes dark after the phone is seized."

"Still may be geography."

She gave him a look. "You don't believe that."

"I don't have to believe it. I have to prove it."

Caleb pulled up a map and marked the kiosk, Civic Bridge, Horizon, Lily's school, and Marissa's house. The locations formed a practical corridor, not a conspiracy chart. People lived, worked, shopped, and bought phones in overlapping places. Jack knew a judge would see that too. The value was not the location alone. The value was the timing, the contacts, the connection to Tessa, and the deactivation after court involvement.

Amelia stood behind Caleb's chair, careful not to look at the sealed report itself. "Ask for surveillance footage."

Mara nodded. "Retail kiosk may overwrite quickly."

Jack turned to Caleb. "Preservation letter today. Kiosk owner, mall security, payment processor. Narrow date range around activation. No accusations."

Caleb started typing.

Amelia looked at Jack. "You were going to say that anyway?"

"Yes."

"Then I'll pretend I helped."

"You often do."

She smiled despite herself and returned to the outer room.

At four, Claire called. Her tone was less combative than usual, which made Jack more attentive. She had received Ellison's version of the meet-and-confer and wanted to know whether Jack intended to seek an order against Tessa before the next hearing. Jack said yes. Claire did not object in principle, though she wanted the order limited to communications involving Lily or the separate device. That surprised him. Then she explained why.

"I do not represent Ms. Laird," Claire said. "I represent Marissa Cole. If a third-party consultant communicated with that device, I need to know that too."

Jack wrote the sentence down. "Does your client know Ms. Laird?"

"I am investigating that."

"That is not no."

"No, it is not."

Jack waited.

Claire continued. "Marissa attended at least one parent-support webinar where Ms. Laird presented. She says she did not communicate with her directly about Lily."

"When was the webinar?"

"Approximately two months before the petition."

"Civic Bridge?"

"Yes."

"Did Dana refer her?"

"I do not know yet."

Jack leaned back in his chair. "You understand that matters."

"I do."

There was a weariness in her answer that did not sound strategic. Jack heard it and adjusted. Claire might still defend Marissa aggressively, but she was no longer pretending the petition had emerged from a clean clinical process. That did not make her an ally. It made her a lawyer with a client who might have been influenced by the same machinery Jack was trying to expose.

"Send me the webinar information," Jack said.

"I will, subject to relevance and privilege."

"Of course."

"I would also like your agreement that Marissa's attendance at a webinar not be characterized as misconduct."

"If that is all it was, agreed."

Claire was quiet for a beat. "Thank you."

After the call, Jack updated the timeline. Marissa attends Civic Bridge webinar. Possible presenter Tessa Laird. He did not draw a line from the webinar to the phone. He wrote it under Parent Influences, not Evidence of Device. The distinction mattered. Marissa might have attended a webinar because she was scared and looking for help. She might have been guided toward language that made Ethan look dangerous. She might have done both without understanding where one ended and the other began.

Nora stepped into the office with another message. "Victor Hale wants a call."

Jack looked up. "With me?"

"With you, Claire, and Mr. Ellison. He says Fairchild may move to quash any subpoena that seeks foundation-funded training materials."

"Did we subpoena Fairchild-funded training materials?"

"Not yet."

"Then he is objecting to tomorrow."

"That was my reading."

Jack almost smiled. "Tell him to put his concerns in writing."

"I did."

"And?"

"He said written correspondence may escalate the matter."

"Then tell him silence is available."

Nora's expression warmed by a degree. "I already did."

Jack returned to the conference room and told the others. Mara wrote Victor Hale anticipatory objection under Fairchild. Caleb looked both amused and unsettled. Amelia heard from the outer room and muttered something about donor lawyers, which Jack chose not to hear. The case had started with a father accused of being unsafe. Now the lawyer for a foundation was objecting before being subpoenaed to training materials that supposedly had nothing to do with Lily. That did not prove Fairchild directed anything. It did show Fairchild cared deeply about where discovery might go.

By six, the motion to compel Tessa's limited production was ready. Jack attached Dana's deposition excerpt, the carrier metadata summary under seal, the public training page, and the meet-and-confer letter. He did not attach the anonymous drive materials. He referenced them only in a sealed attorney declaration as materials under forensic review that had prompted preservation, not as evidence for relief. That restraint cost him nothing legally and preserved credibility with the judge. It also kept the motion focused on authenticated facts.

Caleb read the final draft aloud in pieces while Jack listened. The practice annoyed Caleb at first, but he had learned that hearing a motion exposed soft language the eye forgave. When Caleb reached the paragraph about raw uncertainty, his voice slowed. Jack stopped him and rewrote the next sentence. The old version said the phrase revealed an effort to suppress Lily's voice. The new version said the phrase supported inquiry into whether Lily's written statements were framed or minimized before disclosure to the court. It was less satisfying. It was stronger.

Amelia watched from the doorway. "That rewrite hurt me personally."

Jack did not look up. "You'll recover."

"It's less powerful."

"It's less vulnerable."

"That is not always the same thing."

"In a motion, it usually is."

Mara nodded. "The rewrite survives."

Amelia looked at Caleb. "Do you all talk like this after law school, or does he train it into you?"

Caleb hesitated. "Both."

Nora appeared behind Amelia. "Dinner is here. Arguments may continue after people eat like adults."

They ate around the conference table with the motion stacks pushed to one end. For twenty minutes, the case became background noise instead of the only air in the room. Caleb talked about his landlord raising rent. Mara described a fraud case where a bookkeeper hid invoices in a folder labeled Recipes. Nora explained why every office plant Jack had ever owned died within thirty days. Amelia listened more than she spoke, which Jack noticed because silence from her usually meant either fatigue or thought. Possibly both.

After dinner, Jack filed the motion. The confirmation came back at 8:42 p.m. Judge Harrow's clerk set a remote hearing for the next afternoon. That was fast, and it told Jack the court understood timing mattered. Tessa's communications needed to be preserved before everyone learned exactly where the pressure points were. Procedure could move slowly, but judges knew how to move when a child's record was at risk.

Ethan texted at nine. Lily asked to watch the same cooking show again. She made tea. No court talk. Jack replied with approval and told him to keep the evening simple. He did not mention Tessa, Fairchild, prepaid numbers, or motions.

Ethan's job that night was to give Lily a quiet house, not to carry the full case in his face while pretending he was calm.

The office emptied near ten. Nora left first, then Caleb, then Amelia after warning Jack not to let caution become cowardice. Mara stayed long enough to confirm the preservation letters to the retail kiosk and mall security had gone out by email and certified mail. Jack remained after everyone left, as he often did, with the whiteboard reflecting in the dark conference room glass. The board was cleaner than it had been that morning. Fewer arrows. More dates. Better questions.

He stood before it and read the path aloud in his mind. Lily wrote. Dana copied and reframed. Dr. Warren minimized and omitted. Tessa's language shaped the handling of uncertainty. A separate phone connected to Tessa's number before the petition. Fairchild's lawyer objected before being formally asked. Each piece could still be explained alone. Together, they had begun to form the record Judge Harrow needed.

Jack capped the marker he had not used and turned off the last conference room light. He was not chasing a headline, a conspiracy, or even an opponent. He was following the route by which a child's words had been turned into adult strategy. The closer he came to that route, the more carefully he had to walk it. Otherwise he would become one more adult deciding that Lily's words mattered only after someone else placed them in the right frame.

17

Judge Harrow's remote hearing on the Tessa Laird subpoena lasted twenty-six minutes and did not waste any of them. Jack Sullivan appeared from his conference room with Caleb beside him and Mara seated outside the camera's view. Claire Whitcomb appeared from her office, careful and reserved, no longer eager to fight every fact Jack raised. Grant Ellison appeared for Tessa with a written objection that repeated the phrase nonparty burden seven times. Victor Hale appeared for Fairchild and identified himself only after the judge asked why a foundation lawyer was present in a subpoena dispute involving someone else's communications.

Judge Harrow listened without interrupting until every lawyer had placed his or her position on the record. That was one of her strengths. She let people talk long enough to reveal whether they had law, facts, or only concern dressed as principle. Ellison argued that Tessa's work was public-policy consulting, not case strategy, and that the subpoena threatened to chill advocacy speech. Hale argued that foundation-supported training materials had no proper place in a child custody matter. Claire said very little, which told Jack she was waiting to see how much of the wall around Tessa the court would leave standing.

Jack kept his argument narrow because narrow had been winning. "Your Honor, respondent is not seeking Ms. Laird's entire advocacy history. We are seeking communications tied to a device found in Lily Cole's backpack, communications with Dana Keene about Lily or this proceeding, and any materials used to frame or describe Lily's written statements before they were withheld from the court. The connection is no longer speculative. The carrier records show contact with the device, and Ms. Keene testified that Ms. Laird gave guidance about raw uncertainty before Ms. Keene handled Lily's note."

Judge Harrow looked down at the deposition excerpt. "Mr. Ellison, did your client communicate with the device number identified in the sealed carrier records?"

Ellison adjusted his glasses. "Your Honor, we have not completed our review."

"That was not my question."

"I am not prepared to make a factual representation today."

"Then I will not treat the absence of your representation as evidence in your favor."

Jack did not move, though Caleb's pen paused just long enough to reveal satisfaction. Ellison had made the mistake of bringing a speech to a factual hearing. Judge Harrow did not punish him for it. She simply refused to let uncertainty become a shield. That was how good judges controlled lawyers without raising their voices.

Hale tried to redirect the issue toward Fairchild. "Your Honor, the foundation is concerned that the subpoena seeks proprietary training materials and donor-supported educational content that is unrelated to this child."

Judge Harrow looked at him over her glasses. "Mr. Hale, no subpoena to your client is before me."

"Not directly, Your Honor."

"Then your concern is noted. It will not drive my ruling."

Hale stopped speaking. Jack wrote that down because it was useful, and because Hale's presence had done more for Jack than any argument could have. Fairchild wanted distance from the custody case while appearing at every procedural turn where training, language, and communications might be examined. A judge could notice that without being asked to say it aloud. Jack preferred when judges noticed things on their own.

Judge Harrow granted the motion in part. Tessa Laird had to produce communications with the device number, Dana Keene, Dr. Warren, Marissa Cole, Horizon, Civic Bridge, Family Futures Coalition, and anyone acting on behalf of those persons concerning Lily Cole, Ethan Cole, Marissa Cole, the Cole proceeding, or any anonymized child scenario matching Lily's circumstances. She also had to produce any language maps, draft talking points, meeting notes, or training excerpts actually shared with Dana, Dr. Warren, Marissa, or Horizon within the relevant period. The production would be under seal, reviewed first by counsel for privilege, then lodged with the court if disputes remained. The deadline was forty-eight hours.

Ellison objected to the deadline. Judge Harrow denied the objection. She said emergency petitions required emergency accountability, especially after the court learned a child's written note had not been disclosed. That phrase landed in the room with the kind of calm force lawyers respected. Jack wrote it down exactly. Emergency accountability.

After the hearing ended, Caleb leaned back and exhaled. “That went better than I expected.”

“It went as far as the record allowed,” Jack said.

Mara walked to the whiteboard and added the order under Tessa. “Forty-eight hours gives them one night to panic.”

“Do not assume panic.”

“I assume document review with elevated heart rates.”

“That is acceptable.”

Amelia entered from the hallway, where she had been waiting with her notebook closed and her patience visibly strained. “What did we get?”

Jack gave her the public-safe version. Tessa’s communications tied to Lily, the device, and the handling of Lily’s statements had to be produced under seal. Training materials were limited to what had been shared with people connected to the case. Fairchild did not receive a protective ruling because Fairchild was not the subpoena target. Amelia listened carefully, and for once she did not demand more.

“So the judge sees the path,” Amelia said.

“She sees enough to let us follow it.”

“That is not the same thing.”

“No.”

“It is enough for today.”

“Yes.”

Nora appeared at the door with a printed email. “Claire sent a proposed temporary framework.”

Jack took the pages. “That was fast.”

"She marked it urgent and child-focused, which means she wants you to notice the tone."

"I noticed."

The proposal was better than Jack expected. It kept medical decision-making status quo, required neutral counseling with Dr. Patel, prohibited both parents from discussing litigation-related issues, routed all parenting communications through a monitored co-parenting application, and preserved the current schedule pending the evidentiary hearing. It also included language that neither parent admitted wrongdoing. Jack could live with most of it. The co-parenting application was overdue, and if Marissa or Ethan violated the order, the record would be cleaner.

Jack handed the proposal to Caleb. "Compare it to Angela's recommendations."

Caleb scanned the pages. "Looks close."

"Then we edit for precision, not ego."

Amelia watched him. "That sounded like something every lawyer should tattoo on his hand."

"Most would object to placement."

Mara looked at the proposal. "This helps Lily."

"It may," Jack said. "If the parents follow it."

"They will if the consequences are clear."

"Then make them clear without making the order sound punitive."

Caleb wrote that down. Jack saw him do it and almost told him not every sentence needed preservation. Then he decided it might. A young lawyer who learned that orders should protect rather than threaten was not wasting ink. Family court had enough punitive language already. The better orders made compliance easier than violation.

Ethan came to the office at noon to review the temporary framework. Jack gave him the document and watched his face as he read. Ethan stopped at the clause routing all communication through the parenting app and nodded slowly. He stopped again at the clause prohibiting discussion of therapy materials, drawings, the note, the phone, or court proceedings. That one hurt him more. Jack let him feel it before explaining.

"This protects you too," Jack said.

"It feels like I'm being told I can't talk to my daughter."

"You can talk to her. You cannot make the case part of her relationship with you."

"She brings things up."

"Then you give safe answers and redirect."

Ethan looked back at the page. "She asked yesterday if adults can get in trouble for trying to help."

Jack did not answer quickly. "What did you say?"

"I told her adults make mistakes and other adults help fix them."

"That was good."

"She asked if I made mistakes."

"What did you say?"

"I said yes."

Jack nodded. "That was better."

Ethan looked tired, but not as raw as before. The case had not become easier for him. He had become more aware of the difference between feeling pain and spreading it. That was the kind of progress no court order could require, and it was the kind that could make a child feel safer without knowing why.

Jack marked the framework for Ethan's signature and told him not to sign until they reviewed the final language after Claire's edits.

After Ethan left, Jack called Claire. The conversation was practical and almost civil. They negotiated the parenting-app language, the neutral counseling update schedule, and the exchange procedures. Claire wanted Marissa to receive reassurance that the order did not imply she had harmed Lily. Jack agreed to a neutral non-admission clause, as long as it did not erase the court's finding that the initial record was incomplete. Claire accepted the distinction. It was the first time in days they sounded like lawyers solving a problem rather than opponents defending territory.

Near the end of the call, Claire lowered her voice. "Marissa says she does not know who gave Lily the phone."

"Does she know Tessa Laird?"

"She attended the webinar I mentioned. She says she emailed a general question afterward but does not remember a direct response."

"Produce it."

"I will."

"Did she ever give Lily a number to call if she felt unsafe?"

Claire was silent long enough for Jack to sit back. "I need to ask that carefully."

"That was not a denial."

"No, it was not. I am not going to guess for my client."

Jack respected the answer because it was exactly what he would have said. "Ask. Then call me."

"I will."

The call ended, and Jack looked through the glass wall at Amelia working in the front office. She had found another public page from Civic Bridge, judging by the way she bent over her laptop with predatory focus. He did not tell her about Claire's uncertainty on the safety number. It involved Marissa's potential communication with counsel and Lily's phone, and it needed to stay in the legal lane until verified. Amelia hated lanes. Jack understood them as the difference between a road and a wreck.

By midafternoon, Claire sent Marissa's webinar email. It was not privileged, and it was worse than Jack expected in a quieter way. Marissa had written to Civic Bridge after a parent-support session, saying her daughter was wavering, her ex-husband was undermining the care team, and she was afraid the court would not act unless everyone used the right words. The response came from a program account and was signed only T. It said: Do not argue conclusions. Document language, distress, and resistance. If child reaches out in confusion, keep the frame steady. Do not let uncertainty become the story.

Jack placed the email in the sealed working file. T could be Tessa. Or not. The content could be generic advice. Or not. The phrase keep the frame steady matched too much of the record to dismiss. He forwarded it to Caleb and Mara, excluding Amelia, and asked for a comparison chart against Dana's testimony, Dr. Warren's texts, and the anonymous spreadsheet. Then he called Claire back.

"Who had access to the program account?" Jack asked.

"I asked. Civic Bridge has not answered."

"You need them to."

"I know."

"Did Marissa forward this to Dana or Dr. Warren?"

"She says she does not remember."

"That answer will not hold."

"I know that too."

Jack heard fatigue on her end. It was not sympathy he felt, exactly. It was recognition. Claire was now managing a client who may have participated in more than she understood, a clinic whose declaration had been weakened, a counselor under administrative leave, a consultant resisting discovery, and a foundation lawyer hovering near the edges. She had filed a clean emergency story. The story had not survived the first serious look at how it was built.

At four, Nora told Jack that Dr. Patel had sent the first general counseling update to Angela, copied to counsel by agreement. The update contained no content. Lily attended session, used drawing materials, engaged appropriately, requested predictable transitions, and benefited from reassurance that therapy was not court testimony. Jack read the last phrase twice. Therapy was not court testimony. He wished every adult in the case could be made to write it by hand one hundred times.

He sent Ethan the permitted sentence only: Dr. Patel says Lily attended and engaged appropriately. Ethan replied with a thumbs-up, then a second message: I won't ask her about it. Jack saved the exchange. Compliance had become part of Ethan's record, and if the case continued to shift, that record would matter. Fathers often lost credibility in custody cases by reacting to provocation. Ethan was learning to create evidence of restraint.

The office worked late but not pointlessly. Caleb finished the comparison chart. Mara prepared preservation letters to Civic Bridge and the webinar platform. Jack revised the temporary framework into a proposed stipulation and sent it to Claire, Angela, and the court clerk for review. Amelia reviewed public materials in the front office and occasionally called out dates that Nora told her to write down instead of shouting. The office felt almost functional, which in this case was as close to peace as anyone was likely to get.

At seven-thirty, Ellison sent a letter stating Tessa Laird would comply with the court's order while preserving all objections. The letter also stated that Ms. Laird had never knowingly communicated with Lily Cole. Jack read that sentence three times. Knowingly was the word doing the work. He marked it and handed the letter to Mara. She circled the same word without being asked.

Amelia saw the motion and stood. "What?"

Jack considered how much he could say. "Tessa's counsel says she never knowingly communicated with Lily."

Amelia's eyes narrowed. "Knowingly."

"Yes."

"That means she communicated through something she claims she didn't know was Lily."

"It may mean that."

"Like an anonymized child scenario."

"Maybe."

She gave him a look that said the word had become unbearable. He understood. Maybe had become the bridge between suspicion and proof, and everyone was tired of standing on it.

Still, Jack would not jump simply because the other side left a tempting gap. The gap had to be measured. Then crossed.

By eight, Claire approved the temporary framework with minor edits. Jack sent it to Ethan for review and called him before he signed. Ethan read every page and asked two good questions, both about how to respond if Lily raised forbidden topics. Jack gave him the same language again, and Ethan wrote it down: I love you. You are not in trouble. The adults are handling adult things. You can talk to Dr. Patel or Angela if you feel worried. It sounded simple. It had taken days of legal work to make simple safe.

Judge Harrow signed the stipulation just after nine. The order would remain in place until the evidentiary hearing or further court order. Jack forwarded the signed copy to all counsel and saved it in the custody framework binder. Nora had gone home by then, and Caleb was packing up. Mara was still at the board. Amelia stood near the door with her coat in hand.

"We kept it under control today," Caleb said.

Jack looked at the signed order. "The court kept it under control. We helped."

"That was almost encouraging."

"Do not get dependent on it."

Caleb smiled and left.

Mara followed ten minutes later, leaving Jack and Amelia alone in the conference room. Amelia did not sit. She looked at the whiteboard, then at the signed order on the table. The day had not produced a dramatic breakthrough, and Jack knew she preferred sharper moments. It had produced something better for Lily: structure, neutral counseling, evidence preservation, and a path toward Tessa's records. That was less cinematic. It was more likely to hold.

Amelia said, "You know this isn't just custody anymore."

"I know."

"Then why does every answer still sound like custody?"

"Because that is the court we are in."

"And after?"

Jack closed the binder. "After we protect Lily, we see what the record can bear."

She nodded, accepting that as much as she was capable of accepting delay. Then she left without another argument. Jack turned off the conference room lights and stood for a moment in the doorway. The whiteboard was dark now, the names visible only as shadows through the glass. The case had moved one step closer to Tessa Laird, and the step mattered because it was lawful, documented, and tied to a child the court had sworn to protect. Jack had spent enough years in court to know that truth did not always arrive fast enough to prevent harm. The work was to make sure it arrived in a form no one could easily send away.

18

Tessa Laird's production arrived forty-six hours after Judge Harrow ordered it, which told Jack Sullivan something before he read a single page. Grant Ellison had used nearly every minute the court gave him, and the file structure showed the careful hand of a lawyer trying to comply without surrendering ground. The secure portal divided the materials into device communications, Dana Keene communications, case-related training materials, and a privilege log. The cover letter preserved objections to relevance, burden, privacy, advocacy speech, donor-funded training material, and anything else Ellison thought might matter later. Jack read the objections first because lawyers often revealed their fears in the things they tried hardest to protect.

Caleb logged the production while Mara prepared the sealed review folder. Amelia was not allowed in the conference room because the materials involved Lily's communications, and this time she did not argue from the doorway. She took a seat in the front office with Nora's coffee and a stack of public records from Civic Bridge, though her posture made it clear she considered exile a professional insult. Jack could see her through the glass wall, head down, pen moving across a yellow legal pad. Her restraint mattered, even if neither of them planned to say so.

The first folder contained text exports between Tessa's number and the device found in Lily's backpack. The messages were redacted, though the visible portions were enough to change the room. The recipient was labeled only as Support Device, and the dates matched the period before the emergency petition. Some lines were blacked out for minor privacy, and some were withheld as nonresponsive. Jack disliked both categories because they were necessary in theory and easily abused in practice.

Mara opened the first visible exchange. The message from Tessa's number read: If you feel pressured, use the words we practiced: confused, unsafe, not ready. You do not need to explain everything. Caleb stopped writing for a moment, then forced himself to continue. Jack read the sentence twice and did not speak. The words were not a confession, but they placed an adult's language inside the mouth of a child whose statements had almost changed custody rights.

The next exchange was dated the following morning. Remember, uncertainty can be used against you. Keep the frame steady. The reply was mostly redacted, leaving only two words visible: I'm scared. Jack stared at those words longer than he wanted to because they belonged to a child and had been turned into evidence by adults who had already taken too much from her. The record had become stronger. That did not make the room feel better.

The final exchange was sent the evening the phone was taken into Angela Morrissey's custody. Tessa's number had sent one message after the phone was powered off: Do not use this device until we know what happened at court. The message was undelivered, matching the carrier metadata Chen had already preserved. Jack wrote the Bates number beside the carrier report reference. The sequence mattered because it tied the content to records already authenticated by a neutral examiner.

Caleb looked at the screen. "She knew the phone was connected to court."

"She knew something happened at court," Jack said.

"That is careful even for you."

"It needs to be."

Mara leaned back. "This is from her own production, Jack."

"Yes. That is why we are not going to ruin it by overstating it."

The Dana Keene folder was worse in a quieter way. One exchange occurred the day Mrs. Palmer gave Dana the note. Dana wrote that a student had left an ambiguous handwritten statement with a teacher and that the statement could complicate the support plan if the father obtained it. Tessa replied: Do not let raw uncertainty become the record. It is data for the team, not a message for the opposing parent. Jack placed the page on the table and looked at it as if distance might make the sentence less ugly.

No one spoke for a few seconds. The sentence explained too much. Lily's note had not been treated as the words of a frightened child asking adults to slow down. It had been treated as raw material for a support team, something to interpret, manage, and keep away from the parent who might use it to challenge the frame. The phrase opposing parent did more damage than Tessa probably understood when she wrote it. Ethan was Lily's father, and the court had not yet made him anyone's legal opponent in her life.

Mara attached the exchange to the timeline. "This supports Dana's deposition."

"It does," Jack said.

"It also supports the anonymous drive."

"It points in the same direction. We still do not rely on the anonymous drive unless we authenticate it."

Caleb nodded. "Use the produced records first."

"Always."

The training-material folder contained a document titled Language Support Guide. It was cleaner than the spreadsheet from the anonymous drive, formatted with headings and neutral language. The columns read child expression, stabilization frame, and court-safe description. Some examples were general enough to appear in any training packet. Others tracked Lily's note too closely to ignore.

One line converted I don't want to hurt either parent into child displays loyalty conflict connected to resistant-parent behavior. Another converted I'm confused into ambivalence expected during stabilization. A third converted adults keep finishing my sentences into child struggles with consistent narrative under pressure. Jack did not need the anonymous spreadsheet anymore to understand what the document did. It showed adults how to transform a child's own words into professional language that could move cleanly through school, clinic, and court.

Caleb read the page silently, then looked up. "How do we argue this without sounding like we're attacking every professional who uses clinical language?"

"We do not attack clinical language," Jack said. "We attack replacing disclosure with interpretation."

Mara nodded. "The court should have received both."

"Exactly."

Jack stood and walked to the whiteboard. He wrote two phrases under the Tessa column: child expression and court-safe description. Then he drew no arrow between them. He wanted the board to remind everyone of the danger. The problem was not that adults interpreted Lily's distress. The problem was that the interpretation reached the court while Lily's actual words stayed behind.

Nora opened the door with a message slip. "Claire wants you to call after you review."

Jack took the slip. "She got the same production?"

"That was my impression. She sounded like someone reading while standing on a trapdoor."

"That is vivid."

"I've had coffee."

Jack called Claire after the first review. Caleb stayed in the room and took notes. Claire answered with the controlled tone of a lawyer who had spent the morning learning that her emergency petition had deeper roots than her client had disclosed. She said she had spoken with Marissa and that Marissa was prepared to supplement her declaration. Then she paused long enough for Jack to know the supplement would not be clean.

"Marissa says she attended a Civic Bridge webinar," Claire said. "She received what was described as a youth support number. She gave that number to Lily because she believed Lily needed someone neutral to contact when she felt overwhelmed."

"Did she know the number reached Tessa Laird?"

"She says no."

"Did she know Lily was being told to use practiced words?"

"She says she believed Lily was being helped to express herself."

"That is not the same answer."

"No, it is not."

Jack wrote the words exactly. "Did Marissa disclose the number to Ethan, Angela, the court, or you before the phone was found?"

"No."

Claire's answer came without argument, which made it more important. Jack could hear fatigue beneath her restraint. She had entered the case as counsel for a frightened mother seeking emergency authority. Now she was managing undisclosed support channels, a communications consultant, a weakened clinical declaration, and a child's note that had been omitted before the court could weigh it. Jack did not mistake her fatigue for friendship. He recognized it as the sound of a lawyer recalculating duty.

"Send the supplemental declaration today," Jack said.

"I will."

"Claire."

"I said today."

After the call, Jack summarized only what could be shared inside the legal team. Caleb prepared a supplemental filing shell. Mara updated the timeline and separated the produced

Tessa materials from the anonymous drive references. Nora was instructed to tell Ethan that Jack would call shortly and that he should not contact Marissa or ask Lily any questions. Ethan responded with a single word by text. Okay. Jack saved it because clean restraint deserved a record too.

He called Ethan from his office. "We received records showing the support number Lily had may have connected to Tessa Laird."

Ethan did not answer at first. "Marissa gave it to her?"

"She may have given Lily a number from a webinar. We are waiting for her sworn statement."

"She gave our daughter to people we don't know."

"Do not say that outside this call."

"It's what happened."

"It is not the way we will say it in court."

Ethan's breathing came heavier. "Then how do I say it?"

"You do not. Not today. To Lily, you stay ordinary. You tell her you love her, she is not in trouble, and adults are handling adult things."

"I don't know how long I can keep doing that."

"Today."

Ethan was quiet. "Today I can."

"That is enough."

The call ended only after Ethan repeated the boundaries. No calls to Marissa. No messages to Dana, Horizon, Civic Bridge, Tessa, or the school. No questions to Lily about the phone, the note, the support number, or anything she said to anyone else. Jack knew the list sounded excessive. It was also the fence between a father's fear and a record the court could trust.

Marissa's supplemental declaration arrived at two. Claire had drafted it with obvious care. Marissa admitted attending a Civic Bridge webinar for parents of distressed adolescents and receiving a youth support number through webinar materials. She stated that she gave the number to Lily because she feared Lily would shut down if forced to speak only with her parents. She denied knowing Tessa personally, denied intending to coach Lily, and denied understanding that the support channel would be used to shape Lily's language for court.

Jack read the declaration twice. "This helps her and hurts her."

Mara took the page. "Frightened mother. Bad judgment. Undisclosed channel."

Caleb looked at Jack. "Do we call it coaching?"

"No. Tessa's texts show language coaching. Marissa's declaration shows access and nondisclosure."

"That is cleaner."

"It is accurate."

Amelia knocked on the glass a moment later and held up a public printout. Jack covered Marissa's declaration before letting her in. She noticed the movement and stayed near the doorway, which Jack appreciated. She placed the printout on the corner of the table and stepped back.

"Civic Bridge webinar archive," Amelia said. "Parent-support session. Downloadable handout."

Jack read the page. The handout listed crisis lines, counseling referrals, and a section titled When Your Child Wavers. Beneath it were the phrases that had followed the case from school to clinic to court: keep the safety frame, document resistance, do not center adult discomfort, support consistent language. At the bottom was the youth support number. It did not name Tessa. It named Civic Bridge Youth Support.

Mara compared the number with the device records. "Same number Marissa likely gave Lily?"

"Yes," Jack said.

Amelia's face tightened. "That means the channel was built before Lily ever used it."

"It means the channel was public and available through the webinar."

"And then Tessa used it to tell her what words to use."

"We can show that Tessa's number communicated with the device and sent those messages. We still need to show the route between the public number and Tessa."

Amelia stared at him. "You are exhausting."

"I am trying to stay useful."

She did not argue further. That told Jack the public handout had disturbed her as much as the sealed records had disturbed him. The handout made the system look ordinary. That was what made it powerful. It did not need secret instructions or hidden donors to begin shaping a parent. It only needed a frightened mother to attend a webinar and accept a number labeled support.

By late afternoon, the supplemental filing was ready. Jack attached the Tessa-produced device texts, the Dana exchange about raw uncertainty, the Language Support Guide, Marissa's supplemental declaration, and the public webinar handout. He asked for a limited order requiring Tessa to appear for deposition, preserving Civic Bridge Youth Support records, and prohibiting any third-party communication with Lily absent court approval or authorization from Dr. Patel through

Angela. He also asked Judge Harrow to reevaluate the emergency petition before any change in medical decision-making authority, because the record now showed that Lily's language had been shaped outside the disclosed family and clinical process.

Claire did not oppose the no-contact language. That mattered. Ellison opposed Tessa's expedited deposition but offered dates two weeks out. Victor Hale sent a letter stating Fairchild did not operate the support line, supervise Civic Bridge, direct Tessa's communications, or participate in any contact with Lily Cole. Jack placed the letter in the Fairchild file. Denials were useful when written by careful lawyers. They told him exactly which doors the foundation wanted closed.

At six-thirty, Judge Harrow set the matter for the next morning. The minute order directed counsel to address temporary custody safeguards, third-party communications, and the timing of Tessa Laird's deposition. No live testimony would be taken unless the court ordered otherwise. Jack forwarded the notice to Ethan with a short explanation and then called him because paper was not enough for what this case kept requiring of him. Ethan answered from his backyard, away from Lily and away from any chance she could hear him.

"Lily is inside drawing," Ethan said. "The cooking show is on again."

"Good."

"She keeps checking her regular phone, like she forgot the other one is gone."

"Do not ask why."

"I didn't."

"If it continues, tell Angela."

"I will."

Ethan paused. "What if she misses the people who confused her?"

Jack leaned back in his chair. That was the kind of question the law barely knew how to hold. A child could attach to a person or channel that also pressured her because the same channel offered attention, reassurance, and language when everything else felt unsafe. Removing it did not remove the need. Sometimes it made the need louder until a safer adult helped name it.

"Then Dr. Patel helps her sort that out," Jack said. "Not you, not me, not Marissa."

"That hurts."

"Yes."

"I thought truth would make this feel better."

"Truth usually makes things clearer first."

Ethan was quiet for a moment. "I hate that."

"I know."

After the call, Jack returned to the conference room. Caleb had gone home to sleep before the morning hearing. Mara was still working through preservation letters to Civic Bridge and the webinar platform. Amelia sat in the front office, reading the webinar handout again as if repetition might make it less disturbing. Nora had left a note on Jack's laptop telling him to go home before he became permanent office furniture. He ignored it for the moment and looked at the whiteboard.

The names were no longer floating around Lily. They formed a path. Civic Bridge gave Marissa the number. Marissa gave Lily the number. The device connected to Tessa. Tessa gave words and frames. Dana received the same philosophy and kept Lily's note from becoming the record. Dr. Warren interpreted and omitted. Claire filed the petition the system had produced.

Jack did not write that last sentence on the board because it was too broad for court. Instead, he added one question under Civic Bridge Youth Support: support channel or strategy channel? The answer might be both, and that was what made the next hearing delicate. A support channel could comfort a child and still shape her testimony. A parent could seek help and still become part of a process she did not understand. A court could protect a child's privacy and still ask who entered that child's life through a number no one disclosed. Jack capped the marker and prepared for the morning, because the record was finally strong enough to ask who had custody of Lily's truth before the judge ever heard it.

19

THE NEXT MORNING'S HEARING felt different before it began. Jack Sullivan could see it in the way counsel entered the remote courtroom, in the absence of unnecessary greetings, and in the narrow expressions of people who had spent the night reading documents they wished had not existed. Judge Harrow appeared at nine sharp from chambers, already working from a marked copy of the supplemental filing. Claire Whitcomb sat in her office with Marissa off-screen. Grant Ellison appeared for Tessa Laird, and Victor Hale appeared again for Fairchild, though the court had not ordered him to be there.

Judge Harrow looked at the appearances and paused on Hale's name. "Mr. Hale, I will say again that your client is not the subject of this morning's motion."

Hale nodded. "Understood, Your Honor. Fairchild remains concerned about references to foundation-funded programs."

"Concern noted. It will not expand your role."

Jack wrote that down. The judge had placed a boundary around Fairchild before anyone argued substance. That mattered because Hale's presence had begun to look like pressure rather than assistance. Good judges noticed pressure even when it wore a suit and called itself concern. Jack kept his face neutral, though Mara, seated out of camera range, made a small note on her pad.

Judge Harrow turned to the filings. "The court has reviewed the produced communications from Ms. Laird, the supplemental declaration from Ms. Cole, and the public webinar material. I am not making final findings regarding intent today. I am deciding what temporary safeguards are necessary and what discovery is required before the evidentiary hearing."

Claire spoke first, and her tone carried more caution than combat. She acknowledged that Marissa had given Lily the support number, believing it to be a neutral resource from a parent webinar. She denied that Marissa intended to bypass the court, hide communications, or influence Lily's testimony. She agreed no third party should communicate with Lily outside the neutral therapeutic structure going forward. She also asked the court not to punish Marissa for seeking help during a difficult parenting crisis.

Jack listened without interruption. Claire was doing what she should do: separate Marissa's fear from Tessa's conduct, and Marissa's conduct from the larger network. It was not a bad argument. A frightened parent could make a poor decision while believing she was protecting a child. The problem was that Marissa's poor decision had opened a door through which someone else had entered with practiced words.

When Judge Harrow turned to him, Jack kept his response short. "Your Honor, respondent is not asking for punishment today. He is asking for protection and a complete record. The support number became an undisclosed communication channel with a child at the center of an emergency petition. Through that channel, Ms. Laird's number sent words Lily was later expected to use, and those words overlapped with the language presented to the court as Lily's distress."

Ellison leaned toward his camera. "Your Honor, that statement assumes Ms. Laird knew she was communicating with Lily Cole."

Jack did not answer him directly. Judge Harrow did.

"That is one reason I am ordering discovery."

Ellison stopped. The ruling had not been announced, but the direction was clear. Judge Harrow understood the central question: knowledge. If Tessa knew she was communicating with Lily, the implications were severe. If she did not, the court still had to know how a support system allowed a communications consultant to send practiced language to a child whose case was heading into court.

Judge Harrow ordered Tessa Laird to appear for a limited deposition within seventy-two hours. The deposition would be three hours, under protective order, confined to communications with the device, Dana Keene, Marissa Cole, Dr. Warren, Horizon, Civic Bridge Youth Support, and any language materials applied to Lily's statements. She ordered Civic Bridge to preserve and produce records identifying who monitored the support number, how calls or messages were routed, and whether any adult knew the user was Lily Cole. She also prohibited any third-party support contact with Lily unless approved through Dr. Patel and Angela Morrissey.

Claire requested that the order make clear Marissa had not been found in violation. Judge Harrow agreed. Jack did not object because the court had not made that finding. The order stated that Marissa's nondisclosure would be considered in assessing the reliability of the emergency record, not as a contempt finding. That distinction was legally precise and emotionally unsatisfying. Jack knew Ethan would struggle with it, and he also knew it was correct.

Before ending, Judge Harrow looked directly into the camera. "This court will not permit a child's private uncertainty to be converted into litigation language without scrutiny. Support is not a license to shape testimony. Advocacy is not a substitute for disclosure. Counsel will govern themselves accordingly."

The hearing ended four minutes later. Caleb saved the minute order as soon as it appeared. Mara added deposition deadline under Tessa's name on the board. Nora stepped into the conference room with her arms folded, reading faces before asking questions. Amelia waited in the hallway and entered only after Jack nodded. She looked from the board to Jack.

"Well?" she asked.

"Tessa deposition within seventy-two hours. Civic Bridge records. No third-party contact with Lily."

Amelia's face changed, not into satisfaction exactly, but into recognition that the case had crossed another line. "The judge said yes."

"She said enough."

"What about Marissa?"

"No violation finding. Her nondisclosure goes to reliability."

Amelia looked toward the front windows. "That will make Ethan angry."

"Yes."

"He deserves to be angry."

"Yes."

"And you're going to tell him anger is not strategy."

"Yes."

Nora gave Amelia a look. "You could do his calls now."

"I lack his gift for making people feel corrected and helped at the same time."

Jack ignored them and called Ethan from his office. Ethan answered quickly, as if he had been holding the phone. Jack gave him the ruling in plain language. Tessa would be deposed. Civic Bridge had to produce routing and support-line records. No one outside the approved counseling structure could contact Lily. The court did not find Marissa in contempt, but her nondisclosure would be considered when the court evaluated the emergency petition.

Ethan was quiet, then spoke with controlled force. "She gave Lily that number and didn't tell anyone."

"Yes."

"And the judge won't call that a violation."

"Not today."

"That is insane."

"It is careful."

"It is wrong."

Jack let the words sit. "Maybe it feels wrong because it does not give you the judgment you want yet."

"I want someone to say what happened."

"The court is building the record to do that."

"She gets careful words. I got called dangerous."

"That is true."

The admission slowed Ethan down. Jack heard his breathing change. Sometimes a client did not need reassurance first. Sometimes he needed the lawyer to admit the unfairness without pretending it had already been corrected. Jack had learned that lesson later than he should have.

"You cannot let that unfairness guide your behavior," Jack said. "That is where they hurt you twice."

Ethan's voice lowered. "I know."

"Today you follow the order. You keep Lily's world quiet. You let us take Tessa's testimony."

"I can do today."

"That is still enough."

After the call, Jack returned to the conference room and found Caleb already drafting the deposition notice. Mara had the Civic Bridge subpoena open and was tightening the categories to match the judge's ruling. Amelia sat near the far end with public materials, not sealed records, and for once did not test the boundary. The office had learned its choreography. Nora controlled the door, Caleb built the paper, Mara found the facts, Amelia found the public trail, and Jack kept all of it from collapsing under its own urgency.

By noon, Ellison offered the following afternoon for Tessa's deposition. That surprised no one. He would want the testimony over quickly before more records arrived from Civic Bridge. Jack accepted, with a reservation of rights to reconvene if the production was incomplete. Ellison objected to the reservation. Jack left it in the confirming email anyway. Lawyers objected to many things that remained true.

The Civic Bridge production arrived in stages. The first set contained administrative records for the webinar Marissa attended, including registration, handouts, and support-line routing instructions. The resource number did not go to a hotline staffed by licensed counselors. It routed to a rotating group of trained response volunteers and consultants, including Tessa Laird during the relevant month. The disclosure statement on the public handout called it peer-informed support. Jack read that phrase and placed it beside the messages telling Lily to use practiced words.

Mara traced the routing log. "Marissa's email registered for the webinar. Two days later, the support number was sent to the device."

"By whom?"

"Civic Bridge system text. Automated."

"So Marissa may have entered Lily's number."

"Or someone entered it from her registration link."

Jack looked at the record. "We need to ask Marissa."

Caleb added it to the hearing list. "Through Claire?"

"Yes. No direct contact."

The routing log showed the device number received a welcome message from Civic Bridge Youth Support: We are here when you need steady words. Save this number. The phrase steady words had not appeared before. Amelia, reading the public handout from across the room, looked up when Mara repeated it. She did not need the sealed record to understand the direction. Steady words sounded gentle. In the wrong hands, it also sounded like preparation.

By three, Claire provided a written clarification from Marissa. Marissa admitted entering Lily's regular number into the webinar resource form but denied entering the separate device number. She stated she did not know how the support line reached the device found in Lily's backpack. That answer opened another gap. Lily's regular phone and the separate device had both now touched the support system in some way, or the system had been updated by someone with access to the separate number. Jack marked the issue for Tessa.

Ethan texted at four. Lily asked if I'm mad at Mom. I said adults are working through things and she doesn't have to carry it. Was that okay? Jack read the message and felt the weight behind it. Lily was trying to locate blame because children often believed knowing who was wrong might make the ground stop moving. Ethan's answer had not fed the case back into her. Jack replied: Yes. That was exactly right.

Nora saw the exchange when Jack logged it. "He is learning."

"He is trying."

"That is sometimes better."

Jack looked up. "You are becoming philosophical."

"No. I am tired."

The next hour was spent preparing for Tessa's deposition. Jack's outline was simple: role, Civic Bridge relationship, webinar, support number, routing procedures, device communications, Dana Keene communications, language support guide, knowledge of Lily's identity, knowledge of court proceedings, and preservation. He avoided questions about Fairchild until he could tie them to specific documents. Hale wanted the foundation insulated. Jack wanted to know whether insulation was distance or design.

Amelia stayed late to help build a public chronology of Tessa's roles across Family Futures and Civic Bridge. She found the same language repeated under different program names over several years: steady language, stabilization frame, resistance dynamics, court-safe communication. None of it proved misconduct alone. Together, it showed that Tessa's vocabulary had been institutionalized before it reached Lily. Jack accepted the chronology and placed it in the public-source binder.

At seven, Dr. Patel's general update came through Angela. Lily attended, used drawing materials, and asked whether therapy could be a place where nobody finished her sentences. The update contained no details beyond that one therapeutic-process note, which Dr. Patel included because it related directly to the court's no-pressure order. Jack read it once, then again. The sentence was gentle and devastating. It said more about the case than many of the adult records did.

He called Ethan. "You may receive a general update from Angela. Do not ask Lily about it."

"Is she okay?"

"She is using the space."

"That sounds like a lawyer trying not to say more."

"It is."

Ethan was quiet. "Did she talk?"

"Ethan."

"I know. I'm sorry."

"Let Dr. Patel do her job."

"I will."

After the call, Jack sat alone for a few minutes. The office had begun to empty, though Amelia remained near the front, and Mara was still at the whiteboard. Caleb was copying deposition exhibits and fighting a printer that had chosen the worst possible week to become unreliable. Nora stood over the machine with the grim patience of someone deciding whether technology deserved mercy. Ordinary office irritation helped. It reminded everyone the world had not narrowed completely to Lily's pain.

When the exhibits were ready, Jack reviewed them one last time. He removed two that were more inflammatory than necessary and added one that showed the Civic Bridge support-line routing in plain administrative language. The routing record mattered more than the angriest text because it showed system design. Tessa did not have to sneak into Lily's life if the system delivered children to her under the word support. That was the question for tomorrow.

Amelia stopped at his office door before leaving. "Do you think Tessa knew it was Lily?"

Jack closed the exhibit binder. "I think she knew enough to ask."

"That is not the same."

"No."

"Will that be enough?"

"For deposition, yes. For the hearing, we will see."

Amelia nodded. "I hate how often that is the honest answer."

"So do I."

She left without another comment. Jack appreciated that too. The case was teaching all of them to accept smaller answers until the record could carry larger ones. It was not satisfying work, but satisfying work often belonged to people who were allowed to simplify. Jack was not.

He turned off the office light after ten and left the deposition binder on the conference table for the morning. Tomorrow, Tessa Laird would sit under oath and explain why a support channel sent a child practiced words during an emergency custody fight. She would explain whether she knew the child was Lily, whether she knew a petition was being prepared, and why uncertainty had been treated as something to keep out of the record. Jack did not need her to confess. He needed her to answer carefully enough that the court could see who had been holding Lily's truth before anyone let Lily speak for herself.

20

Tessa Laird arrived for deposition at 9:58 a.m., two minutes early and composed enough to make the timing feel intentional. She wore a cream blazer, dark slacks, and no visible jewelry except a thin gold watch that looked more functional than decorative. Grant Ellison walked beside her with a leather folder under one arm and the guarded posture of a lawyer who had spent the morning reminding his client that calm was not the same as honesty. Jack Sullivan watched them through the glass wall as Nora led them into the conference room. Tessa did not look frightened, angry, or confused. She looked prepared.

Caleb had arranged the exhibits in three binders: public materials, produced communications, and support-line records. Mara sat near Jack with the sealed binder open only to the first page needed for foundation questions. Claire Whitcomb appeared by video from her office, not as Tessa's counsel, but because the testimony could affect Marissa. Rebecca Sloane did not attend, though Dana Keene's testimony sat in the record like a person in the room. Amelia was not permitted inside, and Jack had stationed her in the front office with Nora's warning that the conference room door was not a suggestion.

The court reporter swore Tessa in at ten. Jack began with ordinary background because every deposition needed a floor before the lawyer tried to build anything on it. Tessa described herself as a communications consultant specializing in youth support, family-systems messaging, and nonprofit program design. She had worked with Civic Bridge, Family Futures Coalition, and several school-facing initiatives. She was not a clinician, not a lawyer, and not a mandated reporter through her consulting role. She stated each limit clearly, as if the limits themselves were part of her defense.

Jack moved slowly through her relationship with Civic Bridge Youth Support. The support number, according to Tessa, was designed to provide language assistance to young people and parents navigating high-conflict family situations. Volunteers and consultants helped users identify feelings, organize thoughts, and seek appropriate adult help. Tessa insisted the service did not provide legal advice, clinical treatment, or instructions about court testimony. Her answers were polished. Jack had expected polish, and polish did not bother him as long as the transcript captured its surface.

"Did Civic Bridge Youth Support maintain written protocols?" Jack asked.

"Yes."

"Were those protocols produced in response to the court's order?"

"My counsel handled production."

Ellison objected to form and instructed her she could answer if she knew. Tessa looked at him, then back at Jack.

"I believe relevant protocols were produced," she said.

"Who determined relevance?"

"My counsel and Civic Bridge counsel."

"Did you participate in selecting what was produced?"

"Only to identify categories when asked."

Jack made a note. That answer created a future path if the production turned out incomplete. He did not press it now. The deposition's center was not document review. The center was whether Tessa knew she had entered Lily's life before the court had the chance to hear Lily's own words.

Jack placed the webinar handout in front of her. Tessa identified it as a Civic Bridge parent-support resource. She confirmed the section titled When Your Child Wavers had been used in more than one webinar. She said the phrases were intended to help parents avoid reactive conversations during periods of distress. Jack asked whether keep the safety frame was her phrase. She said she had used it often in trainings and did not know whether she originated it. That was the kind of answer that avoided ownership without denying familiarity.

He then placed the support-line routing record in front of her. Tessa reviewed it with calm attention. The record showed Marissa's webinar registration, the entry of Lily's regular number into the resource form, the automated message from Civic Bridge, and later communications with the separate device. Jack asked who could transfer a support relationship from one number to another. Tessa said users sometimes requested a different contact number. Volunteers could update the profile if the user initiated the change.

"Who updated this profile?" Jack asked.

"I do not know from this document."

"Could you determine that from Civic Bridge records?"

"Possibly."

"Was it produced?"

"I do not know."

Jack looked to Ellison. "We will request supplementation."

Ellison nodded in the careful way lawyers nod when they are not agreeing but know they cannot openly refuse yet. Jack returned his focus to Tessa. She had not denied that Civic Bridge could identify who moved the support contact from Lily's regular phone to the separate device. That was important. The separate device had not entered the system by magic. Someone had entered it, requested it, or accepted it as a new channel.

Jack placed the first device text in front of her. If you feel pressured, use the words we practiced: confused, unsafe, not ready. You do not need to explain everything. Tessa read it, then folded her hands. Jack let the silence last long enough to make the record honest.

"Did you send that message?" he asked.

"Yes."

"To whom?"

"A support-line user."

"Did you know the user was Lily Cole?"

"At that time, no."

"When did you learn the user may have been Lily Cole?"

Tessa paused. "After the court issue with the device."

"Define court issue."

"I learned there had been a dispute involving a phone found during a custody exchange."

"From whom?"

"Civic Bridge staff."

"Which staff member?"

"I believe it was Aaron Pike."

Mara wrote the name. Caleb marked a blank page for follow-up. Jack kept his expression neutral because names were doors, and this deposition was finally giving him one. Aaron Pike had not appeared in any production summary. If he was staff, he should have been in routing records. If he called Tessa after the phone was found, he knew the device mattered.

Jack continued. "Before you sent this message, what did you know about the user?"

"I knew the user was a young person experiencing family pressure and confusion."

"Did you know there was an active custody dispute?"

"I knew there was family conflict."

"That was not my question."

"I did not know the legal status."

"Did you know an emergency petition was being prepared?"

"No."

The answer came quickly. Jack marked it. A quick denial was not always false. It was often the answer a witness had prepared most carefully. He would need records around that date to test it.

Jack placed the next message in front of her: Remember, uncertainty can be used against you. Keep the frame steady. The reply, redacted except for I'm scared, sat underneath it. Tessa read it without visible reaction. Jack asked what she meant by uncertainty can be used against you. Tessa said young people in high-conflict families often felt their confusion was exploited by adults trying to control the narrative. She said she meant that the user did not have to surrender her sense of safety just because she had complicated emotions.

"Was the father the adult you believed might use uncertainty against the user?" Jack asked.

Ellison objected, and Tessa answered after a moment. "I did not know the father personally."

"Did you understand that one parent was being described as resistant?"

"I understood that the user felt pressure from a parent."

"Which parent?"

"The user's father."

Jack let the answer settle. Tessa now admitted she knew the user was a young person, in family conflict, feeling pressure from her father, and receiving support language connected to safety and uncertainty. She denied knowing the legal status and denied knowing Lily's name at the time. That denial might survive if the routing records supported it. It would not survive if any person connected the user to Marissa, Dana, Dr. Warren, or the petition before the messages were sent.

Jack moved to the Dana exchange. He placed the message on the table and read only the portion already authorized: Do not let raw uncertainty become the record. It is data for the team, not a message for the opposing parent. Tessa looked at it longer than she had looked at the device messages. Her face remained composed, though her hands shifted slightly. Jack noticed. So did Mara.

"What did you mean by opposing parent?" Jack asked.

"In that context, I meant a parent using a child's uncertainty to disrupt support."

"Did you know the parent's name?"

"No."

"Did Dana Keene tell you the child was Lily Cole?"

"No."

"Did she tell you the father was Ethan Cole?"

"No."

"Did she tell you the mother was Marissa Cole?"

"No."

Jack turned one page. "Did she tell you the child had written a note to a teacher?"

"Yes."

"Did she tell you the note complicated the support plan if the father obtained it?"

Tessa hesitated. "I recall a concern that raw writing could be misinterpreted."

Jack looked at the exhibit. "The message from Dana says the note could complicate the support plan if the father obtained it. Did you understand that concern before you replied?"

"I understood the concern generally."

"Did you tell Dana not to let the note become the record?"

"I used the phrase raw uncertainty. I did not mean conceal evidence from a court."

"That is not my question."

Ellison objected to tone. Jack waited, then repeated calmly.

"Did you tell Dana not to let the note become the record?"

Tessa looked at the message. "Those are the words I used."

It was not a confession of intent, but it was an admission of language. Sometimes that mattered more. Intent could be argued endlessly. Words had edges. Tessa had told a school counselor not to let a child's raw uncertainty become the record before an emergency petition was filed. Jack did not need to tell the court what that meant yet. He needed the court to see that it happened.

Claire, watching by video, took notes without speaking. Jack wondered what she was thinking as Marissa's position narrowed around the facts. Claire had tried to protect her client from a contempt finding, and rightly so. This deposition was making Marissa's role more complicated. A parent may have entered a child into a support system without knowing the system's consultant would influence the words that reached the court. That did not absolve Marissa. It did create space for fear rather than malice.

Jack placed the Language Support Guide before Tessa. She identified it as a training-derived tool used to help support teams avoid conflicting language. She denied it was designed to coach testimony. Jack asked why one column was labeled court-safe description. Tessa answered that court-safe meant language that avoided inflammatory or confusing phrases in documents that might later be reviewed by legal professionals. The answer was nearly useful to her until Jack placed Lily's note beside the guide under seal and asked whether several examples mirrored Lily's statements.

Ellison objected to the use of Lily's note and instructed Tessa not to read sealed minor content unless the court order permitted it. Jack agreed to withdraw the physical note from the deposition table and asked from the produced guide only. He did not need Tessa reading Lily's words. He had the court's copy, Mrs. Palmer's testimony, and the guide. The safer question was about whether Tessa created examples from actual user language.

"Were examples in this guide ever drawn from real support users?" Jack asked.

Tessa took longer to answer. "Sometimes generalized examples came from patterns we observed."

"Were any examples drawn from the support user later associated with Lily Cole's device?"

"I do not know."

"Who would know?"

"Possibly Aaron Pike or whoever compiled the user themes."

Another door. Jack wrote the name again. Aaron Pike had now surfaced as the person who informed Tessa about the phone issue and possibly managed user themes. He might be a staffer, a program manager, or a convenient name. The next subpoena would find out.

The deposition paused for a break at noon. Tessa and Ellison stepped into Jack's smaller conference room. Claire remained on video with her camera off. Jack took Caleb and Mara into his office and closed the door. For five minutes, no one spoke as they reviewed the notes. That silence was more productive than most arguments.

Mara finally said, "She's holding the line at no name, no legal status."

"Expected."

"Her problem is Aaron Pike."

"Yes."

Caleb flipped through the exhibits. "If Aaron knew the user was Lily and told Tessa, her denial breaks."

"Then we get Aaron."

"Civic Bridge will fight."

"Good. A fight creates a record."

Mara looked at Jack. "Do we ask about Fairchild today?"

"Only if tied to the guide or program funding."

"Enough to preserve the issue?"

"Enough to keep Hale nervous."

They returned to the deposition. Jack asked Tessa about Fairchild funding in careful terms. She confirmed that some Civic Bridge trainings and support programs received grant support from Fairchild. She denied that Fairchild controlled day-to-day communications with support users. She denied reporting individual support matters to Fairchild. She acknowledged submitting periodic program-impact summaries to Civic Bridge leadership, some of which were used in grant reporting. Jack asked whether those summaries included anonymized case examples. She said yes.

"Could Lily's case have appeared in an anonymized program-impact summary?" Jack asked.

Ellison objected. Tessa answered anyway. "Not by name."

"That was not the question."

"It is possible an anonymized scenario resembling her situation was included if it fit program categories."

"When?"

"I don't know."

"Who would know?"

"Aaron Pike may know. Civic Bridge leadership may know."

The name had now appeared three times. Jack did not need more from Tessa on that point. A judge would understand why Aaron Pike mattered. Fairchild might still be able to deny control, but grant reporting created another route through which Lily's circumstances may have been turned into institutional value. Not identity, perhaps. Not a name. A scenario. A metric. A success category. The law did not always know how to measure that kind of harm, but Jack was beginning to.

Near the end, Jack returned to the core question. "Ms. Laird, sitting here today, do you agree Lily Cole's actual written words should have been provided to the court under seal before any emergency decision-making order was requested?"

Ellison objected to foundation, calls for legal conclusion, and hindsight. Tessa waited, then answered carefully.

"I believe children's privacy should be protected."

"That was not my question."

"I am not qualified to say what the court should receive."

"You were qualified enough to tell Dana Keene not to let raw uncertainty become the record."

Ellison objected again, sharper this time. Jack let the objection sit, then asked one final version.

"Do you regret using that phrase?"

Tessa looked down at the exhibit, then back at Jack. "Yes."

The deposition ended ten minutes later. Tessa did not collapse, confess, or become a caricature. She remained composed to the end. That made her testimony more useful, not less. She had denied knowing Lily's name at the time of the messages, denied knowing an emergency petition was being prepared, and denied intent to shape testimony. She had admitted sending practiced words to the support device, advising Dana not to let raw uncertainty become the record, using court-safe language frameworks, and knowing an Aaron Pike who might explain how the support system handled Lily's identity and materials.

After Tessa and Ellison left, Amelia entered before Nora could stop her. "I waited."

Nora appeared behind her. "Barely."

Jack closed the deposition binder. "Tessa gave us Aaron Pike."

Amelia's expression sharpened. "Who is that?"

"Civic Bridge staff. Possibly support-line operations. Possibly user themes and program summaries."

Mara added, "Also the person Tessa says told her about the court issue with the phone."

Amelia sat slowly. "So he may know whether Tessa knew it was Lily."

"Yes," Jack said.

"And whether Lily's situation was used in grant reporting."

"Possibly."

Amelia looked toward the whiteboard. "Fairchild."

"Maybe Fairchild. Definitely Civic Bridge."

For once, she did not object to maybe. The deposition had given them enough movement that even Amelia could accept the next step. Jack watched her write Aaron Pike in her notebook, underline it once, then close the cover. She understood he could not let her chase him independently yet. Jack appreciated that she closed the notebook before he had to say it.

Caleb ordered the rough transcript expedited. Mara drafted a subpoena for Aaron Pike and Civic Bridge operational records. Jack prepared a sealed status notice to Judge Harrow, summarizing the deposition without argument and identifying the need for Aaron Pike's testimony. He did not accuse Tessa of perjury. He did not claim Fairchild control. He placed the admissions in order and let the sequence speak.

At six, Ethan called. Jack gave him a careful summary. Tessa admitted sending language to the support device and admitted telling Dana not to let raw uncertainty become the record. She denied knowing Lily's name at the time. Ethan listened in silence. Then he asked the question Jack expected.

"Do you believe her?"

"That is not what matters yet."

"It matters to me."

Jack leaned back. "I believe she knew enough to be careful and chose to be useful instead."

Ethan was quiet. "That sounds like guilt without saying guilt."

"It is responsibility without final findings."

"I hate legal words."

"I know."

"No, you don't."

Jack looked toward the darkening window. "I know enough."

Ethan did not push further. He reported that Lily had eaten dinner, watched her show, and asked if she could take her drawings to Dr. Patel. Ethan had told her yes and had not asked what they were. Jack praised him for that because praise, used sparingly, could reinforce better choices than warnings alone. Ethan sounded tired but steadier. That counted.

After the call, Jack stood alone before the whiteboard. He added Aaron Pike under Civic Bridge and wrote three questions beneath the name. Who routed the device? Who knew the user was Lily? Who reported the scenario upward? The questions were plain and unpolished. They were also exactly where the case now lived.

The next hearing would not be about whether Lily had been distressed. Everyone agreed she had been. It would be about who handled that distress, who translated it, who benefited from translation, and who decided her own words were too uncertain to become the record. Jack looked at the board for another minute before turning out the light. The path had moved from the child to the counselor, from the counselor to the consultant, and now from the consultant into the machinery that had called itself support. That machinery had a name, an office, and a staff member who had just become the next witness.

21

Aaron Pike did not want to be found, which made him easier to locate than Jack Sullivan expected. People who were truly hard to find usually had money, practice, or both. Aaron had a LinkedIn page, an old staff profile on Civic Bridge's website, and a conference biography that described him as director of youth response systems. He had also removed his name from the current Civic Bridge staff page sometime after Judge Harrow ordered production. Mara found the archived version before breakfast and placed it on the conference table with the kind of calm that meant she had been awake too long.

Jack read the profile twice. Aaron was thirty-nine, a former school social-work administrator, and the operational lead for Civic Bridge Youth Support. His biography said he designed "low-barrier pathways for vulnerable youth navigating complex family systems." The words sounded benevolent enough to survive a grant application. They also described the exact doorway through which Lily had been reached. Jack underlined operational lead and wrote subpoena beside it.

Caleb entered with coffee and the rough transcript from Tessa Laird's deposition. He looked younger when tired, which made Jack briefly aware of how much pressure he had placed on him in the past week. Caleb placed the transcript on the table and opened to the bookmarked pages. Tessa had said Aaron Pike may know who updated the support profile, who handled user themes, and who informed her after the phone appeared in court. Three may know answers were enough to justify one direct subpoena. They were also enough to make Civic Bridge nervous.

Nora appeared at the door. "Civic Bridge counsel called before eight."

Jack did not look surprised. "Name?"

"Leonard Fray. He says Mr. Pike is unavailable for deposition this week due to a preexisting professional commitment."

"Where?"

"He did not say."

"Convenient."

"That was my legal analysis."

Jack took the message slip and handed it to Caleb. "Notice Pike for deposition. Offer tomorrow morning and tomorrow afternoon. Copy Fray, Claire, Ellison, Angela, and the court only if they force motion practice."

Mara looked up. "They will."

"Then we let them choose to look obstructive."

The notice went out by nine-fifteen. Fray responded by nine-thirty with objections to burden, privacy, donor confidentiality, youth-support confidentiality, and the alleged harassment of a nonprofit employee. Jack read the letter without expression. It avoided one important fact: whether Aaron would appear at all. Lawyers who objected loudly around a simple yes or no often needed time to move something behind them. Jack had built enough cases to hear that noise.

At ten, Claire called. Her voice carried the tension of someone trying to remain reasonable while standing near a widening hole. She had no objection to Aaron Pike's deposition in principle, provided the questions stayed tied to Lily, the support number, and the device. She did not want the hearing delayed. Jack agreed on both points. The agreement surprised Caleb when Jack summarized it after the call, and Jack used the moment to teach.

"Opposing counsel is not the same as enemy counsel," Jack said.

Caleb nodded. "Even when they filed the petition."

"Especially then. If Claire sees the petition was built on bad information, give her a path to correct without making every step a public surrender."

Mara leaned back. "That was generous."

"It was strategic."

"It can be both."

Jack did not answer, because she was right and because agreeing would have pleased her too much.

Amelia arrived at ten-thirty with a printout and the look of a reporter who had found a door everyone else thought was a wall. She remained in the doorway until Jack covered the sealed materials. That had become their ritual. He looked up, nodded, and she entered. She placed the printout in the public-source file rather than on top of the sealed transcript.

"Aaron Pike sat on a Fairchild grant-review panel last year," she said.

Jack picked up the page. "For Civic Bridge?"

"For youth response systems across three counties. The panel selected pilot sites and evaluated program outcomes."

"Was Horizon involved?"

"One pilot listed Horizon as a clinical partner."

Mara stood and crossed the room. "Source?"

"Fairchild annual report. Public PDF. Page forty-two."

Jack read the page carefully. Aaron's name appeared under advisory reviewers. Tessa Laird appeared as communications design consultant. Dr. Elise Warren appeared under clinical advisory participants for one regional pilot. The report did not mention Lily, Marissa, Dana, or the Cole case because it predated the petition. It did something else. It showed that the network of people around Lily's case had worked together before, under Fairchild-funded programming, in roles that matched the same pathway now under review.

Caleb looked at the page. "This ties them together."

"It shows prior professional overlap," Jack said.

Amelia's eyes narrowed. "That is your least offensive correction so far."

"It is enough for questioning."

"Then use it."

"I intend to."

By noon, Leonard Fray agreed to a remote meet-and-confer at one. He did not agree to produce Aaron. Jack took the call with Caleb present, Mara listening from the end of the table, and Amelia removed from the room. Fray's voice was deep, measured, and practiced in nonprofit-defense language. He said Civic Bridge took youth confidentiality seriously, would not expose vulnerable users to adversarial discovery, and would not allow a custody litigant to turn a support program into a political target.

Jack let him finish. "Mr. Fray, no one is asking for all youth users. We are asking about one device found in one child's backpack, in one court case, after your support system sent that device language tied to the emergency petition."

Fray replied, "Civic Bridge disputes your characterization."

"Then produce Mr. Pike and the routing records so the record can be clear."

"We have produced routing records."

"You produced summary routing records. Tessa Laird testified Mr. Pike may know who updated the user profile and who informed her after the court issue. That makes him a material witness."

"He is not available this week."

"Why?"

"Professional commitments."

"What commitments?"

"That is not your concern."

Jack looked at Caleb, who was writing quickly. "It became my concern when you used it as a basis to refuse a court-related deposition."

Fray paused. "He is attending a donor compliance retreat."

Mara wrote the phrase in large letters.

Jack kept his tone flat. "Sponsored by whom?"

"I do not see the relevance."

"Fairchild?"

Fray did not answer immediately. "Fairchild is among several stakeholders."

That was enough for the next motion. Jack ended the call after confirming that Civic Bridge would not produce Aaron before the hearing absent court order. He sent a short letter memorializing the refusal within ten minutes. Then Caleb filed an ex parte request for an order compelling Aaron Pike's appearance or, at minimum, requiring him to be available remotely before the continued evidentiary hearing. Jack attached Tessa's transcript excerpts and the public Fairchild annual report page. He did not overargue donor retreat. He simply stated it.

Judge Harrow set a same-day remote status conference for four. The speed told Jack she was done letting third parties control the pace. At three-thirty, the office felt like a machine under strain. Caleb finalized exhibit packets. Mara updated the witness chart. Nora kept reporters off the phone and counsel on the calendar. Amelia worked in the front office, quiet enough that Jack knew she was listening to the office without pretending not to.

Ethan called at three-forty. Jack almost let it go to voicemail, then answered because fathers did not call during court preparation unless they had lost control or were trying not to. Ethan said Lily had asked whether she could leave a drawing at Dr. Patel's office and not bring it home. Jack told him that was between Lily and Dr. Patel, and that Ethan should not ask what the drawing showed. Ethan said he had not asked. Then he said something that made Jack stop pacing.

"She asked if grown-ups can be helpers and still make things worse."

Jack closed his eyes briefly. "What did you say?"

"I said yes. Then I said that's why helpers need other helpers watching."

Jack opened his eyes. "That was good."

"She said, 'Like court?'"

"What did you say?"

"I said, 'Maybe like court.' Then I changed the subject to tacos."

Jack looked through the glass at the conference room, at the binders, transcripts, and printed orders. "That was also good."

At four, Judge Harrow appeared on screen with less patience than usual. Fray appeared for Civic Bridge. Hale appeared for Fairchild again, claiming observer status. Ellison appeared for Tessa. Claire appeared for Marissa and said she took no position except that the matter should not delay Lily's safeguards. Jack appreciated that. It told the judge the dispute was no longer between father and mother alone.

Judge Harrow began with Fray. "Mr. Fray, why is Mr. Pike unavailable?"

Fray repeated the professional commitment answer, then admitted Aaron was attending a Fairchild stakeholder retreat related to youth response programs. Judge Harrow did not look at Hale. She did not need to. Her expression stayed neutral, but her next question was precise.

"Is Mr. Pike reachable by video tomorrow morning?"

Fray hesitated. "Possibly, though the retreat schedule is full."

"This court's schedule is also full. The difference is that mine involves a child whose communications may have been routed through your client's program."

Fray stopped. "Understood, Your Honor."

Judge Harrow ordered Aaron Pike to appear remotely the next morning at nine for a limited deposition of two hours, with Fray present. She ordered Civic Bridge to produce full routing logs, user-profile change records, staff access logs, and any communications between Pike, Laird, Keene, Warren, Marissa Cole, and Civic Bridge staff concerning the user associated with Lily's device. The production deadline was 8 a.m. She warned that failure to comply could result in evidentiary sanctions and referral to the appropriate authority for review of third-party interference in a custody proceeding.

Hale asked to be heard. Judge Harrow allowed one sentence. He used three.

"Your Honor, Fairchild is concerned that compelled production during a donor retreat may unnecessarily implicate foundation activities unrelated to this matter."

Judge Harrow looked directly into the camera. "Then Fairchild should be pleased that I am asking for records tied to the child and not the retreat."

Hale nodded and said nothing else.

After the hearing, the office breathed out. Caleb looked both exhausted and energized. Mara was already drafting the deposition outline. Amelia appeared in the doorway, read the room, and did not ask for details until Jack gave her the public-safe version. Aaron would testify at nine. Civic Bridge had to produce full logs. Fairchild's objections had not moved the court. Amelia smiled for the first time that day, though there was no joy in it.

At six-thirty, the first supplemental Civic Bridge records arrived early. Mara opened them under seal while Jack and Caleb watched. The access log showed the support profile initially created from Marissa's webinar registration, then modified two days later by Aaron Pike. The modified contact number matched the separate device. The note field read: route to TL for language continuity; parent escalation likely; legal readiness pending.

No one spoke. The room did not need dialogue. The record had just crossed from influence into operational handling. Aaron Pike had changed the profile, routed the device to Tessa, and noted legal readiness before the petition was filed. Jack looked at the timestamp, then at the board. The question for tomorrow had changed from whether Aaron knew. The question was how much he was willing to admit before the documents answered for him.

Jack called Ethan after the record was logged. He told him only that the court had ordered a key witness to testify and that the evidence was moving in Lily's favor. Ethan asked whether that meant the emergency petition would be denied. Jack said not yet. Ethan accepted the answer with less resistance than before. Progress had taught him caution, which was not the same as hope but might keep him from being hurt by hope too quickly.

After the call, Jack stood alone in the conference room. The board looked different now. Not because it had more names, but because one path had become visible enough to follow without guesswork. Marissa entered a number through Civic Bridge. Aaron changed the contact to the separate device. Tessa supplied practiced words. Dana withheld the note from the record. Dr. Warren interpreted the note through stabilization language. The court had heard only the final product.

Jack did not add a dramatic line under Aaron's name. He wrote the Bates number from the access log and the phrase route to TL for language continuity. That was enough. The document said what the case needed said. Tomorrow, Aaron Pike would sit under oath and explain why a child's private support profile contained a note about legal readiness before any judge had heard her full words. The answer would matter, but the record had already begun speaking in a language no one could easily reframe.

22

Aaron Pike appeared on the deposition screen from a hotel conference room with beige walls, a glass water pitcher, and a Fairchild-branded folder turned facedown beside his laptop. Jack Sullivan noticed the folder before Aaron moved it out of frame. So did Mara, who wrote one word on her pad without looking up. Caleb checked the remote recording, confirmed the court reporter was ready, and sent the exhibit link to Leonard Fray. The deposition began at nine sharp because Judge Harrow had made punctuality feel less like courtesy and more like survival.

Aaron took the oath with visible discomfort. He was not as polished as Tessa Laird and not as guarded as Grant Ellison. His face carried the fatigue of someone who had been told by too many lawyers what not to say and by too many supervisors what needed protecting. Jack preferred witnesses like that to witnesses who thought they were smarter than the record. Nervous witnesses often revealed the shape of the truth while trying to walk around it.

Jack began with Aaron's role at Civic Bridge. Aaron confirmed he was director of youth response systems, responsible for routing support requests, assigning consultants, overseeing volunteer responses, and preparing internal program summaries. He also confirmed that Civic Bridge Youth Support was not a licensed clinical service, not a legal service, and not a mandated crisis hotline. It provided "language support and resource navigation" to parents and youth in high-conflict family settings. Jack wrote the phrase down because it sounded like something designed to do more than it admitted.

The first exhibit was the webinar registration record. Aaron confirmed Marissa Cole registered for the parent-support session and entered Lily's regular phone number into the resource form. The system automatically sent a welcome message after the webinar. Jack asked whether that message created a user profile. Aaron said yes. He also confirmed that support users could later request to use a different number if privacy or safety was a concern.

Jack placed the profile-change log on the screen. It showed Aaron's user ID, the timestamp, and the change from Lily's regular number to the separate device number. The note field read: route to TL for language continuity; parent escalation likely; legal readiness pending. Aaron looked at the exhibit and then at his lawyer. Fray objected to form before Jack had asked anything.

Jack kept his voice steady. "Did you make this profile change?"

Aaron swallowed. "Yes."

"Who gave you the separate device number?"

"I don't remember exactly."

"That is not an answer that will survive the document."

Fray objected again. Jack waited. Aaron looked down, and the silence lasted long enough to become part of the testimony.

"I believe it came through the support channel," Aaron said. "The user asked to use a different number."

"Was the user Lily Cole?"

"I did not know her name at first."

"When did you know her name?"

Aaron hesitated. "Before the court hearing."

Jack looked at Caleb, who marked the page. "Which court hearing?"

"The emergency hearing."

"Before the petition was filed?"

"Yes."

The answer changed the air in the room. Aaron closed his eyes briefly as if he knew he had crossed a line his lawyer had hoped to keep blurred. Fray objected to the question as vague and asked to clarify the timeline. Jack allowed it because the clearer answer would either help or hurt, and he was prepared for both. Aaron clarified that he learned Lily's name after Marissa sent a follow-up through the webinar account asking whether her daughter's support communications could remain private if court became necessary. That message had not been included in the first Civic Bridge production.

Jack kept his face neutral. "Where is that message?"

Fray leaned toward the camera. "We are reviewing supplemental records."

"That was not my question to the witness."

Aaron looked miserable. "It should be in the parent-support mailbox."

"Did you search that mailbox before production?"

"I searched the exported user file. I did not personally search the full mailbox."

"Who did?"

"Our legal team."

Fray objected and instructed Aaron not to disclose attorney-client communications. Jack did not press that route. He had the missing category now. The next motion would ask for the mailbox record and audit trail. He moved back to the profile note because it was already in evidence and did not need anyone's memory to exist.

"What did you mean by legal readiness pending?" Jack asked.

Aaron rubbed his thumb along the edge of a paper he had in front of him. "It means the parent indicated the situation could involve court."

"Which parent?"

"Marissa Cole."

"Did she ask Civic Bridge to help prepare Lily for court?"

"No."

"Did anyone at Civic Bridge understand that Lily's words might be used in a court filing?"

Aaron looked down again. "We understood there might be legal proceedings."

"That was not my question."

Fray objected to form. Jack paused long enough to reframe.

"Did you understand that language used by Lily could appear in a court filing?"

Aaron's answer came quietly. "Yes."

Jack let the answer rest before moving on. That one word did not make Aaron a villain, and it did not resolve Marissa's intent. It did establish knowledge inside Civic Bridge that the language support given to a child might later become legal language. The support channel was no longer separate from court. It had been aware of court before the petition was filed.

The next exhibit was the routing note: route to TL for language continuity. Aaron confirmed TL meant Tessa Laird. He said Tessa was assigned because she had experience with youth language stabilization in high-conflict parent situations. Jack asked whether Tessa was told the user was Lily Cole. Aaron said he believed she was given initials and family context, not the full name. Jack asked whether she was told the father was the resistant parent. Aaron said yes, based on the support profile. Jack wrote each answer down, though Caleb was already capturing it.

Jack placed Tessa's message on the screen: If you feel pressured, use the words we practiced: confused, unsafe, not ready. "Was this consistent with Civic Bridge protocol?"

Aaron looked at Fray before answering. "It is consistent with helping a youth identify words when overwhelmed."

"Who selected those words?"

"I don't know."

"Were they entered into the support profile before Tessa sent them?"

Aaron scrolled through his own copy of the records. "Some were."

"By whom?"

He looked at the profile log. "Dana Keene provided a summary with those descriptors."

Jack remained still. "Dana Keene sent Civic Bridge a summary?"

"Yes."

"When?"

"Before the profile was routed to Tessa."

That summary had not been produced either. Jack did not need to say that; Caleb's pen had already moved to the missing-records list. Mara looked at Jack, and he gave a slight nod. Another door. Another production failure. Another adult summary standing between Lily and the record.

"Was Lily's handwritten note included in Dana's summary?" Jack asked.

"I don't remember seeing the note itself."

"Was it described?"

"Yes."

"How?"

Aaron looked at the exhibit list as if hoping the answer was on the page rather than in his mouth. "As a teacher note reflecting ambivalence, confusion, and potential loyalty conflict."

"Those are Dana's words?"

"I believe they were in the summary."

"Not Lily's words?"

"I don't recall Lily's exact words being included."

Jack looked at the screen for a moment. The pattern had repeated again. Lily wrote. Dana summarized. Aaron routed. Tessa framed. Dr. Warren interpreted. Claire filed. Each step sounded administrative until the child herself disappeared from the path.

Fray requested a break after ninety minutes. Jack agreed because breaks were normal, and because the testimony already needed organizing. He took Caleb and Mara into a separate room and muted the deposition line. Caleb looked at his notes with the stunned concentration of a young lawyer watching a case open wider than planned. Mara was calmer, though her anger showed in the way she underlined missing parent-support mailbox.

Caleb said, "They withheld the Marissa follow-up and Dana summary."

"Not necessarily intentionally," Jack said.

Mara looked at him. "Jack."

"Fine. They failed to produce responsive records."

"That is better."

"It is safer."

Mara pointed to the timeline. "Aaron knew Lily's name before the emergency hearing. Tessa had initials and family context. Dana provided descriptors. Marissa told Civic Bridge court might happen. Civic Bridge knew Lily's words could be used legally."

Jack nodded. "That is the status notice."

"Sanctions?"

"Not yet. Compel complete production first. Sanctions if they resist or the court wants them."

Caleb looked surprised. "After all that?"

"Yes. Judges do not like sanctions used as punctuation."

They returned to the deposition after the break. Jack shifted to program summaries and Fairchild reporting. Aaron confirmed Civic Bridge prepared anonymized reports for funders showing how youth response systems supported families through urgent interventions. He denied sending Lily's name to Fairchild. He admitted a scenario resembling her case may have been included in an internal impact draft because it fit the program category of "youth stabilized during resistant-parent escalation." That phrase entered the transcript like a stone placed on glass.

"Was that before the emergency hearing?" Jack asked.

"I believe the draft was prepared after the petition."

"Before the first hearing?"

"Yes."

"Who received the draft?"

"Civic Bridge leadership."

"Fairchild?"

"I don't know if that draft went to Fairchild."

"Who would know?"

Aaron closed his eyes for half a second. "Tessa might know. Or our executive director."

"Name?"

"Caroline Venn."

Jack wrote the name. Mara had already begun searching public records silently from her laptop. The case had moved from support-line operations to executive reporting, and Fairchild remained one step away, never touched directly, always close enough for its lawyer to appear. That pattern mattered. It suggested distance by design, or at least distance maintained by people who understood why distance would later be useful.

Jack asked about the phrase youth stabilized. Aaron said it referred to a young person maintaining the safety frame during conflict. Jack asked whether any licensed clinician determined Lily had been stabilized through Civic Bridge. Aaron said no. Jack asked whether Civic Bridge told the court it had communicated with Lily before the petition. Aaron said no. Jack asked whether Civic Bridge told Angela Morrissey after the phone was found. Aaron said no. By then, even Fray had stopped objecting as often.

Near the end, Jack returned to the separate device. "Who provided the physical phone?"

Aaron said, "I don't know."

"Did Civic Bridge purchase it?"

"No."

"Did Tessa?"

"I don't know."

"Did you?"

"No."

"Did Marissa?"

"I don't know."

"Did the user say where it came from?"

Aaron looked at the routing log. "There is a note that says borrowed safe phone."

"Who entered that note?"

"I did."

"Based on what?"

"A message from the user."

"Where is that message?"

Aaron's face fell. "It should be in the user message export."

"It is not in the production."

Fray objected, stating he could not confirm the completeness of the production during deposition. Jack accepted the objection and marked the record. The missing records now included Marissa's follow-up, Dana's summary, the user message about the safe phone, and the full profile history. The production had not been complete. Whether that was incompetence, over-redaction, or concealment would be decided later.

Jack ended with one question. "Mr. Pike, looking back now, do you believe Lily Cole's actual words should have been preserved and disclosed to the court under seal rather than converted into support-team language?"

Fray objected to form and legal conclusion. Aaron answered anyway.

"Yes."

The word was quiet, but the court reporter caught it. Jack did not ask another question. A final answer like that should not be crowded. He reserved the right to reconvene after full production and ended the deposition at one hour and fifty-seven minutes.

When the screen went black, the conference room stayed silent for a few seconds. Caleb looked at the transcript notes. Mara closed her laptop halfway. Jack removed his glasses and placed them on the table. The case had not ended in that deposition, but the original emergency petition had become almost impossible to defend as complete. Lily's words had not merely been lost. They had been processed.

Amelia entered after Nora told her the deposition was over. She did not ask for the sealed details at first. She looked at the faces in the room and sat down carefully.

"Bad?" she asked.

"Useful," Jack said.

"That means bad."

"It means useful."

Mara looked at Jack. "Aaron admitted Civic Bridge knew Lily's language could be used legally before the petition."

Amelia's jaw tightened. "And Fairchild?"

"Program summaries may have been prepared for leadership and possibly funders. No direct Fairchild production yet."

"Possibly funders."

"Yes."

She nodded slowly. "That is where the story goes."

"Not yet."

"I know. Lily first."

Jack looked at her. She said it without sarcasm. That mattered.

By late afternoon, Jack filed a sealed notice with Judge Harrow. It identified Aaron Pike's testimony, the missing production categories, and the need for immediate completion before the evidentiary hearing. He requested an order requiring Civic Bridge to produce the parent-support mailbox message from Marissa, Dana's summary, the safe phone message, complete profile history, and any impact draft concerning Lily's scenario. He did not request sanctions. He did ask the court to reserve the issue. That was often more effective than demanding punishment before the judge had time to become angry on her own.

Claire did not oppose the request for complete production. Her response was two sentences. Petitioner agrees the record should be complete. Petitioner reserves all rights regarding interpretation of any third-party conduct. Jack read it twice and placed it in the file. Claire was distancing Marissa from the machinery without defending the machinery. That was wise lawyering and a sign the center of the case had shifted again.

Ethan called at six. Jack told him only what he could safely tell a client without feeding the anger that might spill into

Lily's living room. Civic Bridge knew court might be involved before the petition. They routed Lily's communications to Tessa. They had not produced everything the court needed. Ethan took the news quietly. His quiet no longer scared Jack in the same way because it had discipline in it now.

"So it wasn't just Marissa," Ethan said.

"No."

"Was she used too?"

Jack considered the question. "Maybe. She also made choices."

"That sounds fairer than I want it to."

"Fair usually does."

Ethan exhaled. "Lily asked for spaghetti tonight. I burned the garlic bread."

"That may be the best news I heard today."

"It was bad."

"Ordinary bad is underrated."

Ethan gave a real laugh, small but present. Jack let the call end there after reminding him to keep the evening simple. Ordinary bad mattered because it belonged to a home rather than a case file. Burned garlic bread did not need a Bates number. Lily deserved as many things as possible without one.

After the office emptied, Jack stood before the whiteboard and added Aaron's testimony beneath the Civic Bridge column. Knew legal use possible. Routed to TL. Dana summary. Missing messages. Impact draft. He did not draw a line to Fairchild yet. He wrote Caroline Venn under Civic Bridge leadership and placed a question mark beside program summaries. The map looked less like a custody dispute each day, but the heart of it remained the same.

Lily had asked whether helpers could make things worse. The answer was now spread across transcripts, texts, logs, and omissions. Helpers had built a pathway around her, and every stop on that path claimed to protect her while moving her words farther from her. Jack closed the marker and looked at the board until the office lights dimmed. The next hearing would not need dramatic language. The record had learned to speak for itself, and for the first time, it was beginning to sound more like Lily than the adults who had translated her.

23

THE COMPLETED CIVIC BRIDGE production arrived at 7:42 the next morning, and by eight the conference room had become a records room with coffee. Jack Sullivan stood at the head of the table while Caleb broke the files into categories and Mara built a new timeline from the metadata. Nora kept the door closed and told Amelia she could wait in the front office, which Amelia did with the patience of a woman sharpening a knife no one could see. The production was larger than expected, and that told Jack the court's warning had worked. Third parties often found documents faster when a judge mentioned sanctions.

The missing parent-support message from Marissa came first. It was sent through the Civic Bridge webinar account four days before the petition. Marissa wrote that Lily was wavering, that Ethan would use any confusion to stop the process, and that she needed help keeping Lily steady if the court became involved. The response came from the support mailbox under Aaron Pike's user ID. It said a youth support path could be created and that a consistent language environment would help Lily avoid being pulled into "counter-narratives."

Caleb read the sentence twice. "Counter-narratives."

Jack nodded. "Add it."

Mara placed it under Civic Bridge. "That is not clinical."

"No," Jack said. "That is communications language."

The Dana summary was worse because it converted Lily's note before Tessa ever saw the support profile. Dana had written that Lily expressed confusion and fear, showed signs of loyalty conflict, and had given a teacher a note that could be misused by the resistant parent. The summary did not attach Lily's words. It did not quote the note. It treated the note as a risk to the process rather than a record of the child's own experience. Jack placed the summary beside Mrs. Palmer's copy and did not need to say what the comparison showed.

The safe phone message came next. The user, identified only by profile number, had written that the separate phone was "the safe phone" and that she was told to use it when she needed to say things without people getting upset. The message did not say who gave it to her. Aaron had entered the note into the profile, then routed the contact to Tessa for language continuity. Jack read the message and felt the familiar pressure behind his ribs. A child had been given a device that made secrecy feel like safety, and every adult in the case now had to pretend not to understand how much damage that could do.

Mara opened the complete profile history. The first entry came from Marissa's webinar registration. The second came from Aaron. The third came from Tessa. The fourth was a system note: user preparing for possible court-related family transition; reinforce steady words. Jack looked at the phrase family transition and almost laughed, not because it was funny, but because bureaucratic language had a way of making devastation look like scheduling. Lily's family was being pulled through court. The system called it transition.

Caleb looked pale. "This is enough for tomorrow."

"For part of tomorrow."

"You think the judge will deny the emergency petition?"

"I think the judge will have to decide whether the petition can survive the record that produced it."

"That sounds like yes."

"It sounds like what I said."

Mara looked at Caleb. "He does that when he refuses to promise the obvious."

Jack ignored her because she was not wrong. Family court did not move like criminal court, and emergency petitions did not always die because one side's record was flawed. The court still had to assess Lily's distress, the parents' conduct, treatment needs, and immediate safety. Jack's job was not merely to expose the flawed process. It was to give Judge Harrow a safe legal path away from a drastic order and toward a structure that protected Lily without rewarding the adults who had shaped the record.

At ten, Claire called. She had received the same production and did not sound surprised enough for Jack to believe she had slept. She said Marissa would not oppose withdrawal of the request for sole temporary medical decision-making authority, provided the parties could agree to a neutral interim plan with Dr. Patel, shared information protocols, and no unilateral treatment escalation. Jack listened without interrupting.

It was the most important shift in the case so far, and it came without a speech.

"Is your client withdrawing the emergency petition?" Jack asked.

"She is willing to withdraw the request for sole authority without prejudice."

"That is not the same."

"No. It is the position I have authority to offer."

Jack wrote it down. "What about the allegations against Ethan?"

Claire was quiet for a moment. "We can stipulate that the prior record was incomplete and that no finding has been made that Ethan endangered Lily."

"That needs to be in the order."

"I expected you to say that."

"It needs to be plain."

"I know."

Jack leaned back in his chair. "Does Marissa understand what she is agreeing to?"

Claire's answer was measured. "She understands the emergency process was influenced by information she did not fully understand at the time."

"That is doing a lot of work."

"It is the truth as far as I can ethically say it today."

Jack accepted that. He did not need Claire to condemn her client. He needed Claire to help build an order that stopped the harm. The rest could be dealt with through testimony, discovery, and, if the facts supported it, later proceedings involving Civic Bridge, Tessa, or others outside the custody case.

After the call, Jack told the room. Ethan would not get the public vindication he wanted, not yet, but the emergency request that had threatened to take his authority would likely be withdrawn or gutted. Caleb looked relieved. Mara looked cautious. Amelia, who had been called in for the public-safe update, looked unsatisfied because she understood compromise was often where public truth went to lose its teeth.

"She gets to withdraw without saying she was wrong," Amelia said.

"She gets to move away from a bad petition without forcing the judge to keep a child in the middle longer than necessary."

"That is generous."

"It is protective."

"For Lily."

"Yes."

Amelia looked at the sealed binders she could not read. "And for the adults?"

"Sometimes protecting a child means adults avoid the punishment the public would prefer."

She did not like it, but she did not argue. That was another form of restraint, and this case had begun to demand it from everyone.

Jack called Ethan before lunch. He chose his office, closed the door, and sat before speaking because Ethan deserved a voice that was not walking through tasks. He explained that Claire had offered to withdraw the sole temporary authority request without prejudice, that the order would include no finding that Ethan endangered Lily, and that neutral counseling would remain in place. He also explained that this would not end the case. Custody, treatment decisions, records, and Lily's long-term structure still needed resolution.

Ethan was silent. "So I don't get a ruling that says they lied."

"No."

"Even after all this."

"You get an order that stops the immediate harm and removes the emergency claim from over your head."

"That is not enough."

"It may be enough for Lily today."

The line stayed quiet. Jack heard the argument Ethan wanted to make and the father in him fighting not to make it. Ethan had been accused publicly, restrained privately, and forced to watch adults admit piece by piece that his daughter's words had been reshaped. Wanting a judgment was human. Wanting it at Lily's expense would be dangerous.

Ethan finally spoke. "Will it say I didn't endanger her?"

"It will say no finding has been made that you endangered her and that the prior record was incomplete."

"That sounds like a lawyer wrote it."

"A lawyer will."

"Can it say I am her father and I have rights?"

Jack looked at the draft stipulation on his desk. "It can say both parents retain joint legal decision-making pending further order."

"That matters."

"Yes."

"Then do it."

Jack returned to the conference room and began drafting the proposed stipulated order with Claire. They worked by email, then by phone, then by tracked changes that made the document look bruised. The order withdrew the request for sole temporary medical decision-making authority without prejudice. It preserved joint legal custody, required mutual written consent or court order for major treatment changes, continued Dr. Patel as neutral therapeutic provider, prohibited third-party support contact without court approval, and required all parent communication through the monitored app. It also stated that the court made no finding that Ethan endangered Lily and that the emergency record initially presented was incomplete as to Lily's written statements and undisclosed support communications.

Claire fought the word incomplete only once. Jack refused to remove it. Judge Harrow had already used the word in substance, and the record supported it. Claire offered partial instead. Jack declined because partial sounded accidental, and the sequence showed more than accident. They settled on materially incomplete, which was worse for Claire and better for truth. Jack appreciated that she did not make him seek the language through a motion.

At three, Angela Morrissey joined the call. She asked for one addition: Lily should be told in age-appropriate language that neither parent had won or lost and that her therapy did not belong to the court case. Jack agreed immediately. Claire did too. Angela also asked that the order require both parents to attend a session with Dr. Patel separately, not for treatment, but for guidance on how to respond to Lily's anxiety without questioning her. That was wise. It turned the parents from competing audiences into supervised listeners.

The final version went to Judge Harrow at four-fifteen as a joint proposed order, with a request that the next hearing be converted into a review and scheduling conference rather than a contested emergency hearing. Jack sent a copy to Ethan before filing and walked him through each paragraph. Ethan had objections born of pain, not law. Jack listened to them anyway. Sometimes people accepted restraint better after being allowed to name what restraint cost.

Judge Harrow signed a modified version at five-thirty. She added one paragraph of her own, directing Civic Bridge and Tessa Laird to preserve all records pending further order and stating that the court reserved jurisdiction to address third-party interference if later evidence warranted it. Jack read that paragraph twice and understood what the judge had done. She had resolved the emergency for Lily without closing the door on the adults who may have distorted the record. That was careful, and it was strong.

Nora printed the signed order and brought it to Jack's office. "Is this good?"

"Yes."

"Good like pancakes, or good like no one violated an order before breakfast?"

Jack looked up. "Better than both."

"Then I'll take it."

By six, Ethan arrived to pick up his copy. He stood in Jack's office and read the order slowly, line by line. When he reached the sentence stating no finding had been made that he endangered Lily, his eyes stayed on the page for a long time. He did not smile. He did not cry. He looked like a man who had been allowed to put down a weight but did not yet trust the floor to hold it.

"It doesn't undo what people heard," Ethan said.

"No."

"It doesn't fix Lily."

"No."

"It gives us room."

"Yes."

Ethan folded the order carefully. "Then I'll use the room."

Jack nodded. "That is the right answer."

After Ethan left, Amelia found Jack in the conference room. The office had quieted, and the whiteboard still held the full path from Marissa's webinar registration to Tessa's texts to Aaron's routing notes. Amelia stood beside it with her arms folded. She had not touched the marker. Her restraint had become one of the strangest measures of the case.

"This is the end of the first act," she said.

Jack placed the signed order into the binder. "This is the end of the emergency."

"That's not the same."

"No."

"They still used a child as a program outcome."

"Maybe."

She turned toward him, tired of the word again. Jack understood. He pointed to Judge Harrow's added paragraph in the order. Amelia read it, then nodded slowly.

"She left the door open," Amelia said.

"Yes."

"For Civic Bridge."

"For anyone the record supports."

"Fairchild too?"

"If the record supports it."

Amelia looked back at the board. "It will."

Jack did not answer. He had learned not to argue with predictions when tomorrow would test them anyway. For now, Lily had a safer order, Ethan had not lost his rights, and the emergency story had been forced to admit it was built on an incomplete record. That was not justice in the final sense. It was enough legal ground to stand on while the next fight took shape.

At eight, Dr. Patel's general update arrived through Angela. Lily attended briefly by phone, asked whether she still had to choose words from the list, and was told she did not. The update contained no further content. Jack sat with that sentence longer than any court order he had read that day. Words from the list. The phrase would not appear in a public filing unless necessary, and perhaps it should not. It belonged first to the people trying to give Lily back her own language.

Jack sent Ethan only what he could safely say. Dr. Patel says Lily does not have to use anyone else's words. Keep tonight ordinary. Ethan replied ten minutes later. We are making grilled cheese. No court talk. Jack saved the message, then closed the file.

The office lights dimmed automatically as the building settled into night. Jack stood before the whiteboard and erased the word emergency from the top corner. He replaced it with merits. The case was no longer about stopping the first disaster. It was about discovering how many adults, programs, donors, and professionals had touched Lily's truth before it reached the court. The emergency was over for now. The custody of truth had only begun.

24

THE DAY AFTER THE emergency order changed, Jack Sullivan made everyone start over. Not from the beginning, because the beginning was now too crowded with noise, but from the first usable question. What custody arrangement protected Lily Cole while the court sorted the adults? He wrote it across the top of the whiteboard before anyone sat down. Mara looked at the erased sections with mild grief, Caleb looked relieved by the cleaner structure, and Amelia stood near the window with the expression of someone watching a house get remodeled before the arson investigation was finished.

The emergency petition was no longer the center of the case. That mattered legally, because the court was no longer being asked to make an immediate drastic order based on fear. It mattered emotionally, because Ethan could breathe without feeling that every hour might become the hour he lost his daughter. It also mattered strategically, because Marissa had stepped back from the hardest accusation without withdrawing every concern. The case had moved from crisis to merits, and merits required slower proof.

Jack divided the board into three columns: parenting structure, decision-making, and third-party influence. Lily belonged in none of those columns and all of them. That was the problem with custody litigation. A child's life had to be organized into categories the court could manage, even when the child experienced it as one continuous room full of adults. Jack wanted the next phase to reduce the number of adults in that room.

Caleb opened the new case schedule. "We have the review conference in six days, Dr. Patel's first parent-guidance sessions next week, and document production from Civic Bridge still ongoing."

"Add Tessa supplemental deadline," Jack said.

"Already did."

"Mara?"

Mara looked up from her laptop. "Civic Bridge produced the profile logs, but not the impact draft or executive communications with Caroline Venn. They say those are under review."

Jack wrote Caroline Venn under the third column. "Then we keep the pressure there."

Amelia folded her arms. "That is where Fairchild comes in."

"Maybe."

She closed her eyes briefly. "I am going to start charging you every time you say that."

"You will need a billing system."

Nora entered with fresh coffee and a stack of mail. "Please do not give Amelia a billing system. She will invoice all of us for emotional damages."

The small laugh that followed did not last long, but it helped. The office had been living inside sealed records, child distress, and careful outrage for too many days. Humor was not escape. It was pressure release. Jack had learned that people working around pain needed ways to remain human, or they began to sound like the documents they despised.

At ten, Claire sent her proposed long-term temporary parenting framework. It was not a final custody proposal, and the email said so three times. It suggested continued joint legal custody, a regular schedule with neutral exchanges for thirty days, parent-guidance sessions with Dr. Patel, and a prohibition on either parent using outside advocacy, counseling, or support resources for Lily without disclosure and written agreement. It also proposed that both parents refrain from public statements and that counsel work toward a confidential parenting plan. Jack read it carefully because it was better than he expected.

He called Claire with Caleb present. The call was businesslike, and for once neither lawyer sounded eager to win the sentence. Jack told her the framework was a start. Claire said Marissa wanted stability for Lily and did not want the case to become a referendum on every organization that had contacted her. Jack said the organizations became relevant when they contacted Lily. Claire did not argue the point. That silence showed how much the case had changed.

"Marissa wants assurance Ethan will not use this to shut her out of treatment decisions," Claire said.

"Ethan wants assurance Marissa will not outsource treatment decisions to undisclosed third parties."

"That is fair."

"It is also the order."

Claire sighed. "I know."

Jack waited a moment before speaking again. "If both parents can agree that Lily does not belong to anyone's framework, the judge will see that."

Claire's voice softened. "I will try to get Marissa there."

After the call, Caleb looked at Jack. "That sounded almost cooperative."

"Do not confuse cooperation with trust."

"I won't."

"Also do not confuse distrust with intelligence."

Caleb made a note. Jack almost told him that sentence did not need preserving, then decided it might be useful. The younger lawyer was watching the case transform from battle into architecture. That was a harder lesson than cross-examination. A lawyer could win an argument and leave a child without a workable life. Jack wanted the opposite.

Ethan arrived at noon for a scheduled review. He looked better, though better in this case meant shaved, rested, and still carrying the strain behind his eyes. Jack gave him Claire's proposed framework and watched him read it. Ethan stopped at the no-public-statements clause and nodded. He stopped again at the outside-resource disclosure clause and tapped the page with one finger.

"This should have been there from the beginning," Ethan said.

"Yes."

"Can we make it stronger?"

"We can make it clear. Stronger is not always better if it becomes hard to follow."

"She gave Lily a number."

"The new language prevents either parent from giving Lily undisclosed numbers, apps, counselors, advocacy contacts, or support channels."

Ethan read that section again. "Good."

Jack studied him. "You understand it applies to you too."

"I do."

"No pastor, mentor, counselor, friend, or online resource for Lily without disclosure and agreement."

Ethan looked up. "I wouldn't do that."

"Say it anyway."

"I won't do that."

Jack nodded. Ethan did not bristle, and that was progress. In the first days, every warning had sounded to him like accusation. Now he understood that a good order protected Lily by restraining everyone, including the parent who had been wronged. The law did not always feel fair when applied evenly after uneven harm. It was still the only way forward.

They spent the next hour refining practical details. Exchange times. School pickup. Therapy transportation. How to handle Lily's drawings. How to respond if she brought up Tessa, the phone, Marissa, court, fear, or guilt. Jack wrote simple language on a card for Ethan to keep in his wallet: I love you. You are not in trouble. You do not have to use anyone else's words. Dr. Patel and Angela are here to help the adults listen better. Ethan read it and put it in his pocket without speaking.

After Ethan left, Amelia came into Jack's office with a public record printout. She had found Caroline Venn's biography. Civic Bridge's executive director had previously worked for

Fairchild as a senior program officer before moving to Civic Bridge. She had overseen grants related to youth response systems, family court innovation, and legal access partnerships. Amelia placed the page on Jack's desk and waited. Jack read it twice.

"This is public?" he asked.

"Yes."

"Verified?"

"Civic Bridge page, Fairchild annual report, and her own conference bio."

Jack placed it in the public-source binder. "Good."

"Good is underselling it."

"It gives us a clean basis to ask why Fairchild's former program officer was running the organization that routed Lily's support contact."

"And maybe reporting impact back to Fairchild."

"Maybe."

Amelia pointed at him. "Invoice number one."

Jack almost smiled. "Put it on Caroline Venn's tab."

By midafternoon, Civic Bridge produced the impact draft. It had been withheld for review and then produced after Jack's follow-up letter citing Judge Harrow's order. The draft did not name Lily, Ethan, or Marissa. It described a youth-support scenario involving a minor in a high-conflict family where a resistant parent created barriers to stabilization, and where coordinated language support helped the youth maintain safety framing before court intervention. The draft listed the scenario under early indicators of program success.

No one in the conference room spoke for several seconds. Jack read the paragraph again, then placed it beside the support logs. The dates showed the draft had been prepared after the petition was filed but before the first emergency hearing. That meant Lily's situation, anonymized but recognizable to the people involved, had been turned into a program success marker before the court had even heard the full record. It did not prove Fairchild had directed anything. It did prove the case had institutional value to someone beyond the parents.

Mara's voice was low. "Program success."

Caleb looked angry. "The petition had not even been heard."

Jack nodded. "Add the date."

Amelia stood in the doorway, not entering because sealed records were on the table. "What happened?"

Jack covered the document. "Civic Bridge produced an impact draft."

Her face changed. "Lily?"

"Anonymized scenario. Before the first hearing. Program success language."

Amelia looked away toward the front windows. "They were counting her before the judge heard her."

Jack did not correct that. It was the plain version of what the document showed. He would not write it that way in a motion, but he would not pretend it was wrong. Lily's fear had been useful before anyone proved what it meant. That fact would matter, if not to custody, then to whatever came after.

Jack called Claire before filing anything. He told her the impact draft had arrived and that he intended to include it in a sealed status update because it bore on third-party influence and the credibility of the process. Claire asked for twenty minutes to review. He gave her thirty. When she called back, her voice sounded subdued.

"I will not oppose lodging it under seal," she said.

"Do you oppose the court considering it for the limited purpose of third-party influence?"

"No. I oppose any suggestion that Marissa knew about this."

"I do not have evidence that she did."

"Then say that."

"I will say the record does not show that."

"That is acceptable."

Jack understood what Claire was doing. She was protecting Marissa from being swallowed by the machinery that had used her fear. That was proper. Jack could respect it without forgetting that Marissa had opened the door, failed to disclose the support number, and allowed a petition to proceed on an incomplete record. People could be used and still responsible for their choices. The court would have to hold both truths at once.

At five, Jack filed a sealed status update attaching the impact draft, Caroline Venn's public biography, and a short request that Civic Bridge produce communications between Venn, Pike, Laird, and any Fairchild contact concerning the anonymized scenario. He did not ask to subpoena Fairchild yet. The record was close but not there. A premature subpoena would let Hale argue harassment and donor intimidation. Jack wanted the judge to see the path before he asked to step onto Fairchild property.

Ethan called after dinner. Lily was with Marissa that night, and the house was too quiet. He had followed the app protocol, sent one neutral message about homework, and received one neutral answer. No argument. No side channel. No emotional commentary. Jack praised him for keeping it that way, then told him nothing about the impact draft because it would only feed anger he could not use.

"Do you think Marissa knows how much this hurt Lily?" Ethan asked.

"I do not know."

"I want her to know."

"She will learn more through Dr. Patel than through you."

Ethan sighed. "That's the kind of answer I hate because it's probably right."

"Probably is progress."

"I'm learning your language."

"Try not to."

Ethan gave a small laugh, then ended the call. Jack sat with the phone in his hand for a moment. Ethan was changing. Not into someone less wounded, but into someone less governed by the wound. That would matter to Lily more than any transcript. The court could restore authority. It could not teach a father how to be safe with his own pain unless he chose to learn.

The office emptied slowly. Caleb left with the parenting framework draft and instructions to make it shorter. Nora left after telling Jack that shorter also applied to workdays. Mara stayed to finish the Venn search. Amelia remained near the front table, reviewing public donor reports with a level of focus that suggested she had found the larger story and was waiting for the legal case to catch up. Jack let her work. The boundary had held so far.

Near nine, Mara found the first direct Fairchild thread in public records, not sealed production. It was an old conference panel transcript where Caroline Venn, then at Fairchild, described youth response systems as "building the language architecture that allows courts to recognize harm before resistant families bury it." The phrase language architecture appeared three times. Jack read the transcript and placed it beside the impact draft. It did not mention Lily. It did not need to. It showed philosophy, and philosophy often became practice through people who thought they were improving the world.

Amelia read the public transcript over his shoulder. "That's the phrase."

Jack nodded. "Language architecture."

"It sounds clean until you see what it did to Lily."

"Yes."

"Can I use the public transcript?"

"Not yet if it ties directly into this case."

"It does not name her."

"No. But your reporting could signal the direction of sealed proceedings."

Amelia stepped back, frustrated but controlled. "After Lily."

"After Lily."

She nodded. "Fine."

Jack stood alone at the whiteboard after everyone left. He added Caroline Venn under Civic Bridge and wrote language architecture beneath her name. Then he placed a question mark between Venn and Fairchild instead of drawing an arrow. The arrow would come only when the record earned it. That discipline had carried them this far. It would have to carry them farther, because the case was no longer only about the parents. It was about a system that had learned to make children legible to courts by teaching them which words counted. Lily's own words were beginning to return, and the more they did, the less the architecture around her looked like help.

25

THE REVIEW CONFERENCE BEGAN with a signed order already in place and a courtroom full of people who understood the emergency had changed shape. Judge Harrow sat on the bench with the latest sealed status update in front of her, along with the parenting framework, the Civic Bridge impact draft, and the public materials tying Caroline Venn to Fairchild's youth response programs. The courtroom was quieter than it had been at the first hearing. There were still observers in the gallery, and at least two reporters sat near the back, but the spectacle had thinned. Cases were rarely less serious when they became quieter.

Jack Sullivan sat with Caleb at counsel table. Ethan remained downstairs in the conference room because Jack had decided there was no benefit to having him stare at Marissa across a public courtroom while lawyers discussed systems that had used their daughter's distress. Claire Whitcomb sat with Marissa beside her, both of them composed in different ways. Marissa looked less certain than before and more tired. Claire looked like a lawyer who had spent the last week trying to move her client away from a collapsing bridge without letting anyone see how close the bridge had come to taking them both down.

Judge Harrow began by confirming the temporary framework. Joint legal custody remained in place. Dr. Patel would continue as Lily's neutral therapeutic provider. Neither parent could introduce new counselors, advocates, support lines, mentors, online communities, or third-party resources to Lily without written agreement or court approval. Parenting communication would remain on the monitored app. It sounded administrative when the judge read it, but Jack knew each sentence existed because an adult had already found a way around ordinary trust.

The judge then turned to the next phase. "The emergency petition has been withdrawn in its prior form, and the court has entered temporary safeguards. That does not end the court's concern. The record reflects that the minor child's written statement was handled through school, clinical, and third-party support channels before it was disclosed to the court. The court must now determine what custody and decision-making structure protects the minor while ensuring neither parent nor any third party controls the child's voice."

That last phrase shifted the room. Controls the child's voice. Jack wrote it down exactly. Claire did too. Even Ellison, appearing remotely for Tessa, seemed to take note. Victor Hale sat in the gallery this time rather than at counsel table, which Jack suspected was not humility but strategy. Fairchild wanted to be close enough to know and far enough to deny.

Judge Harrow set a limited merits schedule. Parent-guidance reports from Dr. Patel would remain general and protected. A custody evaluation would be considered only after the court determined whether one was necessary and who could perform it without connection to Horizon, Civic Bridge, or Fairchild-funded programming. The parties would exchange proposed parenting plans within ten days. Third-party discovery would continue on the narrow issue of influence over Lily's statements and communications. The court made clear that no party had permission to turn the case into a broad policy trial.

Claire asked to be heard on one point. "Your Honor, petitioner is concerned that continued third-party discovery could overshadow Lily's immediate needs. Ms. Cole accepts the court's temporary framework and wants to focus on stabilization."

Jack expected the word and disliked it less this time because Claire used it differently. Stabilization, in her mouth now, meant less movement, fewer adults, and fewer secret channels. That did not erase how the word had been used before, but language could be reclaimed if people stopped weaponizing it. Judge Harrow looked to Jack.

"Respondent agrees Lily's immediate needs come first," Jack said. "The third-party discovery matters because it affects what safeguards are necessary. If outside actors shaped Lily's words and communications, the court needs to know how to prevent that from happening again."

Judge Harrow nodded. "That is the line the court will maintain."

The conference ended with a scheduling order and no dramatic ruling. Jack preferred that. Dramatic rulings often created dramatic appeals. This order moved the case forward, preserved Lily's therapeutic space, and kept the third-party record alive. It gave Ethan room without inviting him to celebrate. It gave Marissa structure without forcing a public confession. It gave the court time to see what the adults had built around the child.

Downstairs, Ethan read the minute order at the conference table. Jack watched his face as he reached the line about neither parent nor third party controlling Lily's voice. Ethan's eyes stayed there for several seconds. He did not ask whether it meant he had won. He had stopped using that word, and Jack counted that as another kind of progress.

"She said it," Ethan said.

"Yes."

"Not the way I would say it."

"That is why it works."

Ethan folded the order and placed it in his folder. "What happens now?"

"We prepare a parenting plan. You attend Dr. Patel's guidance session. You keep following the order. You let Lily be a daughter instead of a witness."

Ethan looked down. "That last part is the hardest."

"I know."

"No, it is. Because everything in me wants to ask what they said to her, what she believed, what she still believes."

Jack leaned forward. "That is why Dr. Patel exists in this order. Lily needs one adult who is not collecting answers for a side."

Ethan nodded slowly. "I don't want to be another side."

"Then do the harder thing."

By early afternoon, the office had shifted from hearing mode to planning mode. Caleb began drafting Ethan's proposed parenting plan, starting with the areas already ordered: joint decision-making, neutral counseling, monitored communication, and no outside resources. Mara worked on the third-party discovery chart, now organized by witness rather than institution. Amelia returned from the courthouse with three pages of notes from the public portions of the hearing and a face that told Jack she had already written the headline in her mind and then refused herself permission to use it.

She sat across from him in the conference room after he cleared the sealed materials. "The judge gave you a phrase."

"She gave the case a phrase."

"Controls the child's voice."

"Yes."

"That is the book."

Jack looked at her. "This is not a book."

"It will be something."

"Not until Lily is protected."

Amelia closed her notebook. "I know. I'm saying the phrase matters."

"It does."

The brief exchange ended there, which surprised Jack. Amelia was learning the discipline of the case, or at least the timing of when not to argue. He had to admit she had earned more room than he expected when the case began. She had found public records no subpoena would have reached quickly. She had also kept sealed facts sealed, which made her useful in a way many reporters refused to be.

At three, Dr. Patel held Ethan's first parent-guidance session by video from Jack's office. Jack did not sit in. He walked Ethan to the small conference room, reminded him that this was not testimony preparation, and left him there with a legal pad he was not supposed to fill with strategy. Dr. Patel's purpose was narrow: teach Ethan how to respond when Lily expressed fear, confusion, loyalty conflict, or guilt. Ethan looked nervous in a way Jack had not seen in court. Court gave him someone to fight. This gave him someone to become.

When the session ended, Ethan came out quiet. He did not give details, and Jack did not ask for them. That was the structure they had all agreed to. Ethan only said Dr. Patel told him Lily needed fewer conclusions and more permission to have unfinished feelings. Jack nodded. It was the kind of sentence a lawyer could not put in an order and every parent in the case needed to understand.

"Can you do that?" Jack asked.

"I can try."

"That is the honest answer."

"She said I should stop telling Lily everything will be okay."

Jack waited.

"She said I should say, 'I'm here with you right now.'"

Jack nodded again. "That is better."

"It feels weaker."

"It is stronger because it does not make promises you cannot control."

Ethan looked at him for a moment. "You should have been a therapist."

"No one deserves that."

Ethan almost smiled. The moment was small, but small moments had become important. He left through the rear entrance because the courthouse reporters had found the office again, and Nora had counted three calls from producers asking whether Ethan would comment now that the emergency request had changed. Jack had declined all of them. Ethan's public silence was part of Lily's private protection.

Near five, Mara found the first gap in Caroline Venn's production. Civic Bridge produced emails between Venn and Aaron Pike about program summaries, but not the attachment labeled Q3 Youth Response Impact Draft. The metadata showed it had been sent to Venn, Tessa, and an address at Fairchild ending in grantsreview. Hale had said Fairchild did not direct Lily contact. He had not said Fairchild never received program summaries. The distinction now mattered.

Jack read the metadata printout. "Do we have the attachment from Civic Bridge?"

"No. Withheld pending relevance review."

"Privilege?"

"No privilege claimed. Just relevance."

"That will not hold."

Caleb leaned over. "This is the first direct Fairchild address tied to the impact draft."

"Yes," Jack said. "Direct receipt, not direction."

Amelia stood just outside the doorway. "May I hear the public-safe version?"

Jack looked at the covered materials, then at her. "Civic Bridge metadata suggests an anonymized program-summary attachment may have been sent to a Fairchild grants-review address. We do not have the attachment yet."

Her eyes sharpened. "Before or after the emergency hearing?"

"Before."

She said nothing for once. That silence said enough.

Jack drafted a meet-and-confer letter to Hale and Fray before filing anything. He asked for the attachment, transmittal email, recipient list, and any response from Fairchild concerning the anonymized scenario, all under seal and limited to the Cole-related impact draft. He gave them until noon the next day. Hale responded within forty minutes, objecting that Fairchild had no way to determine whether anonymized materials referred to Lily Cole without reviewing protected child information it did not possess. Jack admired the sentence for its structure. It denied knowledge while explaining why knowledge could not be tested.

Fray responded less elegantly. Civic Bridge would review and supplement if required. That meant they had it. Jack forwarded both responses to Caleb and Mara with instructions to prepare a motion only if the attachment was not produced by noon. He did not want to fight before giving them a chance to produce. Judges liked lawyers who made refusal clear before asking for help. Jack also liked making opposing counsel choose their own bad record.

At six-thirty, Claire called again. She had heard from Hale, which annoyed Jack but did not surprise him. She wanted to know whether the Fairchild issue would affect the parenting framework. Jack said not unless it showed Marissa knew Lily's situation was being used externally or that Fairchild influenced the custody petition. Claire said she had no evidence of either. Jack said he did not either. That was the truth, and truth sometimes protected the opposing party as much as the client.

"Marissa is scared this will become bigger than Lily," Claire said.

"It already is bigger than Lily in some respects."

"That is what scares her."

"It should."

Claire was quiet. "She also asked me whether Ethan hates her."

Jack looked through the office glass at the darkening hallway. "He is trying not to let hate make decisions."

"That is probably the most I can ask."

"It is."

After the call, Jack sat alone for a moment. The case had begun with two parents at war, and now it looked increasingly like two parents had been pulled into a system that knew how to use war. That did not make them equally responsible. It did not make either innocent of choices. It meant the final order would need to protect Lily from parental fear and institutional appetite at the same time. Most custody orders were not built for that.

By eight, the office had nearly emptied. Nora left a dinner container on Jack's desk with a note that said, "Microwave exists for a reason." Caleb left with the parenting plan draft. Amelia left after handing Mara a list of public Fairchild filings. Mara stayed long enough to send preservation letters to Fairchild's grants-review address and Civic Bridge's executive office. Then she left too, claiming she would sleep better once everyone else stopped creating evidence.

Jack stood before the whiteboard after the building went quiet. The emergency column was gone. In its place were parenting plan, child's voice, third-party influence, and institutional use. He looked at the last phrase for a long time. Institutional use sounded cold, but the coldness suited the evidence.

Lily's story had become a metric before it had become a full record.

He wrote one question beneath the Fairchild section: Did funder receive value from incomplete truth? The wording was not ready for court, and he knew it. It was a working question, meant to guide discovery rather than persuade a judge. The next phase would require even more restraint than the first. Accusing a parent was painful. Accusing an institution with lawyers, donors, and public goodwill required proof that could survive more than moral outrage.

Jack turned out the light and left the question on the board. Lily's night would be quieter because of the new order, and that mattered more than any document waiting in a withheld attachment. Still, the attachment mattered because it might show how far her words had traveled once adults learned to call them impact. The court had protected Lily from the emergency. Now the record had to protect her from becoming someone else's evidence of success.

26

FAIRCHILD PRODUCED THE ATTACHMENT at 11:47 the next morning, thirteen minutes before Jack Sullivan's deadline expired. That timing was not accidental. Lawyers who produced documents at the edge of a deadline usually wanted the record to show compliance and pressure at the same time. The email came from Victor Hale with a cover letter stating that Fairchild disputed relevance, denied operational involvement in Civic Bridge Youth Support, and produced the document only to avoid burdening the court with unnecessary motion practice. Jack read the sentence twice and placed it in the file because unnecessary motion practice often meant the motion would have worked.

The attachment was titled Q3 Youth Response Impact Draft. It was marked internal and bore the logos of Civic Bridge and Fairchild in the footer, though the cover letter insisted the footer reflected grant-program formatting, not joint authorship. Jack did not care about the logo yet. He cared about the dates, recipients, and contents. Mara pulled the metadata while Caleb created a sealed exhibit index. Amelia waited in the front office with the kind of silence that made Nora suspicious.

The draft described three anonymized cases. The second one matched Lily's facts closely enough that everyone in the room understood it. It described a minor experiencing "identity-related distress," a resistant parent whose objections threatened stabilization, a caregiver aligned with the support plan, and a school-clinical referral pathway that enabled rapid intervention. It said the youth support line provided language stabilization before court-related escalation. It listed the result as "successful maintenance of safety frame during emergency legal process."

Caleb looked up slowly. "They called this a success before the first hearing."

"Yes."

"Before the judge had the note."

"Yes."

Mara added the date to the board. "Before anyone outside their circle knew the record was incomplete."

Jack read the paragraph again. The draft did not name Lily. It did not name Ethan, Marissa, Dana, Dr. Warren, or Tessa. It did not have to. The people who received it would have understood what kind of case it meant, and the people who sent it understood why it mattered to funders. Jack had seen institutions do this before in other forms. A person's pain became proof of program need. Then program need became funding. Then funding became influence over the next person's pain.

Nora entered and placed another page beside Jack. "Hale sent a follow-up."

Jack read it. Fairchild requests confirmation that respondent will not publicly characterize this anonymized draft as referring to any specific minor. The foundation remains committed to child privacy and accurate public discourse.

Mara gave a short, dry laugh. "Public discourse."

Jack handed the letter to Caleb. "Log it."

Amelia appeared at the doorway. "I heard Mara laugh. That usually means something ugly."

Jack covered the sealed draft. "Fairchild produced the attachment."

"Can I know public-safe?"

"An anonymized program-impact draft was produced. It appears to align with the facts of this case and was prepared before the first emergency hearing. It was sent to a Fairchild grants-review address."

Amelia's expression changed. "So they did receive value from the case."

"We can show receipt of a draft describing a similar scenario. Value is an argument."

"It is a true argument."

"Still an argument."

She stepped back before he had to ask. "Then make it clean."

Jack appreciated the word from her, because it meant she had been listening to more than the facts. Clean was not weakness. It was the only way to make sure the people who had framed Lily did not get to accuse him of framing Fairchild. He returned to the draft and began marking the sections that mattered to custody rather than institutional exposure. The judge did not need a grant-fraud trial. She needed to know whether a funding ecosystem encouraged the adults around Lily to treat a partial narrative as program success.

At noon, Jack called Claire. He did not want her learning from Hale's summary. Claire answered after one ring, which told him Hale had already called her or she had been waiting. Jack explained that the impact draft had been produced and that it appeared to describe a scenario substantially aligned with Lily's case before the court had received Lily's note or the undisclosed support communications. Claire did not ask him to send it; she had it already through the service list. Her voice was quiet when she responded.

"Marissa did not know about any impact draft."

"I have no evidence that she did."

"Please keep saying that when you describe it."

"I will say what the record shows."

"That is not exactly the same."

"It is the only promise I can make."

Claire accepted that. She then said Marissa was willing to enter a further stipulation that neither parent would participate in any program, interview, educational material, donor report, advocacy campaign, article, podcast, or public presentation involving Lily's situation without court approval. Jack wrote the categories down. It was more than he had planned to ask for at this stage. Claire was moving quickly to protect Marissa from being associated with institutional use of the case, and in doing so she was offering Lily a stronger shield.

"That should include anonymized descriptions," Jack said.

"I agree."

"And indirect participation through counsel, consultants, churches, schools, nonprofits, support groups, or media."

Claire paused. "That is broad."

"It should be."

"I can probably get there."

"Try."

After the call, Jack brought the proposal to the team. Caleb began drafting the stipulation. Mara added public-use restriction under parenting safeguards. Amelia stood in the doorway and did not smile, though Jack knew she understood what the order would mean. It would make her own future reporting harder if she wanted to connect Lily directly to the system. It would also protect Lily from becoming the face of someone else's exposé. Amelia accepted that because, for all her hunger for the story, she had not lost sight of the child.

At two, Ethan came in to review the proposed stipulation. He read it slowly and stopped at the phrase anonymized descriptions. Jack watched his eyes move back through the paragraph. Ethan understood before asking. The order would prevent either parent from allowing Lily's story to be used even without her name. He looked up with an expression Jack had not seen from him before. It was not anger. It was recognition.

"They already did this," Ethan said.

"Yes."

"Used her without naming her."

"That is what the draft suggests."

Ethan set the paper down carefully. "Then I'll sign."

"Read the rest."

"I will. But I'll sign."

Jack let him finish reading because signing without understanding was its own danger. Ethan asked two questions, both practical. Could he talk to his pastor privately about his own pain? Yes, as long as he did not disclose sealed material, Lily's therapy, or details that could identify her case publicly. Could he preach or speak generally about going through family trials? Jack advised against it while the case was active. Ethan nodded and did not argue, which showed how much he had learned.

Before Ethan left, he looked toward the conference room glass. "Do you think Marissa knew they were using Lily?"

"I do not have evidence that she knew about the draft."

"That's not what I asked."

"I know."

Ethan sighed. "You're going to stay with evidence."

"Yes."

"Good. Somebody should."

The answer stayed with Jack after Ethan left. It was the first time Ethan had asked for restraint from him rather than resenting it. Pain had not made him smaller. It had begun, slowly and unevenly, to make him more careful. That mattered more than the stipulation, though the stipulation would be easier to file.

By four, Claire sent back edits. She accepted the ban on public or anonymized use of Lily's situation but wanted language preserving each parent's right to seek private counseling, pastoral care, or legal advice. Jack agreed, adding confidentiality language and a reminder that sealed information remained sealed. Angela reviewed and approved the final form. Judge Harrow signed it at five-twenty, adding a sentence that any violation could affect custody and decision-making. The order was practical, protective, and unusually direct.

The Fairchild question remained. Jack drafted a narrow request for leave to subpoena communications between

Fairchild grants-review personnel, Caroline Venn, Aaron Pike, and Tessa Laird concerning the impact draft and any scenario matching Lily's case. He did not ask for all donor files, all grants, all training materials, or all youth response program records. He asked for one thread, one draft, one set of recipients, and any response. If Hale wanted to fight, Jack wanted him fighting over something Judge Harrow already understood.

Mara reviewed the draft. "This is almost too narrow."

"It is narrow enough to win."

"It may miss something."

"Then we build from what it produces."

Amelia, standing just outside the room, said, "Narrow enough to win is the most lawyer sentence you've said today."

Jack did not look up. "Only today?"

Nora answered from her desk. "Please do not encourage him."

The hearing request went out just before six. Hale responded within minutes with a demand that Jack withdraw the request, calling it an improper attempt to invade donor deliberations and chill philanthropic support for vulnerable youth programming. Jack did not respond immediately. He let the letter sit. Fast anger in writing often gave away more than careful silence.

Caleb read Hale's letter and frowned. "He sounds worried."

"He sounds like a lawyer whose client is being pulled closer to the record."

"Same thing?"

"Not always."

Mara looked at the letter. "He keeps saying donor deliberations. You asked for communications about one draft."

"That is why his response helps."

Jack filed the request without adding a rebuttal. Judge Harrow could read Hale's objection alongside the narrow scope and decide who sounded reasonable. Jack trusted that contrast more than another paragraph from him. Lawyers often harmed strong motions by trying to win them twice. He submitted it and moved on.

At seven, Dr. Patel's general update came through Angela. Lily attended a full session, brought two drawings, and asked whether she could choose her own words even if they changed from day to day. Dr. Patel's note said Lily was reassured that changing words did not make her dishonest. Jack read the update once, then placed it in the protected therapy folder. That sentence had no place in argument unless the court required it. It was too important to use carelessly.

He sent Ethan only the permitted summary. Lily attended and is engaging. Keep communication simple and ordinary. Ethan replied with a picture of the grocery list Lily had written for their next dinner: noodles, cheese, bread, apples, hot chocolate. Jack stared at the list for several seconds. It was a child's handwriting, uneven and ordinary, and it said more about progress than any filing that day. Lily was making a list of things she wanted in a house where adults were trying not to ask her to prove anything.

Amelia came to his office door as he put his phone away. "Good news?"

"Ordinary news."

"That's better?"

"In this case, yes."

She leaned against the doorframe. "I found another Fairchild event transcript. Caroline Venn talks about turning individual cases into scalable proof for court-facing programs."

Jack looked up. "Public?"

"Yes."

"Send it to Mara."

"I did."

"Do not write about it yet."

"I know."

He believed her, and that surprised him less than it would have two weeks earlier. Amelia had become invested in the story, but she had also become protective of the process that might keep Lily from being consumed by it. That did not make her less of a journalist. It made her better at this one.

By nine, the office had emptied except for Jack and Mara. The Fairchild request sat pending. The new public-use order was signed. The parenting plan draft was improving. The record now showed that Lily's case had been used as an anonymized success marker before the court heard her full words. Jack stood before the whiteboard and added the new order under safeguards.

Mara stood beside him. "We're halfway through the book now, aren't we?"

Jack glanced at her. "What?"

"Nothing."

He looked at her for a moment, then back at the board. "You need sleep."

"So do you."

She left after that, and Jack remained with the board a few minutes longer. The case had entered a quieter and more dangerous phase. The emergency had been stopped, the parents restrained, the child protected for now, and the third-party trail was no longer speculative. That meant the next fight would involve institutions with reputations to defend and enough money to make defense feel like virtue. Jack had faced powerful people before. He had learned that the hardest ones to beat were not the ones who knew they were wrong. They were the ones who believed the harm they caused was justified by the good they could report.

27

JUDGE HARROW GRANTED THE Fairchild subpoena request the next morning in a three-page order that read like someone had measured every word before allowing it to leave chambers. The order did not accuse Fairchild of wrongdoing, did not broaden discovery beyond the Cole-related impact draft, and did not permit a search of donor deliberations generally. It required production of communications between Fairchild grants-review personnel, Caroline Venn, Aaron Pike, Tessa Laird, and Civic Bridge leadership concerning the anonymized youth-response scenario that aligned with Lily's case. It also required any response, comment, approval, revision request, or funding note related to that scenario. Jack Sullivan read the order twice and placed it into the binder marked Third-Party Influence.

Victor Hale called within ten minutes. Jack let Nora take the first call because Hale sounded like the kind of lawyer who needed to be told no by someone who enjoyed it. Nora came to the conference room with a message slip and an expression of mild professional pleasure. Fairchild intended to seek reconsideration unless respondent agreed to narrow the order further. Jack looked at the order, then at the slip, and shook his head. Nora nodded, already satisfied.

Caleb looked up from his laptop. "Are we opposing reconsideration?"

"If they file it."

"Should we offer a narrower search protocol?"

"The judge already wrote one."

Mara tapped the order with her pen. "It is narrow."

"That is why it bothers them."

Amelia arrived with public records from the Fairchild annual reports, though she stopped in the doorway as usual. Jack covered the sealed order before speaking. He gave her only the public-safe version: the court had granted limited discovery into the impact draft and communications tied to the scenario. Amelia's eyes brightened in the way they did when the larger story moved closer. Then she looked toward the closed therapy folder on the side table and checked herself. That moment told Jack she remembered the order protecting Lily's story from public use.

"So now Fairchild has to answer," Amelia said.

"Produce records."

"That's an answer."

"Sometimes."

She placed the public annual reports on the side credenza. "Caroline Venn's old Fairchild division oversaw outcome-based grants. Their language is all about measurable court influence."

Jack looked at her. "Public source?"

"Yes. Annual report, conference transcript, grant rubric."

"Give it to Mara."

"I already did."

Mara looked up. "She did."

Amelia gave Jack a small smile. "Growth."

Nora's voice came from the hallway. "Temporary."

The room returned to work. Caleb prepared a production-tracking chart for Fairchild. Mara built a list of likely custodians from public filings and the impact draft metadata. Jack drafted a letter to Hale confirming that respondent would not agree to narrow the order further but would accept reasonable search terms if provided within two hours. He expected Hale to reject that. Still, the offer mattered. Judges remembered which lawyers tried to solve problems before asking the court to solve them.

Hale responded with four search terms so narrow they looked ceremonial. Lily was not named in the draft, so he offered no child names. Cole was absent, so he excluded family names. He proposed searching only the exact attachment title and one internal tracking number. Jack read the email and handed it to Caleb.

"Ceremonial?" Caleb asked.

"Decorative," Jack said.

Mara leaned in. "Search terms should include youth response, resistant parent, safety frame, legal readiness, language continuity, and the grant-review address."

"And Caroline Venn," Caleb added.

Jack nodded. "Also Aaron Pike, Tessa Laird, Civic Bridge Youth Support, and impact scenario."

Caleb typed quickly. "Should we include Lily?"

"No. The document is anonymized, and we do not want them claiming child privacy prevents the search."

Amelia, from the doorway, said, "That is clever."

"It is obvious."

"Not to normal people."

"Normal people have better hobbies."

By late morning, Hale accepted none of Jack's proposed terms but agreed to produce documents responsive to the order under Fairchild's interpretation. Jack did not fight immediately. The order had a deadline. If Fairchild underproduced, the deficiency would be clearer after the production. Lawyers sometimes wasted energy arguing over future misconduct when actual misconduct would arrive with a Bates stamp. Jack preferred Bates stamps.

Claire sent a short email at noon asking whether the Fairchild discovery would delay the parenting plan exchange. Jack answered no. The parenting plan remained the priority. That was partly legal discipline and partly moral discipline. Fairchild could not become more important than where Lily slept, who drove her to therapy, and whether her parents learned not to turn every feeling into proof.

Ethan came in after lunch for the parenting-plan draft. He had written comments in the margins by hand, which Jack appreciated more than tracked changes from a client. His notes were practical and careful. He wanted alternating weekends clarified. He wanted both parents to receive school notices directly rather than through each other. He wanted a specific clause saying Lily could contact either parent during the other parent's time without interrogation or monitoring. Jack read that one and nodded.

"This is good," Jack said.

Ethan looked relieved. "I wasn't sure."

"It focuses on Lily's life, not Marissa's conduct."

"I tried."

"It shows."

Ethan looked down at the page. "I wanted to add that Marissa can't ever give her another number again."

"The order already covers undisclosed third-party resources. We can reference that without sounding like punishment."

"It feels like everything has to not sound like punishment."

"Because if it sounds punitive, the judge may think you are writing for revenge instead of function."

Ethan breathed out through his nose. "Function is hard when you're angry."

"Yes."

They worked through the plan for nearly an hour. Jack added language requiring direct school access for both parents, neutral scheduling of therapy transportation, and equal access to routine medical and educational records. He removed one sentence Ethan had written about "all adults who previously interfered," because it belonged in the third-party discovery file, not the parenting plan. Ethan did not argue after Jack explained why. That alone was a sign of how far he had come since the first hearing.

Before leaving, Ethan paused at the office door. "Lily asked if she can invite a friend over this weekend."

"That is good."

"Normal?"

"Very normal."

"I said I'd check with her mom through the app."

"Good."

"It feels strange asking permission for ordinary things."

"You are not asking permission. You are documenting co-operation."

Ethan considered that. "That sounds better."

"It is also true."

After Ethan left, Jack sent the revised parenting plan to Claire. Her response came two hours later with fewer edits than expected. She agreed to most of the structure and asked for reciprocal language requiring Ethan not to discuss Marissa's mistakes or third-party conduct with Lily. Jack accepted immediately. The order already required it, but repeating the obligation in the parenting plan would help both parents. If the plan became a roadmap rather than a weapon, it might actually protect the child it named.

At four, Fairchild's first production arrived. It contained eighteen documents, far fewer than Mara expected and fewer than the order's scope suggested. The cover letter stated that Fairchild found no communications directing or approving Civic Bridge's handling of Lily Cole or any identifiable minor. Jack set that letter aside and opened the documents. The first fifteen were administrative grant emails. The last three mattered.

The impact draft had been forwarded to a Fairchild grants-review analyst named Nina Sato with the message: This is the early outcome example Caroline mentioned. Shows model effectiveness when school, caregiver, youth support, and legal readiness align quickly. Nina replied: Strong case for renewal. Need to ensure privacy-safe language and avoid appearance of litigation support. Jack read the reply aloud once, then placed it on the table.

Mara moved closer. "Avoid appearance of litigation support."

Caleb looked at the email. "That means they saw the risk."

"It means Nina saw the risk," Jack said.

"And still called it strong for renewal."

"Yes."

The third document was a calendar invitation for a Fairchild-Civic Bridge grant review call scheduled two days before the first emergency hearing. Attendees included Caroline Venn, Aaron Pike, Tessa Laird, Nina Sato, and a Fairchild senior director named Malcolm Reese. The agenda line read: Q3 youth response outcomes and court-facing program language. Jack looked at the phrase and felt the case shift again. Court-facing program language was not donor fluff. It was the bridge between funding and the legal system.

Amelia stood at the doorway. "I can tell by everyone's faces that I hate whatever that is."

Jack covered the documents. "Fairchild produced a small set. Some of it is significant."

"Public-safe?"

"An email discusses an early outcome example and warns to avoid the appearance of litigation support. A calendar entry references court-facing program language."

Amelia gripped her notebook. "Court-facing program language."

"Yes."

"That phrase is public?"

"Not yet. It is under seal."

She took one step back, visibly restraining herself. "I'm going to walk away before I ask for something you won't give me."

"That is wise."

Nora passed behind her. "Write that date down."

Jack did not smile until they were gone. Then he returned to the documents and began drafting a deficiency letter. Eighteen documents could not be the complete production if a grant review call occurred with five attendees and court-facing program language on the agenda. There should be notes, slides, drafts, chat messages, follow-up emails, or at least a denial that none existed. Fairchild had produced the edge of the table and pretended the room was empty.

The deficiency letter went out at five. Jack requested the meeting materials, notes, attendee communications, follow-up emails, and any documents concerning the phrase court-facing program language. Hale responded with a promise to review. That was not enough, but it was not refusal. Jack gave him until noon the next day and copied all counsel. Claire did not respond. Jack suspected she was reading the same phrase and deciding how far Marissa needed to stand from it.

Dr. Patel's update came through Angela at six. Lily had asked whether her parents were allowed to have different feelings about the same thing. Dr. Patel gave no content beyond that, noting only that both parents should avoid correcting Lily's emotional descriptions. Jack forwarded the permitted guidance to Ethan and Claire. Ethan replied, Understood. Claire replied, Thank you. Those two responses were plain enough to feel like progress.

Near seven, Amelia returned to Jack's office. She did not bring documents this time. She closed the door halfway and stayed standing.

"You know Fairchild is the second half of the book," she said.

Jack leaned back. "You keep talking like this is already written."

"It is being written whether anyone admits it or not."

"By the record."

"And by whoever gets to tell it after."

Jack studied her. "You want to be that person."

"Yes."

"Lily is not a symbol."

"I know."

"Do you?"

Amelia's face tightened, but she did not look away. "I have been chasing institutions like Fairchild for eighteen months. I thought the story was influence. Then Lily became real. That changed it."

Jack believed her. He did not fully trust what belief would make her do later, but he believed the sentence. That distinction mattered. Amelia was not harmless. Neither was he. The case had taught him again that people could mean well and still turn a child into proof of something larger than her life.

"At the right time," Jack said, "the public record may matter."

She nodded. "After Lily."

"After the court protects her."

"And if the court protects only part of her?"

Jack did not answer immediately. That was the question that kept good lawyers awake. Courts could restrain parents, order therapy, compel records, and sanction parties. They could not repair every injury done by systems that never appeared as parties. If the public record became the only way to stop future harm, Amelia's work might become necessary. It was not necessary tonight.

"Then we decide what the record can bear," Jack said.

She accepted that and left. Jack returned to the conference room and looked at the new phrases on the board. Early outcome example. Avoid appearance of litigation support. Court-facing program language. The words were cleaner than threats and uglier because of it. No one had needed to say, use Lily. Institutions rarely spoke that plainly. They built categories and let people disappear into them.

Jack packed the Fairchild production into the sealed binder and turned off the conference room lights. The parenting plan was moving toward stability. Ethan was learning restraint. Marissa was stepping back from the machinery she had trusted. Lily was beginning to ask questions in therapy that sounded like her own. Around them, the institutional record was opening slowly, document by document, phrase by phrase. Tomorrow might bring the missing meeting materials, or it might bring another fight. Either way, the case had reached the place where power stopped sounding like accusation and started appearing in calendar invites.

28

FAIRCHILD PRODUCED THE MISSING meeting materials at 11:58 a.m., two minutes before Hale's deadline and exactly late enough to make the point. Jack Sullivan was in the conference room with Caleb and Mara when the secure link arrived. Nora stood at the door with her arms folded because she had taken personal offense at Fairchild's habit of using the last possible minute. Amelia waited in the front office, pretending to work through public filings while watching the glass wall with open impatience. No one in Jack's office had slept enough, and everyone knew the next set of documents would either open the Fairchild issue or close it for now.

The production contained a slide deck, a one-page agenda, a meeting summary, and two follow-up email chains. Hale's cover letter repeated that Fairchild did not direct Civic Bridge's handling of any child, did not participate in litigation strategy, and did not have access to personally identifying information about Lily Cole. Jack placed the letter in the file without comment. Denials mattered, but slides and emails usually mattered more. He opened the deck first.

The first five slides were ordinary grant language. Program goals, access barriers, regional need, and support pathways. The sixth slide changed the room. It showed a flowchart labeled Youth Response to Court-Facing Family Conflict. The path ran from caregiver intake to youth support, then to school coordination, clinical stabilization, and legal readiness. No names appeared anywhere. No case number. No court. The structure was sanitized enough for a boardroom and specific enough for Jack to understand why it had been produced reluctantly.

Caleb leaned closer. "Legal readiness is in the flowchart."

"Yes."

Mara pointed to the lower corner. "Prepared by Civic Bridge. Reviewed with Fairchild grants team."

Jack wrote the footer language on his pad. "Not authored by Fairchild."

"Reviewed with them."

"That distinction will matter."

The next slide contained the phrase they had seen in the calendar invite: court-facing program language. It described how partner organizations could help families present consistent, safety-centered descriptions when urgent intervention became necessary. Beneath that was a bullet point: reduce contradictory child language before formal review. Jack read the line twice. It did not say hide the child's words. It did not need to. Reduce contradictory child language was the polished version of everything that had happened to Lily.

Mara's jaw tightened. "That line goes straight to the judge."

"Under seal," Jack said.

Caleb wrote it down.

Jack moved to the meeting summary. It listed Caroline Venn as presenter, Aaron Pike as program operations, Tessa Laird as communications design, Nina Sato as Fairchild grants review, and Malcolm Reese as Fairchild senior director. The summary noted that the early outcome example demonstrated "rapid alignment among caregiver, school contact, youth support, and clinical partner prior to court escalation." It also recorded a concern from Fairchild: "Ensure examples do not imply funder involvement in case-level legal strategy." Jack underlined the sentence.

"That is the second warning," Caleb said.

"First warning was avoid appearance of litigation support," Jack said. "This is more specific."

Mara looked at the summary. "They knew the appearance was a problem."

"They knew the boundary was a problem."

"That sounds stronger."

"It is stronger because it is true."

Jack called Claire before filing anything. He kept Caleb in the room and summarized the new materials in careful terms. Claire had the production and had already reviewed the same slide. Her voice had the low, controlled tone of someone trying not to let anger become strategy. She said Marissa had never seen the deck and had no knowledge that Civic Bridge or Fairchild discussed her family situation as an outcome example. Jack believed that may be true. It did not erase Marissa's choices. It did mean the case was now moving beyond what either parent had understood.

"Marissa is shaken," Claire said.

"She should be."

"She feels used."

"She may have been."

Claire paused. "You said that carefully."

"I meant it carefully."

"Does Ethan understand that?"

"Not yet."

Jack did not tell Ethan immediately. He first reviewed the materials, prepared the legal summary, and notified Angela Morrissey because any institutional use of Lily's situation might affect how the child should be supported. Angela responded within minutes. She asked that no parent discuss the Fairchild materials with Lily under any circumstances and that Dr. Patel be informed only in general terms unless the court ordered more detail. Jack agreed. Claire did too.

At one-thirty, Jack called Ethan. He closed his office door and sat down because the news needed weight without drama. He told Ethan that Fairchild had produced materials showing Civic Bridge discussed an anonymized outcome example resembling Lily's case with a Fairchild grants team before the first hearing. He explained that the materials did not show Lily's name and did not show Marissa knew about the meeting. He also explained that the materials used language about legal readiness, court-facing program language, and reducing contradictory child language.

Ethan said nothing at first. Jack waited.

"They had a meeting about my daughter like she was a project," Ethan said.

"An anonymized scenario resembling her situation was used in a program discussion."

"I need you not to translate it right now."

Jack looked at the wall across from him. "Yes. They discussed a situation like Lily's as a program example before the court heard her full words."

Ethan breathed out slowly. "Thank you."

"That does not mean you can act on it."

"I know."

"Say it."

"I won't talk to Lily about it. I won't call Marissa. I won't post. I won't call anyone from those organizations."

"Good."

Ethan's voice lowered. "Was Marissa used too?"

Jack respected the question more than he expected. "Possibly. She also made choices that harmed the record."

"I can hold both."

"Try."

The call ended with Ethan steadier than Jack had feared. That steadiness did not make the facts easier. It only meant Ethan was learning how to keep the facts from entering Lily's house through his face. Jack had told him for days to be ordinary, and now he understood how hard that command really was. Ordinary had become an act of discipline.

By midafternoon, Jack filed a sealed supplemental request. He did not ask Judge Harrow to turn the custody case into a proceeding against Fairchild. He asked for three things: permission to question Caroline Venn under oath, production of communications related to the meeting materials, and an order confirming that any institutional use of Lily's situation in grant reporting, training, or program evaluation must cease unless authorized by the court. He attached the slide deck, meeting summary, and Fairchild's own cautionary language. The motion was short because the documents were strong.

Hale opposed within an hour. He called the request an overreach, said the materials did not identify Lily, and argued that respondent was trying to chill philanthropic collaboration in sensitive youth services. Jack read the opposition and found the absence more important than the words. Hale did not deny that the scenario aligned with Lily's case. He did not deny that Fairchild reviewed it before the first hearing. He did not deny that the deck discussed reducing contradictory child language before formal review. Those omissions would matter.

Amelia entered after Jack cleared the table. "I know you filed something."

"You know too much."

"I know movement."

He gave her the public-safe version. Civic Bridge used an anonymized scenario resembling Lily's facts in a Fairchild grant discussion before the first hearing, and the court was being asked to stop institutional use of the scenario. Amelia listened without interrupting. Her face tightened at reducing contradictory child language, even though Jack would not show her the slide.

"That is the system saying the quiet part with better font," she said.

"Yes."

"Can I look at Fairchild's public program materials for the same phrase?"

"Yes. Public sources only."

"I know the boundary."

"You do."

She nodded once and left to work. Jack watched her through the glass for a moment. He had expected Amelia to make the case harder. In some ways, she had. In others, she had become the only person outside the legal team who understood the public architecture around the sealed record. That might matter later. Not yet.

At five, Judge Harrow set a remote conference for the following morning. She ordered Fairchild, Civic Bridge, and all parties to preserve all materials relating to the outcome example and any use of it in reporting, funding, training, or evaluation. She also prohibited any further dissemination of the scenario pending the conference. The order was brief and forceful. Jack printed it and placed it in the binder. Then he sent copies to Claire, Hale, Fray, Ellison, Angela, and Ethan.

Ethan replied by text. I understand. No discussion with Lily.

Jack saved it. Then he sat for a while in his office without opening another file. The case had moved beyond the emergency, beyond the phone, beyond the note, and into the machinery that learned from those things without asking Lily permission to be its lesson. He knew the next hearing would be delicate. The court had jurisdiction over the parents and the child. Its reach over institutions was narrower, more contested, and more vulnerable to appeal. The remedy had to fit the custody case even if the harm reached farther.

Nora knocked once and stepped in. "You should go home."

"I will."

"Tonight?"

"That is usually implied."

"With you, it is not."

Jack closed the Fairchild binder. "Point taken."

She looked at the binder, then back at him. “Is the child safer today?”

Jack considered the question. “A little.”

“Then go home before you start thinking that little is not enough to rest.”

After Nora left, Jack stood before the whiteboard. He added Caroline Venn deposition request, dissemination stop order, and reducing contradictory child language beneath the Fairchild section. Then he stepped back and looked at the whole case. Lily was not a cause. She was not a program example. She was not proof of model effectiveness or a line in a grant renewal deck. The law could not erase every place adults had placed her. It could, if handled carefully, order them to stop.

The office lights dimmed while he was still standing there. Jack let them. The board remained faintly visible in the dark, all names and arrows reduced to gray lines. Tomorrow, Fairchild would argue distance, Civic Bridge would argue anonymity, and Claire would try to keep Marissa from being crushed by a system she had trusted. Jack would argue the only thing that mattered inside that courtroom: a child’s truth could not belong to the adults who found it useful. That was not a cliff to stand on. It was a record to build, one careful page at a time.

29

THE REMOTE CONFERENCE BEGAN with Fairchild trying to sound absent while appearing on every screen. Victor Hale appeared from a conference room with a white wall behind him and no logo visible. Leonard Fray appeared for Civic Bridge with Caroline Venn seated beside him, not as a witness yet, but as the person whose name had moved too close to the center of the record to remain theoretical. Claire Whitcomb appeared for Marissa, quiet and watchful. Jack Sullivan appeared from his office with Caleb beside him and the sealed Fairchild binder open to the slide that no one wanted read aloud in full.

Judge Harrow began by identifying the narrow purpose of the conference. She was not deciding whether Fairchild had committed wrongdoing, whether Civic Bridge should lose funding, or whether any public-policy program was lawful. She was deciding whether the court needed additional orders to protect Lily Cole from further use, disclosure, or shaping of her statements. That distinction mattered, and Jack could see Hale relax slightly when the judge said it. He relaxed too soon.

"The court's concern," Judge Harrow continued, "is not merely that the minor's name was used. The concern is whether her circumstances, statements, and distress were treated as program material while the court was being asked to act on an incomplete record."

Hale leaned toward the camera. "Your Honor, Fairchild never possessed identifying information regarding Lily Cole."

Judge Harrow looked at him. "I understand your position."

"That point is central."

"It is one point. It is not the only point."

Jack wrote that down. He did not need to argue it because the judge had already located the problem. Institutions often believed anonymity solved ethical use. In custody court, anonymity did not answer whether a child's private distress had been converted into leverage, training data, or funding narrative before the court heard her own words. Lily did not need to be named to be used.

Fray argued next. He said Civic Bridge had acted in good faith, providing peer-informed support to a youth in distress and responding to a caregiver's request for resources. He acknowledged the language in the deck was regrettable when viewed with hindsight, but insisted it reflected program evaluation, not litigation strategy. Caroline Venn sat motionless beside him. Her face gave away nothing. Jack watched her rather than Fray because people often react differently when their lawyer says a word they know is too small for the facts.

Claire spoke briefly. She supported the prohibition on any further use of Lily's situation by third parties and requested that the court make clear neither parent may cooperate with such use. She did not defend Civic Bridge's impact draft. She did not defend Fairchild's review. She did not mention Marissa except to say her client accepted the new restrictions. Jack had expected her to retreat to parental innocence. Instead, she stayed with child protection. That was the right move.

When Judge Harrow turned to Jack, he did not repeat the whole record. The judge had read it. Repetition could make strong facts sound like advocacy rather than evidence. He focused on remedy.

"Your Honor, Lily's note was transformed into summaries, support language, and eventually an anonymized impact example before the court received her actual words. Respondent is asking for an order that stops any further use of her situation, requires production sufficient to identify who approved the use, and permits a limited deposition of Caroline Venn on that issue. We do not ask the court to decide institutional liability. We ask the court to protect the child from becoming program material in her own custody case."

Hale objected immediately to the phrase program material. Judge Harrow allowed the objection to be noted and said the phrase was argument, not a finding. Jack accepted that. He had used it intentionally and sparingly. The record supported it, but the court did not need to adopt it that morning. The remedy was more important than the label.

Judge Harrow asked Hale a direct question. "Did anyone at Fairchild ask Civic Bridge whether the anonymized outcome example was connected to an active court proceeding?"

Hale paused. "I cannot answer that without consulting the client further."

"You are here on behalf of the client."

"Yes, Your Honor."

"And you cannot answer whether the client asked if an example concerning court-facing program language involved an active court matter?"

"Not with certainty."

Judge Harrow made a note. "Then that question will be included in the permitted inquiry."

Hale's expression tightened. Jack saw it, and so did everyone else. Fairchild had tried to stand on lack of identifying information. The judge had moved the question to institutional awareness. Did they know, or should they have asked, whether an example used for grant review came from an active child custody proceeding? That was a more dangerous question because it required less access to Lily's name and more attention to the obvious.

The order came from the bench. Caroline Venn would appear for a limited deposition within five days. Fairchild would produce communications concerning the outcome example, including whether any Fairchild employee asked about the status, source, legal posture, privacy safeguards, or consent related to the scenario. Civic Bridge would produce all versions of the slide deck, impact draft, and any dissemination list. The court prohibited Fairchild, Civic Bridge, Tessa Laird, and any related agents from using, sharing, presenting, reporting, or referencing the scenario connected to Lily's case in any format pending further order.

Hale asked whether the prohibition applied to fully anonymized internal compliance review. Judge Harrow allowed internal legal compliance review under counsel's supervision. She did not allow program reporting, donor communications, training, or evaluation use. Fray asked whether Civic

Bridge could continue operating the support line. The judge said yes, but it could not communicate with Lily, reference her case, or use her scenario. Claire asked whether the order applied equally to the parents. The judge said it did, and Jack did not object.

When the conference ended, the room remained quiet. Caleb saved the order summary and exhaled slowly. Mara added Venn deposition to the board. Amelia waited outside until Nora opened the door and gave her permission to enter, which made Amelia look both annoyed and grateful.

Jack gave her the public-safe summary. "The court prohibited further use or dissemination of Lily's scenario. Venn deposition granted. Fairchild has to produce communications about whether anyone asked if the scenario came from an active court matter."

Amelia sat down. "That is bigger than I expected."

"It is narrow."

"It is narrow and big."

"That can happen."

She looked toward the board. "The question is consent."

"One question."

"Who gave them permission to turn her into an example?"

"Yes."

Mara capped the marker. "No one, from what we have."

Jack looked at her. "From what we have."

Mara gave him a tired smile. "There. I said it your way."

By noon, the written order was entered. Jack sent it to all counsel and to Ethan with only a short note: This protects Lily from further use of her situation by outside organizations. Do not discuss it with her. Ethan replied within three minutes. Understood. Thank you. The answer was plain, and Jack heard the discipline behind it. Ethan had learned that gratitude and anger could occupy the same sentence without one controlling the other.

The rest of the day moved into practical work. Caleb revised the parenting plan to incorporate the new no-use order by reference. Mara prepared the outline for Caroline Venn's deposition. Amelia worked through public records on Fairchild's grant structures, looking for language that matched the sealed materials without touching the sealed materials themselves. Nora managed calls from reporters who had noticed another hearing on the docket and wanted to know why a foundation lawyer was appearing in a custody case. She told each of them the firm had no comment, and then wrote down their names in case their questions revealed who was talking.

At two, Claire called. She sounded tired, but less guarded. Marissa had completed her first parent-guidance session with Dr. Patel. No content was shared, but Dr. Patel had recommended that Marissa stop using support language Lily had learned from outside resources and respond in ordinary words. Claire said Marissa agreed. Jack listened and wrote the note in the parent-guidance folder. Ordinary words had become a therapeutic goal, and that fact said almost everything about how far the case had gone wrong.

"Ethan will need the same instruction," Claire said.

"He has it."

"I'm not suggesting otherwise."

"I know."

Claire paused. "Marissa wants Lily to know she is sorry without putting more weight on her."

"Then Dr. Patel can guide that."

"That was my advice."

"It was good advice."

The compliment landed awkwardly, though Jack meant it. Claire did not respond to it directly. The call ended with agreement to exchange revised parenting-plan language by the next morning. The case was still adversarial, but the parents' lawyers were beginning to build around the same child instead of firing across her. It was late. It was still better than never.

Ethan called at four after his own guidance session. He said Dr. Patel had told him Lily needed fewer explanations and more predictable responses. Jack did not ask for therapeutic details. Ethan volunteered only the general advice, and Jack let it stay general. Then Ethan said Lily had asked whether she could use different words with different people. He had said yes, as long as they were her words. Jack wrote that down because it was not evidence, but it was the kind of truth the case had been trying to restore.

"That was a good answer," Jack said.

"She looked relieved."

"Good."

"I wanted to say no one gets to give you words anymore."

"I know."

"I didn't."

"That is why it worked."

Ethan laughed softly. "I'm starting to hear your voice before I say stupid things."

"Then my work here is nearly done."

"Not even close."

Jack smiled after the call ended, though the smile faded quickly. Ethan was right. The emergency had ended, but the case had not. The parenting plan remained unfinished. The Venn deposition could pull Fairchild closer or let it step away. Civic Bridge could still claim good-faith support. Marissa could still argue that Ethan's original objections contributed to Lily's distress. The custody merits would not vanish because the third-party record became ugly.

Near six, Fairchild produced a short supplemental email chain ahead of Venn's deposition. Nina Sato had asked Caroline Venn whether the outcome example involved "a live matter" and whether all consents were in place for grant reporting. Caroline replied: Scenario is privacy-safe, active support context, no identifiers. Use as internal learning only until court posture resolves. Jack read the reply three times. Court posture resolves. It was the first direct Fairchild-Civic Bridge communication showing awareness that a court matter existed.

Mara leaned over the page. "They knew."

"Venn knew," Jack said. "Sato asked."

"Fairchild knew enough to ask."

"Yes."

Caleb looked at the email. "And they still kept it in the deck."

"Internal learning only."

"That doesn't make it okay."

"No. It makes it their explanation."

Jack added the email to the Venn deposition binder. The phrasing would matter. Active support context. Court posture resolves. Internal learning. Each phrase sounded safe until placed beside Lily's note, the support messages, and the petition. Then it sounded like adults waiting to see whether the court would validate their frame before using the child's situation more broadly. Jack would not say that in the first question. He would let Venn explain the words first.

Amelia was allowed to hear only that a supplemental email confirmed Fairchild asked whether the scenario involved a live matter and Civic Bridge responded in general terms. She stared at Jack for several seconds. "That is public-good language hiding private harm."

"Possibly."

She held up one finger. "Invoice number two."

Nora, passing by with a file box, said, "Put interest on it."

The humor lasted only a moment. Amelia returned to her notes, and Jack returned to the binder. He could feel the book, as Amelia might have called it, turning under the surface of the case. Not a written book, not yet, but the deeper narrative that institutions feared: a support system designed to help children had learned to value the stability of its own language over the instability of a child's truth. Fairchild had not necessarily caused that. It may have rewarded it.

By nine, the office was nearly empty. Caleb had gone home. Nora had gone after leaving soup in the refrigerator. Amelia had left with public records and a promise not to publish anything connected to the sealed proceedings. Mara stayed late, as usual, and stood beside Jack at the whiteboard before leaving.

"Venn is the hinge," she said.

"Yes."

"If she says Fairchild wanted success examples before court outcomes, that changes everything."

"If she says it and the documents support it."

Mara looked at him. "You are no fun."

"I am useful."

"Sometimes."

After she left, Jack remained alone in the conference room. He read the new email one more time and placed it in the binder. Lily's life had been called an active support context, as if the right phrase could make the wrong use less personal. The court had now ordered the adults to stop using her that way. The next question was whether anyone had wanted her story because it helped her, or because it helped prove the model worked.

Jack turned out the lights and left the whiteboard untouched. Some days the record needed no new lines. It needed the people reading it to sit with what the existing lines already said. Lily had asked if she could use different words with different people, and Ethan had told her yes, as long as they were hers. That answer, small and private, was closer to justice than anything in the Fairchild binder. The law would have to catch up to it the best way it could.

30

Caroline Venn appeared for deposition in person, which Jack Sullivan took as a strategic choice before she said a word. People like Venn did not travel to a lawyer's office unless they wanted presence to do part of the work. She arrived with Leonard Fray, a slim leather portfolio, and the polished calm of someone accustomed to boardrooms where disagreement was softened by grant language and catered coffee. Her gray suit was plain, her hair pulled back, her expression attentive. She looked prepared to be reasonable, and Jack distrusted that more than open hostility.

The deposition room was arranged with deliberate simplicity. Jack sat across from Venn with Caleb to his right and Mara beside the exhibit binders. Fray sat close enough to Venn to remind her who owned the objections. Claire appeared by video and identified herself for Marissa, though she said she would not participate unless her client's interests required it. Victor Hale appeared for Fairchild by video after Judge Harrow's order allowed him to attend limited portions involving Fairchild communications. Amelia remained in the front office, where

Nora had placed her at a table with public documents and a warning that coffee did not come with discovery privileges.

The court reporter administered the oath at ten. Venn took it without hesitation and folded her hands on the table. Jack began with her background, which was not filler. She had worked at Fairchild for eight years, overseeing outcome-based grants in family systems and youth response programming. She left to become executive director of Civic Bridge three years earlier. She remained in contact with Fairchild personnel through grants, advisory panels, and program reviews. Each answer was ordinary, and each one placed her more firmly between donor money and child-facing operations.

Jack placed the Fairchild annual report in front of her. Venn confirmed her prior role. He placed the Civic Bridge program description beside it. She confirmed her current role. Then he placed the Q3 Youth Response Impact Draft on the table, with the identifying portions sealed and the scenario paragraph marked. Venn read it calmly. She did not look surprised, which told Jack nothing except that Fray had prepared her properly.

"Did you review this draft before it was sent to Fairchild?" Jack asked.

"Yes."

"Did you understand the second scenario to be based on circumstances involving Lily Cole?"

Fray objected to form and privacy. Venn waited for him to finish.

"I understood it to be based on an active support matter," she said.

"That was not my question."

"I did not know the child's full name when I first reviewed the draft."

"When did you know the child was Lily Cole?"

Venn looked down at the draft. "After the court issued orders regarding the support device."

Jack wrote that down. "Before the first emergency hearing, did you know the scenario involved an active court matter?"

"Yes."

The answer was cleaner than Jack expected. He looked briefly at Hale's image on the screen. Hale's face remained still, but the stillness looked more deliberate than natural. Fairchild had argued that its lack of identifying information mattered most. Venn had now admitted that, at least on Civic Bridge's side, the scenario was understood to be active and court-related before the first hearing. That did not prove Fairchild knew the child's name. It proved the program knew the court posture mattered.

Jack moved to the email from Nina Sato. "Ms. Sato asked whether the scenario involved a live matter and whether consents were in place for grant reporting. You replied, 'Scenario is privacy-safe, active support context, no identifiers. Use as internal learning only until court posture resolves.' Did I read that accurately?"

"Yes."

"What did you mean by court posture resolves?"

"That we would not use the scenario externally while legal proceedings were active."

"Did you understand the legal proceedings involved custody?"

"Yes."

"Did you understand the support communications might become part of the custody record?"

"I understood that was possible."

Jack paused, letting the sequence settle into the transcript. Venn was answering carefully, but she was not running from the documents. That made her more credible and more dangerous to Fairchild than a hostile witness would have been. A hostile witness lets institutions blame personality. A careful witness makes the documents carry the weight.

Fray objected when Jack asked whether Venn sought consent from either parent before including the scenario in the draft. The objection was preserved, and Venn answered that Civic Bridge did not treat internal anonymized program review as requiring individual consent. Jack asked whether she sought consent from Lily. Fray objected again, more sharply. Venn's answer was quiet.

"No."

"Did anyone at Civic Bridge consider whether the minor child might object to her circumstances being used as a program example?"

Venn looked at the document for several seconds. "Not specifically."

Jack did not raise his voice. "Why not?"

"Because the draft was internal and anonymized."

"Does anonymity answer whether a child's private distress should be used?"

Fray objected that the question was argumentative. Jack withdrew it because he already had enough. The judge would understand the exchange. Venn's framework was institutional: internal, anonymized, program review. Jack's framework was custodial: child, consent, court, private distress. The legal question was which framework mattered in a family court tasked with protecting Lily.

Jack placed the slide labeled Youth Response to Court-Facing Family Conflict in front of Venn. She confirmed that Civic Bridge created it and reviewed it with Fairchild's grants team. She said the flowchart described general program design, not Lily's case specifically. Jack asked about the pathway from caregiver intake to youth support, school coordination, clinical stabilization, and legal readiness. Venn said the pathway described coordination during urgent family conflict. Jack asked whether Lily's situation moved through that pathway. Venn did not answer immediately.

Fray spoke first. "Object to form. Calls for speculation."

Venn answered anyway. "Parts of it did."

"Which parts?"

"Caregiver intake, youth support, school coordination, and clinical partner consultation."

"Legal readiness?"

Venn's hands tightened slightly. "There was awareness that legal proceedings might occur."

"That is not the same as legal readiness."

"No."

"Was Lily's case treated as legally relevant before the petition was filed?"

Venn looked toward Fray, then back to Jack. "It was understood that the family might seek court involvement."

Jack wrote the exact answer. It was cautious, but useful. She had avoided the phrase legal readiness while conceding the system saw court involvement coming. That was the hinge. The support system was not operating in a vacuum of emotional care. It was operating in the shadow of court before the court had access to the child's own note.

Jack turned to the phrase reduce contradictory child language before formal review. Venn said the phrase was unfortunate and would not be used again. Jack asked who wrote it. She said she believed Tessa drafted that slide with input from Aaron Pike. Jack asked whether Venn approved it before presentation to Fairchild. She said yes. Jack asked whether Fairchild objected to the phrase. She said not that she recalled.

Hale leaned toward his camera. "Objection. The witness cannot testify as to Fairchild's internal reaction."

Jack looked at the screen. "I asked whether anyone objected during the meeting."

Venn answered, "No one objected during the meeting."

That answer would matter more than Hale's objection. Fairchild did not need to direct the phrase to have reviewed it without objection. The question later would be whether silence in a grant-review meeting meant approval, indifference, or lack of understanding. For custody purposes, it was enough that the phrase had been part of the ecosystem around Lily's case and that no one stopped it before it reached the court's attention.

After a short break, Jack moved to program value. Venn acknowledged that outcome examples helped funders assess whether a program was working. She denied that Civic Bridge needed Lily's scenario to secure renewal. She acknowledged that early examples of coordinated response were useful in grant reporting. She acknowledged that a scenario showing alignment among caregiver, school, clinical partner, and youth support would be considered a positive program indicator. Jack let those answers stack without commentary.

Caleb passed him a note. Ask whether incomplete record changes success.

Jack did.

"If the court later found that the child's actual written statement was not disclosed before emergency relief was sought, would that affect whether the scenario should be described as a program success?"

Fray objected. Venn took a slow breath.

"Yes," she said.

Jack nodded. "Why?"

"Because the process would not have achieved the kind of informed stability the program intends."

"Informed stability requires the court to receive the child's actual words?"

"In a court matter, yes."

The answer was the cleanest admission of the day. It did not accuse anyone of malice. It did not give Ethan every word he might want. It did something more useful. It made the program's own standard depend on the same thing Jack had been arguing since Mrs. Palmer's copy surfaced: the court needed Lily's actual words, not only the system's interpretation.

Claire did not ask questions. Hale asked three. He established that Fairchild did not receive Lily's name, did not request communication with her, and did not instruct Civic Bridge to withhold records from the court. Venn agreed to all three. Jack did not object because the answers were likely true and because overblocking them would make him look afraid. The case did not need Fairchild to have called Lily by name.

It needed to show that Fairchild's grant process rewarded an outcome example built from a court-related scenario before the court knew the scenario was incomplete.

Fray asked a handful of repair questions, mostly about good faith, privacy, and the purpose of support programming. Venn said Civic Bridge intended to help vulnerable youth, not manipulate them. She said staff believed they were reducing harm. She said the use of Lily's scenario should have been paused sooner once court involvement was known. That last answer did not help her as much as Fray hoped. It sounded responsible in the present tense and damning in hindsight.

The deposition ended after two hours and forty minutes. Venn thanked the court reporter, gathered her papers, and left with Fray through the rear hallway. Hale disconnected without comment. Claire stayed on the video feed for a moment after everyone else left.

"Jack," she said.

He looked toward the screen. "Yes."

"Marissa needs to see the parts that affect her. Not the sealed child content, but enough to understand the system she trusted."

"I agree."

Claire looked relieved, and then tired. "Send what you can under the order."

"I will."

When the screen went dark, Amelia entered with Nora close behind her. Nora had clearly decided the deposition was over and the reporter could be released from containment. Amelia looked from Jack to Caleb to Mara. No one looked victorious. That told her more than a smile would have.

"Venn?" Amelia asked.

Jack removed the exhibit stickers from the table. "She admitted Civic Bridge knew the scenario involved an active court context. She admitted no one asked Lily for consent to use her situation internally. She admitted the incomplete record would affect whether the scenario should be called a success."

Amelia sat down slowly. "That is enough."

"For what?"

"For the shape."

Jack did not argue. The shape was there now. It was still not everything Amelia wanted, and not everything Ethan deserved, and not everything Lily would need to heal. It was enough for the next hearing. It was enough to ask Judge Harrow for findings that would protect the child from institutional use and reshape the custody plan around unfiltered communication.

By late afternoon, Jack drafted the sealed merits brief. It was shorter than Caleb expected and less dramatic than Amelia would have written. It asked the court to maintain joint decision-making, adopt the proposed parenting plan, preserve Dr. Patel's neutral role, prohibit third-party influence, and enter findings that Lily's actual written statements were not disclosed before emergency relief was sought; that an undisclosed support channel supplied language later echoed in the emergency record; and that Lily's circumstances were used in an anonymized program-impact context before the court had a complete record. Those findings would not punish everyone. They would make denial harder.

Ethan came in at six to review the parts that concerned him. Jack gave him the proposed findings in plain language.

Ethan read them slowly, then asked whether the judge might sign them. Jack said some, not all. Ethan nodded as if he had expected that. He looked most closely at the sentence about Lily's actual written statements not being disclosed before emergency relief was sought.

"That sentence matters," Ethan said.

"Yes."

"It says what happened without calling anybody evil."

"That is why it may survive."

Ethan looked up. "I used to want evil."

"I know."

"I still do sometimes."

"That is human."

He placed the page on the desk. "Lily needs safer more than I need evil."

Jack said nothing for a moment because the sentence deserved room. Ethan had not become calm. He had become aligned with the thing he said he wanted most. That was different. That was stronger.

After Ethan left, Jack returned to the conference room. Amelia was packing her notes. Mara was updating the board. Caleb had the merits brief open and was removing every extra adjective Jack had circled. Nora had already gone home, leaving behind a note reminding Jack that soup did not reheat itself. The office felt tired in a cleaner way than it had before the deposition. The facts were still ugly, but the legal path was less fogged.

Amelia stopped at the door. "You think the judge will make findings?"

"Some."

"Enough?"

"For custody, maybe."

"For Fairchild?"

"Not in the way you mean."

She nodded. "Then the public record waits."

"Yes."

"After Lily."

Jack looked at her. "After Lily."

When she left, Jack stood before the board and drew a box around three phrases: actual words, support channel, program impact. He did not connect them with arrows. They no longer needed arrows. The evidence had done that work. The next hearing would ask the court to place those phrases into findings, not as slogans, but as protection.

Jack closed the marker and turned off the lights. Lily had not been in the room for any of the depositions, hearings, filings, or arguments that had defined her week. That was one of the few things they had done right. The adults had spent days trying to recover the words other adults had taken from her. Now the court would have to decide whether those words would shape the next order or whether the system that translated them would be allowed to call itself help and move on.

31

THE MERITS HEARING BEGAN on a Thursday morning with fewer cameras outside and more consequence inside. Jack Sullivan arrived before the courtroom opened and found Caleb already waiting in the hallway with the hearing binders stacked on a bench beside him. The binders were slimmer than they had been a week earlier because Jack had cut anything that did not serve the order he wanted. That was harder than adding pages. A strong record still needed a lawyer willing to leave some of it alone.

Ethan arrived ten minutes later in a dark suit and plain tie, looking nervous but composed. Jack had told him not to wear anything that made him look like he was trying to win a press conference. He had listened. He carried only a folder, a bottle of water, and the card Jack had written for him with the words Lily needed to hear if she became anxious. He tapped the folder against his leg until Jack looked at him, then stopped.

"She slept okay last night," Ethan said.

"Good."

"She asked if court means people are still fighting."

"What did you say?"

"I said court means adults are trying to make better rules."

Jack nodded. "That was safe."

"It felt incomplete."

"Most safe answers do."

Claire Whitcomb arrived with Marissa a few minutes before the bailiff opened the courtroom. Marissa did not look at Ethan, and Ethan did not look away fast enough to pretend he had not noticed. Jack stepped slightly between them, not as a barrier, but as a reminder. The court had built a structure for the parents because neither of them could be trusted to improvise in hallways. That did not make them bad parents. It made them parents under strain.

Judge Harrow took the bench at nine-thirty. The courtroom stood, then settled into the tense quiet of people ready to hear a decision that would not feel like enough to anyone. The judge had already read the sealed merits briefs, the deposition excerpts, Dr. Patel's protected general updates, the proposed parenting plans, and the stipulated safeguards. She did not need a full trial that morning. She needed argument, limited testimony only if required, and enough clarity to convert the temporary framework into a workable order.

The first witness was not Lily, and Jack was grateful for that. Neither side had asked to call her, and Judge Harrow had made clear she would not allow it absent extraordinary need. Instead, Angela Morrissey testified briefly about process, not content. She confirmed Lily was engaging with Dr. Patel, that both parents had complied with the no-discussion order since the emergency ruling, and that the child benefited from predictable exchanges and reduced adult explanation. She did not reveal therapy content. She did not disclose drawings. She protected Lily by saying less.

Claire asked Angela whether Marissa had followed the current order. Angela said yes. Jack asked whether Ethan had followed the current order. Angela said yes. Judge Harrow asked whether either parent had attempted to use therapy as evidence. Angela said no. That answer mattered because the case had finally created one place where adults had not yet taken more than they were allowed.

After Angela stepped down, Judge Harrow heard argument on the parenting plan. Claire went first and conceded that joint legal decision-making should continue under specific limitations. She asked that Marissa not be treated as unsafe based on third-party conduct she did not fully understand. She acknowledged Marissa's nondisclosure of the support number was a serious error and said Marissa accepted the court's restrictions. Her argument was careful, and Jack thought it was probably the best one available.

Jack stood when the judge turned to him. He did not attack Marissa as if she had designed Civic Bridge. He did not excuse her either. He told the court Ethan needed equal decision-making authority, direct access to school and medical information, structured communication, and protection from any future attempt to route Lily's distress through undisclosed systems. He asked the court to adopt findings that did not punish the parents but preserved the truth of what happened. He used the phrase materially incomplete once and only once.

"The court does not need to decide every institutional question today," Jack said. "It does need to recognize that Lily's actual written words did not reach the court before emergency relief was requested, that an undisclosed support channel supplied language later reflected in the record, and that third parties treated her circumstances as program material before the court had a complete view. Those findings are necessary because the remedy must prevent repetition, not merely resolve blame."

Judge Harrow looked down at her notes. "And if the court enters those findings, what practical custody order follows?"

"Joint legal decision-making, no unilateral treatment changes, neutral therapeutic oversight, direct record access for both parents, monitored parenting communication, no undisclosed third-party support resources, and a review hearing after Dr. Patel has had enough time to work with Lily and both parents."

Claire did not object because most of that language had already been negotiated. The fight was no longer over whether the safeguards were needed. The fight was over the findings that explained why. Findings could follow a family long after an order was signed. Jack understood Claire's concern. He also understood that without findings, the same adults could later reframe the whole case as a misunderstanding caused by an emotional father.

Judge Harrow asked both parents to stand, not to testify, but to hear the order directly. Ethan rose beside Jack. Marissa rose beside Claire. Neither looked at the other. Judge Harrow removed her glasses and spoke in a voice that filled the courtroom without sounding theatrical.

"This court finds that Lily Cole's initial emergency record was materially incomplete," she said. "The court further finds that the minor child's written statement to her teacher should have been disclosed under seal before emergency relief was requested. The court makes no finding at this time that either parent intentionally misled the court. The court does find that the use of undisclosed third-party support channels created a serious risk that Lily's words would be shaped, filtered, or interpreted before the court could evaluate them."

Ethan lowered his head slightly. Marissa closed her eyes for a moment. Claire wrote the language down. Jack did not move because the words were still coming, and every word mattered.

Judge Harrow continued. "The court further finds that the minor child's circumstances were referenced in an anonymized program-impact context before the court had a complete record. That use was inappropriate in the context of an active custody proceeding. The court orders that no parent, counsel, consultant, provider, school employee, nonprofit, foundation, or related agent may use, publish, report, train from, present, or otherwise disseminate the minor child's circumstances without further court order."

Hale was not at counsel table, but Jack knew the order would reach him before lunch. The language was broader than Jack had requested in one respect and narrower in another. It protected Lily without turning Fairchild into a party to every remaining custody issue. That was likely the strongest order the court could make without creating appellate vulnerability. Jack wrote the key phrases as the judge spoke, though the minute order would arrive later.

The custody order followed. Joint legal custody remained in place. Major medical, psychological, educational, and counseling decisions required written agreement or court order. Dr. Patel remained the neutral therapeutic provider, with general updates only. Both parents would attend separate guidance sessions and follow written communication protocols. Exchanges would remain neutral for thirty days, then transition to school-based or agreed public exchanges if Dr. Patel and Angela believed Lily could tolerate the change.

Judge Harrow addressed the parents directly after reading the order. "Lily does not need either of you to explain this case to her. She needs consistency, ordinary care, and room to speak without being managed. If she uses different words in different places, that does not make her dishonest. It makes her a child trying to feel safe in more than one room."

The courtroom stayed quiet. That sentence reached farther than the legal order. Jack saw Ethan's face change, and he saw Marissa's shoulders drop. The judge had given both parents a way to understand Lily without claiming her words for either side. It was not therapy, but it was close to wisdom, and family court needed more of that than its calendars usually allowed.

The hearing ended with a review date set six weeks out and a status conference on third-party compliance scheduled in two weeks. Jack gathered his papers slowly. Claire approached before Ethan could leave. She asked to speak attorney to attorney, with the parents out of earshot. Jack agreed. They stepped to the side of the courtroom while Caleb walked Ethan toward the hallway and Claire's associate stayed with Marissa.

"Marissa wants to apologize eventually," Claire said.

"Not directly to Lily without Dr. Patel."

"I know."

"Not to Ethan in a way that asks him to comfort her."

Claire nodded. "I know that too."

Jack looked toward Marissa, who was standing at counsel table with one hand on the back of a chair. She looked less like an adversary and more like someone seeing the wreckage after the fog lifted. That did not absolve her. It did make her human, and human problems were always harder to order around than legal ones.

"She can start by following the order," Jack said.

"That is what I told her."

"Then we agree."

Outside the courtroom, Ethan stood near the elevators with Caleb beside him. Reporters waited near the far end of the hall, but the bailiff had kept them back. Ethan looked at Jack, searching his face for the meaning of the order beyond the words. Jack handed him the printed notes he had made, then spoke quietly.

"You kept joint decision-making. The court found the emergency record was materially incomplete. The court barred use of Lily's circumstances. The next six weeks are about stability."

Ethan nodded. "She said Lily can use different words."

"Yes."

"That might be the best thing that happened today."

"It may be."

Ethan looked down the hall toward Marissa, then back at Jack. "I don't know what to feel."

"Then do not decide yet."

"That sounds like Dr. Patel."

"She is probably better at it."

Ethan gave a small, tired smile. Then he put the order notes into his folder and walked with Caleb toward the side exit. He did not stop for reporters. He did not look back for Marissa. He had learned that leaving quietly could be an act of protection. Jack watched him go and felt a measured relief that still carried the weight of everything unresolved.

Back at the office, the team read the written order when it arrived at 2:18 p.m. Nora printed three copies and placed one in the custody binder, one in the third-party binder, and one in Jack's hands. Amelia stood near the conference room door, waiting for the version she could hear. Jack gave her the public-safe summary. The court entered findings that the emergency record was materially incomplete, protected Lily from further institutional use, and preserved joint custody with safeguards. Amelia wrote only a few words down.

"That order matters beyond this case," she said.

"Eventually."

"I know."

"Do you?"

She closed her notebook. "After Lily."

Jack nodded. The words had become a promise between them, though neither had named it that.

At five, Dr. Patel sent a general note through Angela. Lily had been told, in age-appropriate language, that the adults had made rules so she did not have to choose words from anyone else's list. The note said Lily asked whether that meant she could say she did not know yet. Dr. Patel responded that not knowing yet was allowed. The update contained nothing more. Jack read it twice and placed it in the protected folder.

He called Ethan and gave him only what he was allowed to share. "Dr. Patel says Lily understands she does not have to choose words from a list. If she says she does not know, you let that be enough."

Ethan was quiet. "That sounds like Lily."

"Yes."

"I can let that be enough."

"Good."

After the call, Jack stayed in his office while the building grew quiet. The case had not ended, but the first half had closed in a way that protected Lily more than it punished anyone. That was not the kind of victory people cheered. It was the kind that gave a child space to become less afraid of her own voice.

He walked into the conference room and erased the phrase emergency petition from the board. Under the next phase, he wrote three words: stability, compliance, accountability. Then he capped the marker and stepped back. The custody order had given Lily room. The third-party order had stopped her use. The accountability question remained, and it would move slower because powerful systems rarely fell in the same room where they were first exposed. Jack knew the next fight would be harder to keep inside family court. He also knew the record was finally strong enough to follow wherever the law allowed.

32

The first week after the merits order was quieter than Jack Sullivan trusted. Quiet in family cases rarely meant peace. It usually meant people were measuring the new rules, testing the edges, and deciding whether compliance cost less than resistance. Ethan followed the order with the focus of a man who understood one careless message could undo a month of restraint. Marissa followed it too, though her messages in the parenting app carried the careful tone of someone writing under supervision.

Jack reviewed the app exchanges every morning with Caleb. Homework. Therapy transportation. Lily's school project. A request to switch pickup by fifteen minutes because of traffic. Nothing in the messages was warm, and Jack did not expect warmth. Functional communication was the first stage of repair, and some parents never reached it.

On Wednesday, Lily's school sent both parents the same email about a history presentation. Ethan forwarded it to Jack even though Jack had direct access through the order. The message from Ethan said only, I received it directly. That was all. Jack understood the weight behind it. For weeks, information had reached Ethan filtered, delayed, or not at all. A school email about a presentation had become evidence that the new structure was working.

Mara came in at nine with the third-party compliance chart. "Fairchild certified no further dissemination."

"Who signed?"

"Hale."

"That is a lawyer's certification."

She handed him the page. "Civic Bridge certification is signed by Caroline Venn. Tessa's is signed by Ellison. Horizon's is signed by Dr. Warren."

Jack read each certification. They were narrowly written, as expected. No further use, dissemination, presentation, reporting, or training involving the scenario connected to Lily Cole without court order. Each one preserved objections, denied wrongdoing, and claimed compliance. That was enough for the moment. Family court orders often began as paper boundaries before they became real boundaries through enforcement.

Caleb entered with a draft status report. He had organized it into three sections: parenting compliance, therapeutic structure, and third-party compliance. Jack liked the structure. He removed two adjectives, changed "disturbing" to "concerning," and changed "pattern" to "record." Caleb watched him make the edits with visible resignation.

"You cut all the force out of it," Caleb said.

"No. I cut the argument out of the facts."

"That feels like the same thing."

"It is not."

Mara looked at Caleb. "He is right, which is annoying."

Jack handed the draft back. "Facts with restraint look stronger to a judge who already understands the problem."

By late morning, Amelia arrived with a folder of public records and a bakery box she claimed was not a peace offering. Nora accepted the pastries and announced that motive did not affect admissibility when powdered sugar was involved. Amelia had found three public Fairchild grant summaries using phrases that matched the sealed deck: court-facing language, family stabilization pathways, and scalable proof. None of them mentioned Civic Bridge directly, but the funding category matched. Jack allowed Mara to review them as public-source background only. He did not want the custody file contaminated with speculation dressed as context.

Amelia sat across from Jack after the documents were logged. "There are other cases."

Jack looked at the folder. "Publicly?"

"Not names. Patterns."

"Patterns are not cases."

"They become cases when someone opens the right door."

"Not this week."

She leaned back. "You think I am trying to run ahead."

"You are."

"I am trying not to."

"That is also true."

The exchange stopped there. Amelia had learned not to push past the boundary once it was named clearly. Jack had learned that her instincts were often right even when her timing was dangerous. The public story was gathering outside the sealed case like weather at the edge of the map. The court could not ignore it forever. It also could not let it define Lily.

At noon, Claire called about Marissa's parent-guidance session. She said Dr. Patel had given both parents the same instruction: avoid asking Lily whether she felt safer, better, clearer, confused, pressured, or ready. Those words had become loaded. The better question, Dr. Patel said, was whether Lily wanted soup or a sandwich, whether she needed help with homework, whether she wanted quiet or company. Jack wrote the guidance down and sent it to Ethan with no commentary. He replied, Understood. Sandwiches are easier.

Jack almost smiled at that. A month earlier, Ethan would have written three paragraphs about how Marissa had destroyed his daughter's sense of safety. Now he wrote about sandwiches. That did not mean he had forgiven anyone. It meant he understood the difference between what he felt and what Lily needed. Jack had built entire defenses around clients who never learned that distinction.

The calm broke at two-sixteen. Nora brought in a message from Daniel Mercer, Lily's principal. A local education blogger had called the school asking whether San Aurelio Unified had participated in "youth language coaching connected to a sealed custody case." Mercer had not answered. He wanted to know whether the court order allowed the district to issue a general statement. Jack told Nora to get Mercer on the phone immediately and asked Caleb to pull the school confidentiality provisions.

Mercer sounded strained when he came on. "I did not confirm anything."

"Good."

"They knew enough to ask the wrong question in the right hallway."

"Who called?"

"Name was Paula Raines. Runs a local school accountability site."

Jack wrote it down. "Did she mention Lily?"

"No. She mentioned a sealed custody case and a counselor placed on leave."

"Do not issue any statement without district counsel and court guidance."

"That's why I called."

"You did the right thing."

Mercer exhaled into the phone. "I wish that felt better."

After the call, Jack contacted Sonia Patel, district counsel, and then Claire. He sent a notice to all counsel stating that a third party appeared to be seeking information connected to the sealed proceedings and that no party, witness, school employee, nonprofit, consultant, or related agent should comment. He copied Angela because any breach could affect Lily. Then he asked Mara to find out who Paula Raines was and whether she had ties to Fairchild, Civic Bridge, or any advocacy group connected to the case. He did not assume a leak. He did not dismiss one either.

Amelia was still in the front office when she saw the movement. She waited until Jack walked past, then stood. "Something leaked."

"Something may have."

"Was it me?"

Jack stopped. "No."

"You are sure?"

"You have not had the sealed facts she asked about."

Amelia absorbed that. "What did she ask?"

"Enough that I cannot tell you more."

She nodded, though frustration crossed her face. "Let me search public sources."

"Public only. No calls to Mercer, Dana, Civic Bridge, Fairchild, or anyone connected to Lily."

"I know."

"Say it."

She gave him a look. "Public sources only. No contacts tied to the child, the school, the family, or the sealed case."

"Good."

By four, Mara had a profile. Paula Raines ran a local site that mixed school-board coverage, parental-rights commentary, and open-records stories. She had recently posted about nonprofits influencing school counseling policies. One post referenced Fairchild by name, accusing the foundation of funding "soft legal activism through school wellness programs." Jack read the posts with care. Raines was not necessarily linked to Fairchild. She may have been circling the same ecosystem from a different direction.

Caleb looked at the screen. "She could blow this open."

"Not if she has no names."

"She has school, counselor, sealed custody case."

"That is enough to hurt Lily if someone feeds her more."

Jack drafted a short ex parte notice to Judge Harrow, not asking for punishment, asking for clarification and reinforcement of the sealing and no-comment orders as to school personnel and third-party witnesses. Claire joined the request. Sonia Patel joined on behalf of the district. Even Hale sent a one-line response saying Fairchild had not communicated with Raines and supported protection of child privacy. Jack did not know whether he believed the first half. The second half was useful.

Judge Harrow issued a same-day minute order by five-thirty. It reminded all parties, counsel, witnesses, consultants, organizations, and agents that sealed information could not be disclosed or hinted at publicly. It directed the district to make no comment beyond a generic statement that student privacy laws prevented discussion of any matter involving a student. It warned that any violation could result in contempt, evidentiary sanctions, custody consequences, or referral to appropriate authorities. The order was stern because the risk had changed. A leak did not have to name Lily to find her.

Jack sent the order to Ethan and called him before the internet could do what the internet did. Ethan answered from his car in a parking lot. Jack told him a blogger had made inquiries at the school, that the court had reinforced the sealing order, and that Ethan was not to search, comment, message, or call anyone about it. Ethan said nothing for several seconds. Jack could hear traffic in the background.

"She is going to find Lily," Ethan said.

"We are working to prevent that."

"What do I do if Lily hears something?"

"You say, 'Some adults are asking questions they should not ask. You are safe tonight. You do not have to answer anyone. I will talk to the grown-ups who handle that.' Then you contact Angela or Dr. Patel through the proper channel."

"I hate this."

"I know."

"I won't search it."

"Good."

"I already want to."

"Wanting is not doing."

Ethan gave a tired breath. "That should be on another card."

Jack ended the call after confirming Ethan was calm enough to drive. Then he called Claire. Marissa had already heard through the school parent network that "some custody thing" might involve a district counselor. Claire had instructed her not to respond to anyone. Marissa was frightened and, according to Claire, ashamed. Jack accepted the report without comment. Shame could lead people toward repair or toward concealment. The next forty-eight hours would show which way Marissa leaned.

At seven, Amelia returned from her public-source search with a printout. Paula Raines had posted that afternoon: Sources say a local school district is hiding involvement in a sealed family-court matter tied to outside nonprofits. More soon. There were no names. No school. No child. The words were vague enough to avoid contempt and sharp enough to invite speculation. Jack read it and felt the old familiar dislike of public pressure entering private litigation.

"She has a source," Amelia said.

"Maybe."

"She says sources plural."

"People do that."

Amelia sat down. "This is why the public record matters. Someone else will write it worse."

"That does not authorize you to write it now."

"I know."

"Do you?"

"Yes." Her voice softened. "I am not arguing for Lily's case. I am saying the vacuum is dangerous."

Jack agreed with that, which made the problem harder. Silence protected Lily. Silence also allowed speculation to grow in the shape of whatever people feared most. A careful public statement might stop rumors, or it might confirm there was something worth digging for. In family court, privacy often had to tolerate unfair narratives because correcting them did more harm than the lie.

Jack called Angela and proposed that the parents receive written guidance for Lily in case she heard rumors at school. Angela agreed and asked Dr. Patel for language. Within an hour, Dr. Patel provided three sentences for both homes: Some adults are asking about things that are private. You do not have to answer questions about your family. The adults who help you know what to do. Jack sent it through counsel and the parenting app. Both parents acknowledged receipt.

The office quieted after that, but no one felt finished. Caleb updated the status report to include the attempted media inquiry. Mara added leak risk to the third-party compliance chart. Nora taped Judge Harrow's no-comment order near her desk with a handwritten note beneath it: Talk less. Live longer. Amelia took a picture of the note and asked if she could quote Nora someday. Nora said only after her death and preferably under a better headline.

Jack stayed late, reading Paula Raines's post again. It did not violate the court order on its face because Raines was not bound by it unless she had received sealed material from someone who was. The law could restrain parties and witnesses, not every person with a website and a theory. That was the weakness in every sealed child case once the outer world found the scent. The court could build walls around records. It could not build walls around curiosity.

Before leaving, Jack stood at the whiteboard and added one more column: exposure risk. Under it he wrote Raines, school inquiry, rumor network, parent guidance. Then he drew a line back to Lily's protected space and stopped. The case had shifted again, not away from custody or accountability, but toward containment. Someone outside the courthouse wanted the story. Jack's task was to keep Lily from becoming the door they used to enter it.

33

Paula Raines posted again before sunrise, and this time the phrasing was closer to the sealed record than Jack Sullivan liked. The post did not name Lily, Ethan, Marissa, the school, or the case number. It did say a district counselor had helped route a child's uncertainty through an outside nonprofit before a family-court emergency hearing. It also said a major foundation had reviewed the situation as a program outcome while the court record remained incomplete. Whoever spoke to Raines understood enough to be dangerous and careful enough to avoid the obvious line.

Jack read the post at his kitchen table with coffee he had forgotten to drink. He did not call Ethan first. He called Nora, then Mara, then Caleb, each with short instructions and no commentary. By seven-thirty, the office was open, the conference room lights were on, and the whiteboard had exposure risk circled in black. Nora came in carrying a pastry bag and the expression of someone prepared to deny all comfort to anyone who earned it.

Mara arrived with screenshots already archived. "She has sealed concepts, not sealed documents."

"That may be enough," Jack said.

"Enough for contempt?"

"Only against someone bound by the order, and only if we can trace it."

Caleb set down his laptop. "Can the court order Raines to take it down?"

"Not on this record."

"She is inviting people to identify the child."

"Yes. That is why we move fast."

Jack drafted an emergency request for a protective conference. He did not accuse Raines because she was not a party and because the First Amendment was not a decorative obstacle. He asked Judge Harrow to require all bound persons and entities to file declarations stating whether they had communicated with Raines or anyone connected to her site, whether directly or through intermediaries. He also asked for a temporary order prohibiting parties, witnesses, counsel, organizations, and agents from confirming, denying, correcting, or contextualizing any public reporting connected to the sealed case. The difference mattered. People often leaked through denial as easily as disclosure.

Claire joined the request within twenty minutes. Sonia Patel joined for the district. Hale opposed the declaration requirement as burdensome and unnecessary, while offering a voluntary statement that Fairchild had not disclosed sealed information. Fray said Civic Bridge would comply if ordered. Ellison said Tessa had no contact with Raines. Each response sounded written for a future reader as much as the judge. Jack expected nothing less.

Ethan called at eight-fifteen, which meant he had seen the post or someone had sent it to him. Jack answered from his office with the door closed. Ethan's voice was controlled, but thin in the way a voice gets when anger is being held in place by both hands. He asked whether the post was about Lily. Jack did not answer the question as asked because a direct answer could confirm what the court was trying to protect.

"It appears to describe issues connected to this case," Jack said.

"That means yes."

"It means we are treating it as a risk."

"People at school will guess."

"We are asking the court for immediate protection."

Ethan went quiet. "Lily has school today."

"I know."

"Should I keep her home?"

"Not without agreement or guidance. That could make her feel something is wrong or make the school rumor worse. Let Angela and Dr. Patel help decide."

Ethan exhaled hard. "I hate every option."

"That is not the same as every option being equal."

Jack heard the line land. Ethan said he would wait for guidance and not call the school, not message Marissa outside the app, and not search Raines's comments. Jack had him repeat those three things. It sounded childish, and it worked. People in family court often needed plain instructions because pain made intelligence unreliable.

By nine, Angela had coordinated with Dr. Patel and the school. Lily would attend school under ordinary routine. If another student asked about family court, school staff would redirect without confirming anything. Dana Keene remained on leave, and Mercer would brief only the minimum staff needed. The plan was imperfect. Every child-protection plan in a public school was imperfect once adults outside the building began circling a sealed case.

Judge Harrow set an emergency protective conference for eleven. The remote link filled with lawyers, each appearing from offices that looked more orderly than the facts. Raines was not present because no one had moved to join her and the court had not ordered her appearance. Judge Harrow began by saying the court had reviewed the public posts and would not restrain nonparties without proper process and constitutional analysis. Then she turned to the people she could reach.

"This court can and will regulate those bound by its orders," she said. "No party, attorney, witness, consultant, provider, organization, foundation, employee, agent, or intermediary subject to this court's orders may confirm, deny, hint, correct, elaborate upon, contextualize, or otherwise respond to any public reporting concerning this sealed matter without further order."

Hale asked for clarification that Fairchild could protect its reputation if publicly accused by name. Judge Harrow said Fairchild could issue a generic statement affirming its commitment to privacy and declining comment on any legal matter involving a minor. It could not discuss the existence, nonexistence, accuracy, inaccuracy, or context of any specific case-related allegation. Hale looked dissatisfied. Jack considered that a useful sign.

The judge ordered declarations from all counsel and institutional witnesses within forty-eight hours. Each declaration had to state whether the declarant had communicated with Raines, her site, any school board source, any media outlet, or any third person for the purpose of public disclosure concerning the case. The order also required preservation of texts, emails, direct messages, call logs, Signal messages, and social-media messages from the date of the first emergency hearing forward. Jack watched the faces as the judge read that list. Most remained still. Caroline Venn's counsel looked down.

The conference ended without fireworks. Fireworks were for people who did not understand how damaging preservation orders could be. The declarations would either close the leak path or expose it. The preservation requirement would make later denials more expensive. Jack saved the order and sent Ethan the only message he needed: Court reinforced privacy. Follow Dr. Patel's guidance. No searching, no comments, no changes to school routine unless instructed.

Ethan replied, I understand. Lily asked for extra pencils this morning. I sent them.

Jack stared at the message longer than he expected. Extra pencils meant school. School meant routine. Routine meant the adults had not yet allowed the public noise to take the whole day from her. In a normal case, no lawyer would care about pencils. In this one, they were a measurable form of mercy.

At noon, Amelia came in with her laptop and a face that made Nora tell her to sit before speaking. Amelia had traced Raines's public comments and found that the post had first been amplified by an account tied to a local parent group. That group had shared several Fairchild-critical articles in recent months and had hosted a webinar with a former Civic

Bridge volunteer. The volunteer's name was Mina Torres. Mara searched the name and found it in Civic Bridge's old public staff listing under youth support fellows.

Jack looked at the screen. "Was Mina Torres involved in Lily's profile?"

Mara checked the sealed logs. "No access entries under that name."

"Former volunteer?"

"Likely."

Amelia leaned forward. "She may know the system without knowing Lily."

"Or someone used her as a bridge."

Caleb frowned. "Can we subpoena her?"

"Not yet. First declarations, then targeted inquiry if needed."

Amelia closed her laptop halfway. "She is public. I can call her."

"No."

"She is not bound."

"You are bound by your agreement with this office."

"I did not sign anything."

Jack looked at her. "You gave your word."

That stopped her. Not because it was legal, because it was not. It stopped her because the word mattered to her. She looked away, then nodded once. Jack did not soften the moment. Boundaries only worked when people felt them before they reached the edge.

The declarations began arriving that afternoon. Claire filed hers first, stating she and her firm had no contact with Raines or anyone connected to public reporting. Marissa's declaration came with it, short and shaky in tone even through formal language. She denied contacting any media, blogger, parent group, or third party for public disclosure. She also stated that after hearing rumors in the parent network, she did not respond. Jack believed parts of it and reserved judgment on the rest, as habit required.

Sonia Patel filed for the district with declarations from Mercer and two staff members. Mercer's was clean. He confirmed Raines called, that he declined to comment, and that he notified Jack. The district's communications director confirmed no statement had been issued. Dana Keene's declaration did not arrive with the district's. Sonia sent a separate note saying Dana was represented by private counsel and would file independently. Jack read that twice.

Mara saw his face. "Dana."

"Maybe."

"She has motive."

"She has exposure."

"Same neighborhood."

"Not the same house."

Caleb added Dana to the leak chart. Jack did not object. Dana had been the first person to treat Lily's note as a risk to be managed. She had the language, the school connection, and enough reason to make the system look larger than her own conduct. That did not prove she leaked. It made her declaration one of the most important.

At four, Rebecca Sloane filed Dana's declaration. Dana denied speaking to Raines, the parent group, any reporter, or any person for the purpose of disclosure. She admitted receiving a text from an unknown number asking whether she was "the counselor in the Civic Bridge custody mess." She did not respond. She attached a screenshot. The number was blocked. Mara took the screenshot and began tracing what little could be traced.

Hale filed Fairchild's declarations last. They were polished and broad, stating no Fairchild employee had knowingly disclosed sealed information or communicated with Raines about the Cole matter. Nina Sato's declaration disclosed one detail the cover letter had not highlighted. Two weeks earlier, before Judge Harrow's expanded sealing order, she had received an inquiry from a "community education writer" asking generally about court-facing youth grants. She responded with a link to public grant materials and declined to discuss any matter involving minors. The writer used the name Paula Raines.

Jack read the declaration twice, then passed it to Mara. "There is the first contact."

Mara scanned it. "Public grant materials."

"Maybe true."

"Maybe enough for Raines to frame the post."

"Maybe not enough for the sealed concepts."

Caleb looked at the timeline. "Raines contacted Fairchild before the latest post."

"Yes."

Amelia, who had returned to the doorway, said quietly, "Raines was already looking at Fairchild. The leak may not be one leak. It may be convergence."

Jack looked at her. The word was useful. Raines had public material, Fairchild grant language, a former volunteer community, a school rumor, and perhaps one sealed hint from someone who did not understand how much one hint could reveal. Leaks were not always dramatic handoffs in parking lots. Sometimes they were five small disclosures that became one recognizable shape.

By early evening, Judge Harrow had the declarations but had not yet ruled further. Jack sent a status note identifying the known contact with Fairchild, the unknown-number text to Dana, and the need to preserve Raines-related communications without naming Raines as a party. He did not ask for subpoenas yet. He asked for a follow-up conference after the preservation period closed. The judge set it for the next week.

Dr. Patel's update came at seven. Lily attended school without reported incident. She used the extra pencils in art class. She asked Angela whether adults on the internet could make court rules. Angela told her no, adults on the internet do not make the rules for her family. The update ended there. Jack read the last sentence and felt some of the day's pressure ease. It was not a legal finding, but it was true enough to matter.

He sent Ethan the permitted summary: School was okay today. Keep tonight ordinary. Ethan replied with a photo of a pencil sharpener and the words, We are prepared. Jack smiled for real this time. Then he forwarded the permitted summary to Claire, who answered, Thank you. Marissa will keep tonight quiet. That response mattered too. Both homes had received the same instruction. For one evening, both appeared willing to follow it.

After the office emptied, Amelia remained in the conference room with Jack's permission, reviewing only public documents. Jack stood at the board, considering whether to add Raines beneath exposure risk or keep her outside the core case.

He finally wrote public pressure and placed Raines beneath it, separate from the custody merits. That was legally cleaner. It was also emotionally honest. Raines was not the original harm. She was what happened when original harm became discoverable by people with their own agendas.

Amelia watched him write. "You are not going after Raines."

"Not unless she receives or publishes sealed identifying information."

"She will keep pushing."

"Probably."

"That means someone else may feed her."

"Then we watch the people bound by the order."

Amelia nodded. "Convergence."

Jack tapped the marker cap against the board. "Yes."

The word stayed in the room after Amelia left. Convergence. Public records, private mistakes, institutional language, school rumors, and sealed proceedings moving toward one another until a child's life became visible through the gaps. Jack turned off the lights and left the board as it was. The next fight was not only about who leaked. It was about whether the court could keep Lily ordinary in a world that had learned to profit from turning children into examples.

34

The following Monday began with compliance on paper and unease everywhere else. Jack Sullivan arrived to find the declarations binder on his desk, placed there by Nora with a yellow note that said, Everyone swears they behaved. That was the problem with declarations. They could narrow a question, preserve a record, and expose an omission, but they rarely satisfied the part of a lawyer that had learned people lied most confidently when they used formal language. Jack carried the binder into the conference room and set it beside the whiteboard.

Caleb had already prepared the summary chart. Claire, Marissa, Ethan, Mercer, Sonia Patel, Dana, Fairchild, Civic Bridge, Tessa, Horizon, and the school district all denied leaking sealed information. Nina Sato admitted a general public-materials response to Paula Raines before the second post. Dana admitted receiving an anonymous text. No one admitted giving Raines enough to tie the school counselor, nonprofit, foundation, and family court together. That meant the leak was either indirect, carefully laundered, or not a leak in the legal sense at all.

Mara entered with coffee and a thin folder. "I have the unknown number from Dana's screenshot."

Jack looked up. "Registered?"

"Prepaid carrier. No subscriber without subpoena. Number activated six days before the text and inactive two days after."

Caleb frowned. "That sounds deliberate."

"It sounds temporary," Jack said. "Deliberate is a conclusion."

Mara placed the folder down. "Temporary with excellent timing."

Jack accepted that wording. The text to Dana could have been a journalist, a parent activist, a former Civic Bridge volunteer, or someone inside the case trying to see whether Dana would panic. Without records, it was smoke. Smoke mattered because fires existed, but courts did not issue orders on smoke alone unless a child was standing in it. Lily was close enough that Jack was willing to move, but not so close that he could ask the judge to burn procedure.

The follow-up protective conference was set for eleven. Before that, Jack met with Ethan by phone because Lily was with Marissa that morning and Ethan had already sent three app messages he wanted reviewed before sending a fourth. Jack read the draft. It asked whether Marissa had heard any school rumors and whether she knew who might be talking to the blogger. Jack told him not to send it. Ethan made a frustrated sound that was not quite a word.

"It is a reasonable question," Ethan said.

"It is also a question that turns the parenting app into discovery."

"She might know."

"She might. Your parenting app is not where we find out."

"So I just ask about Lily's lunch and pretend this isn't happening?"

"You ask about Lily's lunch because Lily's lunch is what the app is for."

Ethan was quiet for a moment. "That sounds ridiculous and right at the same time."

"Many family court rules do."

Ethan deleted the message while Jack stayed on the line. Then he sent a short note asking whether Lily needed her blue sweater for the school assembly. Marissa replied twelve minutes later that Lily had it in her backpack. Jack watched the exchange appear in the app log and felt the strange satisfaction of a small disaster avoided. A sweater was not the case. That was precisely why it mattered.

At eleven, Judge Harrow appeared on the remote conference link with the declarations already reviewed. She did not look pleased, which Jack expected. Judges disliked leaks, and they disliked being asked to chase rumors through a custody case even more. She summarized the record: a public writer had reported information resembling sealed issues; bound persons denied disclosure; one Fairchild employee acknowledged responding to a general inquiry with public materials; a district counselor received an anonymous text; no party had established a direct violation of the sealing order. Then she looked into the camera and spoke to everyone at once.

"The court will not conduct a media investigation inside a custody proceeding absent evidence that a person bound by this court's orders disclosed protected information. The court will strengthen the protective protocol because the risk to the minor remains real. The court will not expand this case into a generalized inquiry into public commentary."

That ruling was exactly what Jack expected and less than everyone feared. The judge ordered all future filings containing third-party institutional materials lodged under seal with redacted service copies where appropriate. She required counsel to meet and confer before sharing any institutional production with clients, limiting disclosure to what each parent needed to understand obligations and decisions affecting Lily. She also ordered that any future media inquiry to a party, school, provider, nonprofit, or foundation be logged and reported to counsel within twenty-four hours. It was practical, not satisfying.

Hale asked whether Fairchild could respond to public criticism about its grant programs generally. Judge Harrow repeated that generic statements were permitted, case-specific responses were not. Fray asked whether Civic Bridge could correct inaccuracies if Raines published false claims about its support line. The judge gave the same answer. Claire asked whether the parents could tell close family members not to discuss rumors. Judge Harrow allowed brief privacy requests without case details. Jack did not object to any of it because the order needed to be livable.

After the conference, Amelia came into the office with two printed posts from Raines. The first repeated the earlier allegations. The second asked whether "a prominent legal figure" was pressuring witnesses to hide nonprofit influence in family court. Amelia looked annoyed enough that Nora offered her coffee without insult. That alone made Jack notice the room had become very tired.

"She is trying to pull you into it," Amelia said.

Jack read the post and set it down. "She wants a reaction."

"She may get one from someone else."

"Then we make sure it is not from here."

"She is framing privacy as cover-up."

"That is common."

"It works."

"Yes."

Amelia sat back. She understood the trap. If Jack publicly defended privacy, Raines would say he was hiding the system. If he publicly criticized the system, he would confirm the sealed case existed. If anyone corrected the details, they would give her better details. The safest answer for Lily made the public narrative worse. The law often required that kind of bargain.

At one, Marissa's declaration became the next issue. Claire called and said Marissa wanted to amend it. She had remembered a conversation at a grocery store with another school parent after the first emergency hearing. Marissa had not mentioned Lily by name, according to Claire, but she had said the school counselor situation was "bigger than our family" and that outside organizations had "made everything confusing." The parent was named Elise Donnelly. Claire sounded angry at her own client and careful not to say so.

Jack put the call on speaker with Caleb present. "When did this conversation occur?"

"Two days after the first merits order."

"Before Raines posted?"

"Yes."

"Did Ms. Donnelly have any connection to Paula Raines?"

"I do not know."

"Did Marissa know Ms. Donnelly was involved in any parent group?"

"She knew she attended school board meetings."

Jack closed his eyes briefly. "We need the amended declaration today."

"I know."

"And the name of any group Ms. Donnelly participates in, if Marissa knows."

"I will get it."

Claire paused before continuing. "She says she was overwhelmed and talking too much. She understands that does not excuse it."

Jack accepted the statement without comment. It was not enough to prove Marissa caused the posts. It was enough to create a plausible path from parent-network rumor to public writer. A grocery-store conversation could do what sealed records did not. It could give a person the confidence to connect public materials to a private family. The harm was informal, which meant it was harder to punish and easier to repeat.

Ethan had to be told, but carefully. Jack called him after receiving Claire's amended declaration. He explained that Marissa had disclosed a conversation with a school parent that may have contributed to rumor, and that the court would be notified. Ethan's first reaction was silence. His second was a laugh without humor.

"She just talked in a grocery store," Ethan said.

"That is what the declaration says."

"She always does this. She tells people enough to make herself the worried mother."

"Ethan."

"I know. I'm not going to message her."

"Good."

"I want to."

"I know."

He breathed for a moment. "Was Lily named?"

"Not according to the declaration."

"That does not make it better."

"No. It makes it legally different."

"That is the worst kind of different."

Jack could not argue with that. Legal difference mattered because law required boundaries. It did not always comfort people inside the facts. Ethan had a right to be angry. He did not have a right to put that anger in front of Lily, into the parenting app, or onto a public page where the whole case could burn.

Mara searched Elise Donnelly while Caleb prepared a supplemental notice. Donnelly appeared on the board of a local parent transparency group that had reposted Raines twice. She had spoken at school board meetings against foundation-funded counseling programs. Her public posts criticized Fairchild and Civic Bridge by name. None of that made her a wrongdoer. It did mean Marissa had spoken loosely to exactly the kind of person who could turn a vague comment into a public thread.

Amelia read the public information from across the room. "That explains convergence."

Jack nodded. "Public records, Raines, parent group, Marissa's grocery-store conversation."

"And maybe no sealed document leak."

"Maybe."

"That is almost worse."

"It is harder."

She looked at him. "Because no one person did enough to be the villain."

"Correct."

The supplemental notice went to Judge Harrow at four-thirty. Claire joined it, attaching Marissa's amended declaration. Jack requested no sanctions, only that the court consider whether additional parent guidance or restrictions were necessary. That restraint cost Ethan something, and Jack knew it. A sanctions motion might satisfy the wound and fail the child. A targeted correction might actually reduce future harm.

Judge Harrow responded with an order requiring both parents to attend an additional guidance session with Dr. Patel on privacy, public conversation, and community rumors. She also ordered that neither parent discuss the case, the school counselor, nonprofit involvement, court orders, or Lily's distress with other parents, extended family, congregants, coworkers, or community members except for confidential legal, therapeutic, or pastoral support. The order was broad, but grounded in the amended declaration. It did not punish Marissa by name. It made the rule unmistakable.

Claire called Jack after the order. "Marissa is embarrassed."

"She should be."

"She is worried Ethan will use this against her."

"He wants to."

"That is honest."

"I am stopping him."

Claire was quiet. "Thank you."

"Do not thank me. Keep her quiet."

"I will."

The call ended without warmth, but with something like professional trust. That was often all opposing lawyers could offer in a case where both clients were hurt and both could still harm the child by defending themselves too loudly. Jack did not need Claire to like him. He needed her to keep Marissa inside the order. He suspected she needed him to do the same with Ethan.

At seven, Dr. Patel's general update came through Angela. Lily had asked why adults whisper after court. Dr. Patel's note said the parents should not answer with explanations. They should say, "Some things are private, and you are not responsible for adult conversations." Jack sent the language to both sides through counsel. Ethan replied that he understood. Claire confirmed Marissa would use the exact language if needed.

Nora left shortly after, telling Jack the office could survive one night without him guarding the copier. Caleb left with the amended compliance chart. Mara stayed another hour tracing Donnelly's public links, then concluded there was no basis for formal action yet. Amelia left last, pausing by Jack's door with her bag on her shoulder.

"You know," she said, "Raines may be wrong about details and still right that the public deserves to know the system exists."

Jack looked up from the binder. "Yes."

"That answer is new."

"No. It is just not the answer for tonight."

She nodded. "After Lily."

"After Lily."

When she left, Jack sat alone with the amended declaration. A careless conversation in a grocery store had become a public pressure point. That was how fragile sealed custody cases were. They did not always break because someone smuggled documents out of a courthouse. Sometimes they broke because a frightened parent told the wrong person a little too much while reaching for sympathy between the produce aisle and the checkout line.

Jack stood at the whiteboard and added Elise Donnelly beneath convergence. Then he wrote community rumor beside parent guidance. The next six weeks were supposed to be about stability, and now stability included teaching adults not to feed the world pieces of a child's private pain. The law could issue orders. It could not make people wise. That remained the harder work, and it was the one Lily needed most.

35

The additional parent-guidance order changed the tone of the case more than Jack Sullivan expected. It did not create new facts, and it did not undo the grocery-store conversation that had helped the public rumor find shape. It did something quieter. It forced both parents to admit that privacy was no longer a preference or a courtesy. It was part of Lily's safety plan, as real as neutral exchanges and therapy appointments.

Ethan arrived for his session with Dr. Patel looking like a man prepared to be corrected. Jack walked him to the small conference room and reminded him that parent guidance was not a deposition. Ethan gave him a look that said he knew the words and still disliked needing them. Dr. Patel appeared on the screen at noon, calm and plainspoken. Jack left before the session began, because Lily needed one corner of the case where her father's lawyer was not listening.

Marissa's session took place two hours later, through Claire's office. Jack knew only that it happened because Claire confirmed compliance. That was all he was entitled to know. He had to remind Caleb of that when Caleb asked whether

Dr. Patel would tell the court if Marissa minimized the grocery-store conversation. Jack told him the court would receive only general compliance information unless a safety issue required more. Family court could not turn therapy into a surveillance device every time lawyers wanted cleaner answers.

By three, both sessions were complete. Angela sent a brief update stating that both parents had received guidance on privacy, rumor management, and responding to Lily without explanation. The recommended parent language was simple: "Some adults talk when they do not know the whole story. You are not responsible for that. You can tell us if something makes you uncomfortable." Jack forwarded it to Ethan and Claire. Ethan replied within two minutes. Marissa replied through Claire within ten. Compliance had become a rhythm, and Jack hoped habit would become restraint before another mistake tested it.

Mara came in with the latest Raines post printed on one page. It was less specific than the last one and more accusatory in tone. Raines claimed court insiders were using privacy rules to shield institutions from scrutiny. She did not identify Lily or the school. She did not mention the grocery-store parent by name. She was working around the sealed case, pressing at the edges, trying to make the wall itself look guilty.

Caleb read the post and frowned. "Can we do anything?"

"Not unless she crosses a legal line."

"She is making the court look corrupt."

"Courts survive adjectives."

"What about the child?"

Jack took the paper from him. "That is the only question that matters."

The office shifted into protective review. Nora logged calls. Mara monitored public posts without engaging. Caleb checked whether any new public comments identified the school or child. Amelia, who had arrived with more public Fairchild material, was placed under what Nora called "voluntary containment" in the front office. She objected to the word voluntary. Nora told her the pastries were voluntary too, and Amelia stayed where she was.

At four, Mercer called again. A parent had asked the front office whether the school was involved in a court scandal. The office staff gave the district-approved privacy response and reported it to him. No student names were used. No staff confirmed anything. Mercer sounded exhausted in the careful way school administrators sound when every sentence could become a board complaint.

"Do you need a revised statement?" Mercer asked.

"No," Jack said. "Use the approved one and document every inquiry."

"This is affecting staff."

"I know."

"Dana's name is moving around the parent groups."

"Do not comment on personnel matters."

"I know the rule. I am telling you the building knows there is smoke."

Jack looked through the glass wall toward the conference room. "Keep the fire away from the children."

Mercer was quiet for a moment. "That is what I am trying to do."

After the call, Jack notified Sonia Patel and copied Claire. He did not copy Ethan directly because school inquiry details had to travel through counsel and the app only if needed for parenting. Ethan needed to know anything affecting Lily's day, not every rumor moving through the adult world. That distinction had become the hardest part of client management. Parents often believed access to every detail proved they were protecting their child. Sometimes it only gave their fear more material to work with.

At five, Claire sent a message that Marissa had received a text from Elise Donnelly apologizing if she had "made things worse." The message did not mention Raines, Lily, or the case by name. Claire attached a screenshot and said Marissa had not responded. Jack forwarded it to Mara and Caleb, then called Claire. Her voice carried the strain of a lawyer who had told her client exactly what not to do and then watched the world approach her client anyway.

"Tell her not to respond," Jack said.

"She has not."

"Preserve the phone."

"Already instructed."

"We may need Donnelly's communications."

"I assumed."

Claire paused. "Marissa is frightened that this will be used to take Lily from her."

"That is not what we are doing today."

"Today?"

"Claire."

"I know."

Jack heard the exhaustion on both sides of the line. Marissa's fear did not erase the harm caused by her loose conversation. It also did not mean Ethan's side should turn every error into a custody weapon. The judge had entered structure, not a death sentence for one parent's judgment. Jack wanted accountability. He did not want to create the very fear-driven spiral that had started the case.

Mara traced Donnelly's public activity. The timing was ugly. Donnelly had reposted Raines twelve minutes after the first post, then deleted two comments in which other users asked whether she had inside information. Screenshots of the deleted comments were captured by another local account and reposted later. None of that proved Donnelly was the source. It proved she was close enough to public speculation to justify a narrow subpoena if the court allowed it.

Jack drafted a targeted request by six. He asked Judge Harrow for leave to issue a limited subpoena to Elise Donnelly seeking communications with Paula Raines, Raines's site, any school parent group, or any third party concerning Lily's school, a sealed custody matter, Civic Bridge, Fairchild, Dana Keene, or Marissa Cole, from the date of Marissa's grocery-store conversation forward. He proposed a protective protocol requiring production to counsel only, with any child-identifying information redacted before broader circulation. It was intrusive, and he knew it. It was also the cleanest way to find whether rumor had become disclosure.

Claire did not oppose. That mattered. Sonia Patel supported the request because the school had a privacy interest. Hale filed a statement taking no position while denying Fairchild involvement. Fray objected mildly to including Civic Bridge in the subpoena language, then withdrew the objection after Jack agreed the subpoena would not request Civic Bridge's internal records from Donnelly beyond her own communications.

The court granted leave at eight-thirty that night. The order was narrow, sealed, and urgent.

Ethan called minutes after Jack sent him a short update. Jack had told him only that the court allowed a limited subpoena related to community-rumor communications. Ethan wanted to know whether Marissa caused the blogger posts. Jack said the record did not establish that. Ethan did not like the answer, and Jack could hear him walking while trying not to raise his voice.

"She talked to someone who reposted it," Ethan said.

"She disclosed a conversation to a school parent who appears connected to the public discussion. That does not prove she caused the posts."

"Why does every sentence have a fence around it?"

"Because your daughter lives inside the consequences of loose sentences."

That stopped him. Jack did not say it harshly. He said it because Ethan needed to hear it from someone who did not care whether the sentence comforted him. Ethan was quiet for nearly ten seconds.

"You're right," Ethan said.

"I know you are angry."

"I am."

"Then do the thing angry people rarely do well."

"What?"

"Nothing."

Ethan gave a tired laugh. "That is terrible advice."

"It is excellent advice for tonight."

When the call ended, Jack looked at the whiteboard and knew the next phase had entered a different kind of danger.

The case had started with distorted language inside systems. It had moved through emergency custody, institutional use, and sealed findings. Now it was in the community, where proof thinned and rumor thickened. Family court had tools, but not limitless ones. Every subpoena, order, and hearing had to justify itself against the privacy of a child whose life had already been overhandled.

Amelia remained after the others left, sitting in the conference room with a public Fairchild report and no appetite for the pastry Nora had left beside her. Jack watched her for a moment before entering. She looked up, and for once she did not speak first.

"You think the public story is slipping away from the facts," Jack said.

"Yes."

"And you think that creates harm."

"Yes."

"You still cannot publish Lily's case."

"I know."

He sat across from her. "There may be a way to write about the public funding structure without referencing this case."

She held his gaze. "There is."

"Later."

"After Lily."

"After this rumor issue is contained."

She nodded. "I can wait."

Jack believed she meant it. He also knew waiting would get harder if Raines kept posting and other outlets picked it up. Amelia had spent her career believing sunlight stopped institutional rot. Jack had spent his career watching sunlight burn children when adults forgot who was standing in it. They were both right, which made the boundary harder rather than easier.

Near ten, Dr. Patel sent one more brief note through Angela because Lily had heard a student say something about "court people" at school. Lily had not been named, and the comment had been vague. Lily asked whether every adult was mad at every other adult. Dr. Patel's guidance was to keep answers short and present-focused. The recommended response was: "Some adults are working through hard things, and you are allowed to have a regular day."

Jack sent the guidance to Ethan and Claire. Ethan replied, I will use those words. Claire replied, Marissa confirms the same. Jack saved both replies. For one more night, both parents had the same script, not to shape Lily, but to keep adult fear from spilling onto her. The difference between those two uses of language mattered. It may have been the difference at the center of the whole case.

Before leaving, Jack stood at the whiteboard and added Donnelly subpoena under convergence. Then he wrote one more phrase beneath Lily's protected space: regular day. It looked almost foolish beside Fairchild, Civic Bridge, Raines, Venn, Dana, and the court orders. That was why he left it there. The whole apparatus existed, or should have existed, for the chance that Lily Cole could have a regular day without being asked to carry the truth everyone else kept mishandling.

36

ELISE DONNELLY'S SUBPOENA RETURN arrived two days later in a password-protected file that looked too small for the trouble it had caused. Jack Sullivan downloaded it in the conference room with Caleb and Mara present, then waited while Nora logged the receipt and printed the protective order cover sheet. The production contained seventeen text messages, four direct messages from a parent group account, and one email thread with Paula Raines. It did not contain a confession, which Jack had not expected. Most harmful disclosures did not arrive wearing a label.

Donnelly's first message to Raines came three hours after her grocery-store conversation with Marissa. It said a parent at San Aurelio told her the counselor issue was tied to a custody case and outside nonprofits. Donnelly did not name Marissa, Lily, or Ethan. She did mention Dana Keene, Civic Bridge, and Fairchild. Raines replied within nine minutes, asking whether the case involved a child whose statements were changed before court. Donnelly answered, "That sounds like what she meant, but I do not know details."

Caleb leaned back from the table. "That is the bridge."

"Yes," Jack said.

Mara tapped the second page. "Raines already had the changed-statements theory before Donnelly confirmed anything."

"She had enough to ask the right question."

"From where?"

Jack looked at the page. "That is the next problem."

The direct messages from the parent group account showed Raines had been circulating public Fairchild materials for weeks. She had been asking parents whether school counseling programs were tied to family-court interventions. Donnelly sent her public board-meeting clips, annual reports, and posts about Dana's administrative leave. That explained part of the convergence. It did not explain Raines's knowledge that a child's statements had been changed before court. That phrase sat too close to the sealed record to be comfortable.

Jack called Claire first. He summarized the subpoena return without editorializing. Claire already sounded braced for bad news. She asked whether Marissa's grocery-store conversation had caused the posts. Jack said it helped connect Raines's existing investigation to this case. Claire did not argue the distinction. She understood the difference between being the source and being the accelerant.

"Will you seek sanctions?" Claire asked.

"Not against Marissa on this record."

"Thank you."

"That is not absolution."

"I know."

"Dr. Patel's privacy guidance has to continue."

"It will."

Jack hung up and sat with the subpoena return for a moment before calling Ethan. He knew Ethan would hear only one part at first: Marissa talked, Donnelly passed it on, Raines posted. The rest would come later, if he let it. Jack closed the door before placing the call.

Ethan answered from work, voice low. "Did something happen?"

"We received Donnelly's subpoena response."

"Was Marissa the leak?"

"The response shows Donnelly contacted Raines after speaking with Marissa. It does not show Marissa gave sealed details or named Lily. It does show the conversation helped Raines connect public information to this case."

"That sounds like yes in a suit."

"It is no in law and partly yes in life."

Ethan was quiet. "I hate how honest that is."

"Good. Honest is useful."

Ethan asked whether the court would punish Marissa. Jack said probably not beyond the privacy guidance already ordered. Ethan did not like it, but he did not erupt. He asked whether Lily had been named in the messages. Jack said no. He asked whether the school had been named. Jack said no. Then Ethan said he would not message Marissa. Jack did not have to ask him to repeat it this time.

By noon, Jack filed a sealed status update attaching the Donnelly return. He asked for no sanctions and requested only that the privacy orders remain in place, that Donnelly be instructed not to disclose or discuss further information connected to the case, and that Raines-related inquiries continue to be logged. He also asked the court to permit a narrow follow-up subpoena to Raines only if she published identifying information or claimed access to sealed records. It was a restrained request because restraint was the best way to keep the judge focused on Lily rather than adult outrage.

Judge Harrow issued a short order by three. Donnelly was placed under the no-disclosure order for information learned through Marissa or any school-parent network relating to the sealed case. She was not sanctioned. The court found the current record did not establish intentional disclosure of sealed information by Marissa or Donnelly. It also found the communication created a foreseeable privacy risk and reinforced the parents' obligation to avoid community discussion. Jack read the order and knew Ethan would hate the word foreseeable more than intentional. Courts often chose the word they could prove.

Raines posted again at four-seventeen. This time, she complained that local parents were being silenced by "private family-court orders designed to protect powerful institutions." She still did not name Lily, Ethan, Marissa, or the school. She did not mention Donnelly. She made the privacy order sound like a conspiracy, which was predictable and effective. The comments beneath the post filled with guesses. None were accurate yet, which offered little comfort.

Amelia brought the post to Jack herself. "This is getting picked up by two larger accounts."

Jack read the names. One covered education activism. The other covered nonprofit accountability. Neither had mainstream reach, but both could move a story into the bloodstream of people who did not care whether a child lived inside it. He set the page down and rubbed the bridge of his nose. The court could manage parties. It could not manage the internet with a minute order.

"What do you want to do?" Amelia asked.

"What I want and what is lawful are not the same."

"She is using the sealed order as proof of cover-up."

"Yes."

"And if no one says anything, she keeps defining it."

"Yes."

Amelia waited. She was not pushing yet. Jack appreciated that because he was considering something he had resisted for days.

"We may need a neutral public statement," he said.

Her expression changed. "From whom?"

"Not from Ethan. Not from Marissa. Not from the firm. Possibly from the district, with court approval, limited to student privacy, no confirmation of any case, and no institutional defense."

"That will not stop her."

"It may reduce school speculation."

"It may."

Jack called Sonia Patel and raised the idea. Sonia had already drafted something similar but had not wanted to move without court approval. The proposed statement said the district does not comment on student matters, does not disclose information related to any student or family, and follows all applicable privacy laws and court orders. It also stated that rumors about individual students or families should not be shared or repeated. It did not mention counseling, custody, nonprofits, or Fairchild. Jack thought it was bland enough to be safe and direct enough to serve Lily.

Claire approved it. Hale did not oppose, likely because Fairchild was not mentioned. Fray preferred language saying the district could not verify any allegations about outside partners. Jack objected to that because it introduced outside partners into a statement that did not need them. Judge Harrow approved Sonia's version without Fray's addition. By six, the district posted the statement on its website and sent it to school families. It was not a sword. It was a shield, thin but better than bare skin.

Ethan saw it before Jack called. "That's about us without saying us."

"It is about privacy."

"Will people know?"

"Some will assume."

"Will Lily know?"

"She may hear there was a school privacy message. Use Dr. Patel's language if she asks."

Ethan sighed. "Some adults are talking without knowing the whole story."

"Yes."

"You are not responsible for adult conversations."

"Yes."

"You are allowed to have a regular day."

"Yes."

He was quiet. "I wish adults believed that too."

Jack did not answer because Ethan was right.

That evening, Lily had dinner with Ethan under the regular schedule. He sent no photos, no updates beyond the required app note that pickup and drop-off occurred on time. At eight-thirty, he sent Jack a private text: She asked why people like secrets. I said privacy is different from secrets because privacy protects people. Was that okay? Jack stared at the message and felt the case, for one moment, move away from filings and toward something useful.

He replied, That was good. Do not add more unless she asks.

Ethan answered, I didn't. We watched cooking videos.

Jack saved the text. It would not go in a filing unless it had to, and he hoped it never would. Not everything good belonged in evidence. Some things needed to stay in the life they were meant to protect.

At nine, Amelia came to Jack's office with her coat over her arm. "The district statement helped a little. Comments are slowing."

"For now."

"You sound disappointed by improvement."

"I distrust it."

"That is a cheerful way to live."

"It is a professional way to survive."

She sat in the chair across from him. "I drafted something."

Jack looked at her.

"I am not publishing it. It is about public funding structures and court-facing youth programs. No Lily. No San Aurelio. No custody case. No references that would point back here."

"Send it to me before you do anything."

"I figured you would say that."

"I am saying it as a condition of you staying in this building."

She nodded. "Fair."

Jack studied her for a moment. "Why wait?"

"Because the story is better if it does not hurt a child."

"That answer is better than the one you would have given two weeks ago."

"I know."

After she left, Jack turned back to the Donnelly messages. The leak had not resolved into a single betrayal. It had become something messier and more believable: a frightened parent saying too much, a community activist connecting dots, a blogger already hunting the pattern, institutions leaving public language like breadcrumbs, and a sealed case sitting in the middle of it all. The law could respond to each piece. It could not make the pieces stop wanting each other.

Before leaving, Jack updated the whiteboard. Under exposure risk, he wrote: no direct sealed leak established. Under community rumor, he wrote: Donnelly bridge. Under Lily's protected space, he left regular day where it was and added privacy, not secrets. It was not legal language, but it was the language Ethan had used correctly at the dinner table. Jack looked at it for a long time. Sometimes custody law worked best when it stopped trying to sound like law and gave a parent the right sentence at the right moment.

37

THE DISTRICT STATEMENT SLOWED the rumors for almost two days, which was longer than Jack Sullivan expected and shorter than Lily deserved. By Friday morning, the larger accounts had moved on to a school-board fight in another county, and Paula Raines's last post sat mostly unanswered except by the same handful of names. Quiet returned, not clean quiet, but the cautious kind that comes after adults realize the court is keeping a ledger. Jack took the improvement without trusting it. In family court, a quiet week was not peace until it repeated.

Ethan's app exchanges with Marissa became almost mechanical. Pickup confirmed. Homework folder received. Therapy time acknowledged. School assembly noted. The messages were plain, stiff, and mercifully boring. Jack told Caleb that boring parenting communication was often the first sign a child might get a life back.

Claire sent a revised parenting plan late Friday morning. It accepted nearly all of Jack's last draft and added one provision requiring both parents to attend a joint parent-guidance session only if Dr. Patel recommended it. Jack agreed with the concept but changed the wording so the session could not occur unless Dr. Patel believed it would help Lily and both parents were ready to participate without discussing blame. Claire accepted the edit within thirty minutes. That speed told Jack she wanted the plan done before another public flare-up changed the landscape again.

Mara reviewed the third-party compliance log while Jack worked through the parenting plan. Fairchild had certified compliance. Civic Bridge had certified compliance. Horizon had certified compliance. Tessa had certified compliance. The declarations were complete, the dissemination order was in place, and the open question of institutional accountability now sat outside the immediate custody mechanics. Jack did not mistake that for closure. He only recognized when one part of a case needed to wait while another part moved.

At noon, Amelia asked to see him. She came into his office with the article draft she had mentioned, printed and marked in pencil. She did not hand it to him right away. That hesitation mattered because Amelia rarely hesitated around paper. Jack closed the custody binder and held out his hand. She gave him the draft without speaking.

The article was about court-facing youth programs, foundation-funded family services, and the growing use of language frameworks in school and custody-adjacent settings. It cited public annual reports, conference transcripts, grant rubrics, and archived program descriptions. It did not mention San Aurelio, Lily, Ethan, Marissa, Dana, Civic Bridge's support device, Judge Harrow, or the sealed custody case. It did not reveal what had happened in court. It pointed to a system without using a child as the proof.

Jack read it twice while Amelia sat across from him. The first reading was for risk. The second was for motive. The piece was careful, sharper than a legal memo, and disciplined in places where he knew she wanted to strike harder. He marked three sentences that came too close to the sealed case by echoing language from the protected record. Amelia leaned forward when he turned the page, but she did not interrupt.

"These three need to change," Jack said.

She took the marked pages. "Because of Lily?"

"Because someone who knows the sealed record could hear the echo."

"That is not the legal standard."

"No. It is the ethical one."

She looked at the first sentence, then the second, then the third. "I can rewrite them."

"Good."

"You think it is publishable?"

"I think it is safer after those edits."

"That is not the same."

"It is the answer I have."

Amelia nodded and placed the pages back in her folder. She looked disappointed and relieved at the same time. Jack understood that feeling. Discipline often felt like losing until enough time passed to see what it protected. Amelia had waited longer than many reporters would have. She had also written the first public thing that might expose the architecture without dragging Lily into the light.

After Amelia left, Ethan arrived for the final parenting-plan review. He had Lily that evening and had brought the plan in a folder with notes clipped to the front. He looked tired, but the frantic edge was gone. Jack noticed he had written fewer objections and more questions. That mattered. Questions could be worked with. Objections often came already married to fear.

They went through the plan paragraph by paragraph. Ethan agreed to the schedule, the decision-making protocol, the therapy boundaries, the school access provisions, and the no-public-discussion clause. He paused at the language allowing both parents to seek confidential pastoral or therapeutic support for themselves. He asked whether Marissa could use that to start telling the story again. Jack explained that private support was allowed; disclosure of Lily's private information, sealed materials, and identifying case details was not. Ethan read the section again, then nodded.

"I want support too," he said.

"You are allowed to have it."

"I just don't want her turning support into another audience."

"That is why the language limits details."

He tapped the page. "Then keep it."

Jack watched him sign the stipulation. The signature did not mean forgiveness. It did not mean trust. It meant Ethan understood that Lily needed a stable plan more than he needed every paragraph to announce what had been done to him. That was the difference between a good client and a good father. Ethan was trying to become both.

Claire sent Marissa's signature an hour later. The stipulation went to Judge Harrow with Angela's approval and Dr. Patel's limited recommendation that the structure remain predictable for at least ninety days. Judge Harrow signed it before the end of the day. The parenting plan was now an order. Joint legal custody remained, treatment decisions required agreement, therapy stayed protected, school records went to both parents, exchanges stayed neutral, and neither parent could discuss the case in community spaces, online spaces, or with Lily except under the approved guidance.

Nora brought the signed order into Jack's office. "Does this mean we are done?"

"No."

"I asked because I enjoy disappointment."

"It means the custody structure is stable for now."

"That sounds like lawyer celebration."

"It is."

She placed the order on his desk. "Try cake sometime."

Jack sent the order to Ethan with a short message: This is the operating plan. Follow it exactly. Ethan replied, I will. Then, a minute later, another message came through. Lily wants to make pancakes for dinner. Does that violate any court order? Jack laughed before he could stop himself. He wrote back that pancakes were permitted unless used as a third-party support channel.

Ethan replied with a thumbs-up and the words, No non-profit syrup.

Jack saved the message because it was the first genuinely light thing Ethan had written since the case began. It would never belong in a pleading. It belonged to a father standing in a kitchen with a daughter who wanted breakfast at night. The law had spent weeks making space for that ordinary decision. Jack hoped everyone involved had enough sense not to ruin it.

At six, Claire called. Her voice was softer than usual, though still professional. Marissa had read the final order and wanted to know whether she could write Ethan a message acknowledging she had made mistakes. Claire had advised against sending anything directly without lawyer review and asked whether Jack would accept a draft for possible later use. Jack agreed, with conditions. No request for forgiveness, no explanation, no defense, no mention of Lily's therapy, no emotional burden placed on Ethan.

Claire exhaled. "That is what I told her."

"Then send it when you have it."

"She is trying."

"I hope so."

"She is also terrified."

"She should work through that with someone who is not Lily or Ethan."

"I said that too."

The call ended, and Jack sat with it for a moment. Marissa had become harder to hate as the case matured. That did not lessen the damage. It made the future more complicated. A parent could be frightened, manipulated, reckless, apologetic, and still dangerous if she sought relief from the person she had hurt. The parenting plan gave Marissa a path. Whether she could stay on it remained an open question.

Mara entered with the final compliance chart. "For now, all orders are being followed."

Jack looked at the chart. "For now."

"I knew you would say that."

"It is accurate."

"It is bleak."

"It is accurate."

She placed the chart in the binder. "Fairchild has gone quiet."

"That is not the same as gone."

"No. Amelia's public piece may stir them."

"Possibly."

"Are you going to let her publish?"

Jack leaned back. "I do not control her."

Mara gave him a look.

"I can ask her to wait until Monday."

"Will she?"

"I think so."

Amelia did wait. She sent the revised article that night with the three sentences changed and a note that said, "No echoes." Jack read the revised version at home after dinner he barely tasted. It was clean enough. It would still make Fairchild uncomfortable. It might make other parents ask better questions about programs in their schools. It did not point to Lily. Jack replied with two words: Safer now.

The article went live Saturday morning. By noon, it had been shared by education-policy accounts, legal reform advocates, and nonprofit watchdogs. Paula Raines reposted it with a comment accusing mainstream journalists of arriving late to stories parents had already exposed. Amelia did not respond. Jack noticed that and respected it. She had chosen the public record over public argument.

Hale sent a letter by three, addressed to Amelia's editor and copied to Jack for reasons that were transparent and irritating. Fairchild denied any implication that its grants supported litigation coaching or improper influence over family courts. The letter demanded correction of any suggestion that foundation funding directed case-level conduct. Amelia's article had not said that. Jack suspected Hale knew it, and the letter was meant to discourage follow-up.

Amelia called Jack herself. "I am not retracting."

"I did not think you would."

"The editor wants legal review."

"Good."

"Fairchild copied you."

"I saw."

"Why?"

"To remind me they know I read it."

"That is petty."

"It is also strategic."

Amelia paused. "Did I hurt Lily?"

Jack answered carefully because the question deserved more than reassurance. "Not from what I can see. You did not identify the case. You did not use sealed facts. You wrote from public records."

"That is not a no."

"It is the honest answer."

She accepted it. "I can live with that for today."

On Sunday evening, Ethan sent one message through the proper channel. Lily had completed homework, made pancakes, and asked whether Wednesday therapy was still at the same time. Marissa replied that it was and that she would pack the art folder in Lily's backpack after her next overnight. Ethan answered thank you. No accusations. No corrections. No tone.

Jack read the exchange on Monday morning and forwarded it to Caleb as an example of what compliance looked like when adults stopped performing their pain. Caleb replied with a line Jack had not expected: This is the first thing in the file that feels like a child's life. Jack sat with that for a moment. The young lawyer was learning the point.

By the end of Monday, the signed parenting order had been distributed, Amelia's article had not triggered any direct reference to Lily, Raines's posts had slowed again, and no new school inquiries had been reported. The case was not over. Accountability remained unresolved. Fairchild's response to Amelia's article suggested pressure was building outside the courtroom. Marissa's apology draft had not arrived. The review hearing was still weeks away.

Jack stood at the whiteboard before leaving and erased three items: temporary framework, Donnelly subpoena, district statement. He left stability, compliance, accountability, exposure risk, and regular day. Then he added one more phrase beneath parenting plan: working order. It was not a final victory. It was what family court could give when everyone had done just enough right after doing too much wrong. Lily had a working order, and for the first time since she mouthed help me across a courtroom, the adults around her had a structure that might let help feel ordinary.

38

Marissa's apology draft arrived Tuesday morning through Claire, and Jack Sullivan knew before opening it that the document would matter less for what it said than for what it asked Ethan to carry. Apologies in custody cases often arrived dressed as repair while quietly requesting absolution, sympathy, or a rewritten history. Jack printed it, read it once, then read it again with a pen. Caleb watched from the other side of the conference table, waiting for the first mark. Jack circled the second sentence and slid the page toward him.

The draft began plainly enough. Marissa acknowledged that she had trusted people she should have questioned, failed to disclose the support contact, and allowed fear to guide decisions that affected Lily and Ethan. Then it began to explain. It described feeling alone, overwhelmed, frightened of losing Lily, and confused by professional language that made every hesitation sound dangerous. By the fourth paragraph, the apology had become a guided tour of Marissa's fear. Jack understood the fear. He also understood that Ethan was not the person who should be asked to hold it.

Claire called ten minutes later. She sounded as if she already knew what Jack would say. He told her the draft needed to be shorter, cleaner, and free of explanations that required Ethan to comfort Marissa. Claire did not argue. She said she had warned Marissa that apology was not the same as testimony. Jack appreciated the phrase and wrote it down because clients often confused the two. An apology should name harm and stop talking before it became self-defense.

"What can stay?" Claire asked.

"The first paragraph, part of the second, and the line that says she will follow the order."

"That leaves very little."

"That is why it might work."

Claire was quiet for a moment. "She wants him to understand she was scared."

"He knows she was scared."

"He does not believe it excuses anything."

"It doesn't."

"I know."

Jack leaned back in his chair and looked through the office glass toward Nora's desk. "Let her write the long version for her therapist. Send Ethan the short version."

Claire exhaled. "That may be the best advice in this case."

"It is not legal advice."

"It may be better."

After the call, Caleb asked whether Ethan had to receive any apology at all. Jack said no, and that was why the review mattered. A bad apology could reopen the wound and create another app dispute. A proper apology could reduce pressure if Ethan was ready to receive it without turning it into cross-examination. The law did not require emotional repair, and judges could not order humility into being. The best lawyers could do was prevent broken attempts at repair from becoming fresh evidence.

At noon, the revised draft came through. It was five sentences. Marissa acknowledged that her failure to disclose the support contact and her conversations with others contributed to harm. She stated that Lily should not have been placed in a position where adults shaped or repeated her words. She acknowledged that Ethan had been hurt by an incomplete record. She said she would follow the court order and Dr. Patel's guidance. She did not ask for forgiveness.

Jack sent it to Ethan with a note: You are not required to respond. If you choose to respond, send nothing until I review it.

Ethan called instead. "I read it."

"I assumed."

"I don't know what to do with it."

"You do not have to do anything today."

"She didn't say everything."

"She shouldn't."

"She didn't say she lied."

"The court did not find that she lied."

Ethan was quiet. "I still wanted it."

"I know."

The line stayed open, both men listening to the space between law and pain. Jack could hear office noise behind Ethan, a printer or copier humming somewhere nearby. He imagined Ethan standing in a hallway at work, holding a phone, trying to decide whether five sentences could carry weeks of humiliation and fear. They could not. That did not make them worthless.

"What would you write back?" Ethan asked.

"If I were you, nothing today."

"And later?"

"Thank you for acknowledging this. I agree we both need to follow the order and focus on Lily."

"That sounds like a corporate memo."

"It is safe."

"It does not say what I feel."

"That is the point."

Ethan gave a small breath that was not quite a laugh. "I hate your point."

"You keep saying that before following it."

"I know."

Ethan did not respond that day. Jack considered that a good decision. Silence, when chosen instead of swallowed, could be a form of control. It gave Ethan space to feel what the apology could not fix. It also gave Lily one more evening without her parents turning adult regret into a new exchange.

By midafternoon, Amelia came in with Fairchild's response to her article and a new public filing from a policy nonprofit defending outcome-based grants. The filing was not connected to the custody case, but the language echoed Fairchild's letter: privacy-safe evaluation, family stabilization, coordinated systems, misinformation risks. Amelia placed the documents on Jack's desk and did not sit until he gestured to the chair. She looked tired in a way that suggested the public story had begun to move faster than she liked.

"They are building the counter-narrative," she said.

Jack glanced at the documents. "Public response."

"It is coordinated."

"Maybe."

She raised an eyebrow. "Invoice three."

Jack ignored it. "Does any of it mention Lily, San Aurelio, the court, or the sealed case?"

"No."

"Then it stays outside."

"For now."

"Yes."

Amelia leaned back. "Fairchild is trying to make the whole issue about attacks on vulnerable youth programs."

"That is predictable."

"It is effective."

"Yes."

The word carried more weight than she expected, and she stopped pushing. Jack understood the strategy Fairchild was using because it was the same structure they had seen in the sealed record. Define the frame early. Make disagreement sound dangerous. Position critics as threats to vulnerable people. It worked because there were genuinely vulnerable people in the system, and because some critics really were reckless. The truth had to move through that mess without becoming part of it.

Mara joined them with another public record. Fairchild had announced a listening session on youth privacy and program evaluation for the following week. The announcement did not mention Amelia's article, Raines's posts, or Civic Bridge. It spoke in broad terms about public confusion and the need for responsible dialogue. Jack read it and saw the outline of a reputational containment strategy. Fairchild would not answer the sealed facts. It would host a conversation about the values surrounding them.

Caleb looked at the announcement. "Can they do that under the order?"

"Yes," Jack said, "as long as they do not reference Lily's scenario."

"They are obviously responding to the pressure."

"Obvious is not the same as prohibited."

Amelia pointed to the page. "They are going to use privacy as a shield and a podium."

"Probably."

"Can the court stop that?"

"Not without a case-specific violation."

That answer frustrated everyone in the room, including Jack. Courts were powerful inside their jurisdiction and limited outside it. Fairchild had learned how to live in that boundary. Its lawyers were careful enough to avoid direct violation and confident enough to shape the broader conversation. Jack could not stop a foundation from speaking about public policy. He could only stop it from using Lily.

At four, Angela sent a general note from Dr. Patel. Lily had asked whether apologies make people safe. Dr. Patel did not disclose the context, and Jack did not ask. The guidance to both parents was brief: do not teach Lily that apologies erase harm; tell her safe behavior is shown over time. Jack forwarded the guidance to Ethan and Claire. Then he sat with the sentence because it applied to everyone.

Ethan replied first. I understand. Safe behavior over time.

Claire replied that Marissa would follow the guidance.

Jack thought about Marissa's five sentences and Ethan's silence. Apology was a beginning only if behavior followed. The court order had made that principle enforceable in part. Dr. Patel had made it understandable. Lily had asked the right question because children often did. Adults built systems to avoid simple questions, then acted surprised when a child found the center.

That evening, Ethan sent Jack a proposed response to Marissa. It was two sentences: Thank you for acknowledging what happened. I agree we need to follow the order and focus on Lily. Jack approved it without changes. Ethan sent it through counsel, not the app, because the apology had moved lawyer to lawyer and did not belong in the parenting communication stream. Claire confirmed receipt and said Marissa would not respond further. That was wise.

Nora watched Jack print the confirmation. "So nobody wrote a novel in the app."

"Correct."

"Miracles continue."

"Do not document that."

"I document everything."

By seven, the office had settled into the long quiet that came after a crisis did not become another crisis. Jack reviewed the parenting order, the Fairchild compliance file, Amelia's article, Raines's last posts, and the new listening-session announcement. The case now had two tracks. The custody track was stabilizing. The public accountability track was forming outside his control. The tension between them would define the next stage.

Amelia stopped by his door before leaving. "I am going to attend Fairchild's listening session."

"As a reporter?"

"Yes."

"Do not ask about Lily's case."

"I won't."

"Do not ask questions using sealed phrases."

"I know."

"Send me your question list before you go."

She looked ready to argue, then did not. "Fine."

Jack appreciated the restraint. He also knew attending the session would put Amelia in the same room as people whose language had wrapped itself around Lily's case without naming her. She would hear the public version of the system. He would need to compare it against the sealed version without letting the two contaminate each other. That was legally awkward and narratively inevitable.

Before leaving, Jack stood at the whiteboard and added Fairchild listening session under accountability. Under parenting plan, he wrote apology handled. Then he looked at Lily's protected space and the phrase safe behavior over time. It belonged there, not as evidence, not as argument, but as the simplest standard left in the room. Marissa would have to live it. Ethan would have to live it. Fairchild, Civic Bridge, and every adult who claimed to help children would have to be judged by it too, whether in court, in public, or in the quieter place where a child decided who could be trusted with her words.

39

FAIRCHILD HELD THE LISTENING session in a downtown conference center that looked designed to make controversy feel like civic partnership. The lobby had glass walls, framed photographs of smiling students, and a registration table staffed by volunteers in navy blazers. Amelia Grant arrived as press, wearing a plain black jacket and carrying only a notebook, a recorder, and the question list Jack Sullivan had reviewed the night before. She had argued over two of his edits and accepted all of them. That was progress in the same way a restrained objection was progress.

Jack did not attend. He watched from his office through the public livestream with Caleb and Mara seated at the conference table. Nora had insisted on putting the feed on the large screen because she said if Fairchild planned to teach everyone how not to answer questions, they might as well learn comfortably. The event title appeared in clean white letters on a blue background: Youth Privacy, Program Evaluation, and Responsible Public Dialogue. Jack wrote the title down because every word had been chosen to sound harmless. Harmless words often carried the heaviest equipment.

Malcolm Reese opened the session for Fairchild. He was polished, silver-haired, and careful in the way people become after years of speaking in rooms where every sentence might later appear in a grant file. He said Fairchild supported youth-serving organizations across the region and believed deeply in privacy, transparency, and responsible evaluation. He warned against misinformation that could discourage families from seeking help. He never mentioned Civic Bridge, San Aurelio, Lily, Ethan, Marissa, or family court. He did not have to mention them for the room to understand the pressure that had brought everyone there.

Mara watched with her arms folded. "He is framing critics as a risk to children."

"Yes," Jack said.

Caleb looked at the screen. "Is that unfair?"

"Not entirely."

"That makes it harder."

"That is why it works."

The first panelist was a university researcher who spoke about anonymized data and program improvement. Her remarks were reasonable, which made the event more effective. She explained that youth programs needed outcome measures to know whether they helped or harmed. She also said consent, context, and governance mattered when real lives became data points. Jack underlined that last part. Fairchild had invited someone competent enough to give the session credibility and broad enough not to answer the question at the center of the Cole case.

The second panelist came from a youth advocacy nonprofit. She spoke about the need for consistent language when children faced stressful systems. Jack felt Caleb glance at him when the phrase appeared. The panelist used examples from housing, immigration, and school discipline, not custody. She said adults should help children find words without replacing their words. That sentence was good. It was also close enough to the case to sting.

Amelia appeared on the livestream during the question period, seated near the aisle. Jack saw her raise her hand after three audience questions about data privacy and school partnerships. Malcolm Reese called on her by name, which meant Fairchild knew who she was. Her face remained neutral. Jack had to admit she looked calmer than he felt.

"My question is about governance," Amelia said. "When a foundation funds programs that prepare youth-serving organizations to communicate with courts or court-adjacent systems, what safeguards prevent a program from treating an unresolved individual matter as a success before an independent process has reviewed the underlying facts?"

The room shifted. It was a clean question. It used no sealed facts, named no case, and asked the public version of the private problem. Reese took a sip of water. Jack saw him do it and wrote down the pause.

"That is an important question," Reese said. "Fairchild does not direct case-level activity. We fund organizations that operate under their own professional standards, legal obligations, and governance structures. We encourage partners to evaluate programs responsibly and to avoid presenting unresolved matters in ways that could compromise privacy or fairness."

Mara looked at Jack. "That is almost an answer."

"It is an answer to the safest part of the question."

Amelia followed once, as agreed. "Does Fairchild require grantees to distinguish between internal learning, grant renewal materials, and public impact reporting when a matter is unresolved?"

Reese nodded as if the question pleased him. "We are strengthening those expectations. Responsible evaluation requires clear boundaries, and we support additional safeguards where public concern shows those safeguards need clarification."

Jack leaned back. That answer did more than deny. It conceded improvement without admitting fault. It also used the phrase strengthening expectations, which meant Fairchild wanted to own reform before anyone proved the reason reform was needed. That was smart institutional practice. It was also precisely why courts needed records instead of statements.

The session continued for another hour. Amelia asked nothing further. Raines attended remotely through the public comment portal and submitted a question accusing foundations of using privacy rules to bury court-involved scandals. The moderator did not read it aloud, but the question appeared briefly in the comment feed before disappearing. Nora rewound the livestream and captured a screenshot. She looked pleased with herself in a way that suggested the screenshot was now part of her personal archive of small victories.

By the end of the session, Fairchild had announced a new working group on privacy safeguards in youth program evaluation. The group would review grant language, grantee reporting practices, and internal learning protocols. Malcolm Reese said it was not a reaction to any specific matter. Jack wrote that sentence down too. Institutions never reacted to specific matters until litigation forced them to name the matter. They reacted to public concern, evolving standards, best practices, and community dialogue. The specific person stayed invisible.

Amelia called from the parking garage fifteen minutes after the livestream ended. Jack put her on speaker with Caleb and Mara present. She sounded tired, not excited. That told him she understood what had happened.

"They are going to reform around the problem without naming it," she said.

"Yes."

"They are going to become the leaders in fixing the thing they helped reward."

"Probably."

"I asked it clean."

"You did."

"Did I hurt anything?"

"Not that I saw."

She exhaled. "That answer counts."

Jack glanced at Mara, who gave a small nod. "Send us your notes. Public notes only."

"I know."

After the call, Jack reviewed Reese's answers again. Nothing in the session violated Judge Harrow's order. Nothing identified Lily or even Civic Bridge. The public language moved around the sealed facts like water around stone. That did not make it useless. It gave Jack something else: Fairchild's own public statement that unresolved matters should not be presented in ways compromising privacy or fairness. He could use that carefully, not as proof of wrongdoing, but as a public-policy acknowledgment consistent with the protective order already entered.

Claire called at four. Marissa had seen clips from the session because another parent sent them to her, and she was anxious about whether the public discussion was tied to her. Claire had told her not to engage and not to ask other parents about it. Jack approved. Then Claire said Marissa had completed a second apology draft for herself only, not for Ethan, as Dr. Patel suggested. That detail did not belong in the case file, and Jack did not write it down. It mattered anyway.

"Is she following the order?" Jack asked.

"Yes."

"Then that is enough for today."

"She wants to know whether Ethan thinks she is part of Fairchild's conduct."

"Ethan is focused on Lily."

"That is not an answer."

"It is the only one she is entitled to receive."

Claire accepted it, though he could hear the strain in her silence. Marissa wanted to separate herself from the institutions because the institutions now looked ugly in public. That desire was human. It could also become another way of asking Ethan to help her feel less responsible. Jack would not let the case turn there if he could prevent it.

Ethan called at six after Lily's exchange. He had not watched the session and had no interest in it, which Jack considered a healthy sign. Lily had brought the art folder from Marissa's house, and Ethan wanted to know whether he could look through it with her. Jack told him yes, if Lily invited him, and no, if he was looking for messages about the case. Ethan understood the difference immediately. That was another sign of progress.

"She drew a dog with wings," Ethan said.

"That sounds promising."

"She said it is not an angel dog. It just likes high places."

"Then it is a dog that likes high places."

"I almost asked what it meant."

"What did you ask instead?"

"I asked what its name was."

Jack smiled. "Good."

"She said Pickle."

"That is also promising."

The call ended with Ethan sounding lighter than he had all week. Jack put the phone down and sat for a moment. A dog with wings named Pickle had more healing in it than three hearings. That was not sentiment. It was evidence of a kind no court could admit cleanly. Lily was making images that did not have to testify.

Mara came to Jack's office with a printed transcript from the listening session. She had highlighted Reese's answer about unresolved matters, privacy, and fairness. She also highlighted the announcement of the working group. Jack read both and placed them in a folder labeled Public Statements. That folder was separate from the sealed record. Separation mattered because a legal record built from the wrong sources could contaminate itself and invite a fight the child did not need.

Caleb entered behind her. "Can Fairchild use the working group to claim the issue is moot?"

"In public, yes. In court, not as to past conduct."

"Will the judge care?"

"She will care if compliance becomes a question. She will not let us litigate public relations."

Caleb nodded. "So the custody case stays custody."

"As long as we can keep it there."

That remained the central discipline. The custody case existed to protect Lily, not to reform philanthropy, punish school politics, or expose every court-facing program in the state. Those larger questions were real. Amelia's article and Fairchild's session had pushed them into public view. Jack's case had to remain smaller because children are harmed when adults make their cases bigger than their lives.

By eight, the office had emptied except for Jack and Nora. She appeared at his door with her purse over one shoulder and a paper plate covered with foil. "Leftover cake."

"From where?"

"Do not cross-examine cake."

He accepted the plate. "Thank you."

She looked toward the conference room screen, now dark. "Did the foundation say anything useful?"

"Yes."

"Did they mean it?"

"Those are different questions."

Nora nodded. "That usually means no."

Jack waited until she left before returning to the whiteboard. Under accountability, he wrote Fairchild public safeguards statement. Under Lily's protected space, he wrote Pickle. He almost erased it because it did not belong beside legal categories. Then he left it. The board had carried worse things. It could carry one winged dog.

Before leaving, Jack read Amelia's revised notes from the session. They were careful, factual, and did not reference the sealed case. Raines had already posted that Fairchild's listening session proved pressure was working. Fairchild had posted that responsible dialogue was essential to protecting youth privacy. Both were using the same event to tell different stories. Lily, at least for that evening, was not in either one.

Jack turned out the lights and stood in the hallway a moment longer. The case had reached the point where public accountability and private protection were moving on parallel tracks, close enough to influence each other and separate enough to require discipline. Fairchild had begun to adjust its language. Amelia had begun to write without using Lily. Ethan had begun to parent without searching every drawing for evidence. Those were not endings. They were working signs that the truth, once returned to the right owner, did not always need to shout.

40

THE SIX-WEEK REVIEW HEARING arrived with none of the noise that had surrounded the first emergency appearance. No reporters waited at the elevators, and no one in the hallway whispered loudly enough to be heard by people pretending not to listen. Jack Sullivan arrived with one binder instead of five. That felt like progress, though experience kept him from trusting the feeling too far. Quiet cases could still break open if one parent decided the new peace felt too much like losing.

Ethan arrived with Caleb, carrying a copy of the parenting order and the same plain folder he had used since the merits hearing. He looked steadier now, less like a man bracing for impact and more like one learning the rhythm of difficult weather. Jack noticed the change because courts noticed changes too, especially in parents whose first appearances had been marked by fear. Ethan's restraint had become part of the record. That mattered more than any speech Jack could make about him.

Marissa arrived with Claire and stayed near the opposite wall. She looked tired, but not frantic. When she saw Ethan, she gave a small nod that asked for nothing. Ethan returned it with the same restraint. The exchange lasted less than a second. Jack counted it as another ordinary thing the adults had managed not to ruin.

Judge Harrow took the bench at nine-thirty and began with the compliance report. Both parents had followed the parenting plan. Exchanges had occurred on time. School communication had gone directly to both homes. Dr. Patel reported continued engagement, with no therapy content disclosed and no request to modify confidentiality. Angela Morrissey reported that Lily appeared to benefit from predictable transitions and reduced adult discussion. It was the kind of report family courts rarely celebrated because it sounded too simple. Jack knew how much work had been required to make it sound that way.

Claire addressed the court first. She said Marissa accepted the current framework and wanted it continued with a gradual reduction in neutral-exchange requirements if Dr. Patel and Angela agreed. She did not ask to restore sole decision-making authority. She did not revisit the original emergency allegations. She acknowledged the privacy orders remained necessary and said Marissa would continue parent guidance as recommended. The argument was careful, and it stayed within the order rather than trying to rewrite why the order existed.

Jack stood when Judge Harrow turned to him. He agreed the framework should continue and said Ethan supported a measured transition from neutral exchanges only when the professionals believed Lily was ready. He asked that the findings from the merits hearing remain undisturbed and that the third-party no-use order remain in place. He did not ask the court to punish anyone. There was no need that morning. The law had already drawn the lines, and for six weeks the lines had held.

Judge Harrow reviewed her notes. "Mr. Sullivan, is respondent asking for any change in legal decision-making?"

"No, Your Honor."

"Any change in therapy confidentiality?"

"No."

"Any request to expand discovery in this custody matter?"

"Not today."

The judge looked at him for a moment, as if weighing the last two words. Jack had used them intentionally. Accountability questions remained, especially around Fairchild and Civic Bridge, but the custody case did not need to carry every institutional consequence. The child's order was working. Good lawyering sometimes meant resisting the urge to keep pressing when the current structure was doing what it was designed to do.

Judge Harrow continued the existing parenting plan for another ninety days, with authority for Dr. Patel and Angela to recommend a transition from neutral exchanges to school-based exchanges if Lily tolerated the change. She kept joint legal custody in place and preserved all restrictions on third-party resources, public discussion, and institutional use of Lily's circumstances. She also set a limited compliance review for the third-party no-use order, separate from the parenting review. The separation mattered. Lily's life would not be held hostage to Fairchild's paperwork.

Then Judge Harrow addressed Ethan and Marissa directly. "The court's concern remains the same. Lily needs a childhood that is not organized around adult explanations. If she asks questions, answer only what she asks. If she expresses uncertainty, do not correct it. If she seems ordinary, let ordinary be enough."

Neither parent spoke. Both nodded. Jack watched Ethan's face at the word ordinary. He knew Ethan would remember the pancakes, the pencils, and the winged dog named Pickle. Those things had become anchors in a file otherwise crowded with adult language. The judge may not have known about all of them, and that was right. Some ordinary things stayed ordinary only if lawyers left them alone.

After the hearing, Claire approached Jack in the hallway. "Marissa is willing to continue the order as written."

"That is good."

"She has not contacted Donnelly."

"I appreciate the update."

"She also wants to know if Ethan would consider a future joint guidance session if Dr. Patel recommends it."

"That is already in the plan."

"I know. She wanted me to say she is not pushing it."

Jack nodded. "I will tell him only if needed."

Claire accepted that. The old version of the case would have turned the request into leverage. The current version allowed it to remain a future possibility. That did not mean trust had returned. It meant counsel had learned to stop feeding every fear into the record.

Downstairs, Ethan read the minute order at the same conference table where he had once asked whether he would lose his daughter. The question looked different now. He had not lost Lily. He had also not recovered the old ease of being her father. Some damage did not vanish when a judge signed the right order. It had to be replaced slowly with new habits, repeated until the child stopped measuring every room for danger.

"So another ninety days," Ethan said.

"Yes."

"That feels like a long time."

"It is a short time for repair."

He nodded. "She asked if we could hike again."

"That is good."

"I said maybe, when we check the schedule."

"Better than promising."

"I know. I wanted to say yes."

"She needs promises you can keep."

Ethan looked down at the order. "That should be on the card too."

Jack almost smiled. "You are collecting cards."

"They help."

The day should have ended there. It almost did. By two in the afternoon, Jack was back at the office, Caleb was filing the order, and Mara was preparing for the limited third-party compliance review. Amelia had gone to a follow-up interview about public grant safeguards, carefully outside the sealed case. Nora had declared the morning "legally boring in the best possible way" and ordered sandwiches. Then a certified letter arrived for Ethan through Jack's office.

Nora brought it in with a look that removed any hope of sandwich optimism. The envelope came from a civil litigation firm in Sacramento. Jack opened it with Ethan's authorization already on file for case-related correspondence. The letter was addressed to Ethan Cole and copied to Jack. It was a notice of potential civil claims from Fairchild Family Foundation, alleging that Ethan or persons acting in concert with him had contributed to defamatory public narratives suggesting Fairchild engaged in litigation coaching, manipulation of minors, or improper interference in custody proceedings.

Caleb read over Jack's shoulder. "They are threatening him?"

"They are warning him."

"That is worse?"

"It is more careful."

Mara took the letter and scanned the second page. "They do not accuse him of a specific statement."

"No. They accuse him of contribution to narratives."

"That is fog."

"Fog can still be expensive."

Jack called Ethan before sending the letter electronically. He told him a Fairchild-related civil firm had sent a legal notice and that he was not to respond, post, call anyone, or discuss it with Lily. Ethan went quiet in the way Jack had learned to respect. Silence was now where Ethan put the first fire instead of throwing it into the room.

"I didn't say anything," Ethan said.

"I know."

"I followed every order."

"I know."

"They can do this?"

"They can send a letter. Whether they have a claim is another question."

"This is punishment."

"It may be pressure."

"That is a lawyer word for punishment."

"Sometimes."

Ethan breathed hard once, then steadied. "What do I do?"

"Nothing until I review it fully. Save every communication. Do not mention Fairchild to anyone. Keep tonight ordinary."

He laughed once, bitter but controlled. "They send a threat letter, and I make dinner."

"Yes."

"What should I make?"

Jack looked at the letter on his desk. "Something that does not involve nonprofit syrup."

Ethan's laugh came easier the second time. It did not make the threat less real. It did tell Jack the man had not lost the discipline the last ninety minutes had tested. Ethan said Lily wanted grilled cheese again. Jack told him grilled cheese was legally sound.

After the call, Jack read the Fairchild letter line by line. It did not name Amelia, Raines, Donnelly, or any specific post. It referenced "public narratives" and "statements made by parties or their associates." It demanded preservation and requested assurance that Ethan would cease any direct or indirect dissemination of false claims. Ethan had already been under stronger court orders than anything the letter requested. That made the notice feel less like legal necessity and more like intimidation by implication.

Mara sat across from Jack. "They know he has not spoken."

"They know what the public docket shows and what our orders say."

"They also know he is vulnerable."

"Yes."

Caleb looked angry. "Can we bring this to Judge Harrow?"

"Maybe. It concerns pressure on a parent in an active custody case."

"Anti-SLAPP?"

"Too early. No complaint filed."

"Defamation?"

"No statement identified."

"So it is just a shot across his bow."

Jack placed the letter in the new civil-threat folder. "Yes."

He called Claire next because Marissa had likely received nothing, and he wanted to prevent Fairchild from turning the parents against each other by contacting one side only. Claire listened carefully. She had not received a similar letter. Neither had Marissa. That detail mattered. If Fairchild wanted to protect its reputation, a letter to Ethan alone made little sense unless it believed he was tied to public criticism or saw him as the easier pressure point. Claire agreed the court should be informed.

"I do not want this destabilizing Lily," Claire said.

"Neither do I."

"Marissa should not know details unless necessary."

"She may need to know that Fairchild contacted Ethan if it affects the case atmosphere."

"I can prepare her without inflaming her."

"Do that."

For once, there was no edge between them. Both lawyers understood what the letter could do. It could make Ethan feel hunted, make Marissa fear association, and make the parents retreat into defensive versions of themselves. Fairchild may not have intended all of that. In litigation, intent mattered less than foreseeable pressure.

Jack drafted a sealed notice to Judge Harrow before the day ended. He attached the Fairchild letter and stated that Ethan had not made public statements, had complied with all orders, and viewed the notice as potentially chilling and destabilizing within the active custody matter. He did not ask for sanctions. He asked for a protective clarification that no third party should communicate legal threats to a parent concerning public narratives tied to sealed matters without notice to counsel and, where appropriate, the court. Claire joined the request in part, supporting protective clarification without taking a position on Fairchild's civil rights.

Hale responded within an hour. Fairchild had sent a standard preservation and cease-disparagement notice in response to defamatory public claims. It did not intend to interfere with custody proceedings and had copied counsel precisely to avoid improper contact. Jack appreciated the polish. It did not answer why Ethan alone received the notice. It also did not identify a single statement by Ethan.

Judge Harrow set a brief compliance conference for the next morning. The order said the court would address the intersection of third-party civil communications and active custody protections. That was careful language. It did not accuse Fairchild. It told them the letter had entered the wrong room.

At seven, Dr. Patel's routine update came through Angela. Lily had asked whether hiking trails remember people. The note provided no context and no therapy content. It only recommended that both parents support age-appropriate outdoor routines if Lily wanted them and avoid turning activities into symbolic milestones. Jack sent the allowed guidance to Ethan and Claire. Ethan replied that he would ask Lily whether she wanted a short walk this weekend, not a big hike.

Jack closed the message and looked back at the Fairchild letter. The contrast was almost unbearable. A child asked whether trails remembered people, and a foundation sent a legal warning to her father about narratives. Both existed in the same case. Only one belonged anywhere near Lily.

Before leaving, Jack updated the whiteboard. Under stability, he wrote ninety-day order. Under accountability, he wrote Fairchild civil notice. Under Lily's protected space, he wrote short walk. He stood there long enough for the office lights to dim around him. The custody order was working, and that made the pressure around it more visible. Powerful institutions often waited until a person stood up straighter before reminding him how expensive standing could become. Jack had no intention of letting Ethan bend, and no intention of letting Lily feel the hand that had been placed on her father's shoulder.

41

The compliance conference lasted twenty-three minutes and told Jack Sullivan more about Fairchild than a longer hearing would have. Victor Hale appeared for the foundation with a civil litigator beside him, a woman named Adrienne Bell who introduced herself in a tone designed to make the room understand that Fairchild had options beyond family court. Judge Harrow acknowledged her appearance and immediately limited it. The issue was not defamation law, donor reputation, or public advocacy. The issue was whether a civil threat letter sent to a parent in an active custody matter risked destabilizing a child-protection order.

Hale said the letter had been standard, cautious, and routed through counsel. Bell said Fairchild had the same right as any private entity to protect itself from false statements. Neither identified a statement made by Ethan. Jack wrote that down, though he had already written it in his notice. The absence was becoming the point. Fairchild wanted the benefit of pressure without the burden of specificity.

Claire supported Jack's request in her narrow way. She said Marissa did not join any accusation against Fairchild, but she agreed that civil communications directed at either parent could interfere with the court's structure if they created fear, blame, or renewed conflict. That was the right frame, and it mattered that it came from Marissa's side. Judge Harrow listened without interrupting, then looked toward Hale's screen.

"Counsel, if Fairchild believes a parent has made a defamatory statement, it may pursue lawful remedies in the proper forum," Judge Harrow said. "This court will not adjudicate that claim. This court will, however, protect its orders from being undermined by outside pressure on a parent."

Bell began to respond, but the judge raised one hand slightly. It was not dramatic. It was enough.

"The foundation is ordered not to send further legal demands, preservation notices, cease-and-desist letters, or similar communications to either parent concerning public narratives related to this sealed matter without contemporaneous notice to counsel and leave of this court while custody orders remain under review. Communications may be made through counsel for legitimate preservation issues if they identify the basis for the request and do not imply misconduct without facts. The court makes no finding of bad faith today."

Jack wrote the language down as fast as he could. It was not everything he might have wanted, but it was enough. The judge did not strip Fairchild of legal rights. She forced the foundation to stop using those rights in a way that could reach Lily through her parents' fear. That was the cleanest remedy available inside the family case.

Bell asked whether the order applied to Fairchild's responses to media outlets. Judge Harrow said no, provided Fairchild did not reference the sealed case, the parents, Lily, or any facts that would identify them. Hale asked whether Fairchild could preserve documents internally. The judge said yes. Fray asked whether the same rule applied to Civic Bridge. The judge said any nonparty subject to her orders should assume the same principle applied and seek clarification before sending legal threats connected to the case.

The conference ended, and Jack sat still for a moment after the screen went dark. Caleb looked relieved. Mara looked thoughtful. Nora, standing in the doorway with a mug in her hand, looked like she had decided Fairchild could benefit from several more orders and possibly a locked drawer.

Caleb spoke first. "That was strong."

"It was measured."

"Measured can be strong."

Jack nodded. "Good. You are learning."

Mara looked at the order notes. "Fairchild can still sue later."

"Yes."

"Will they?"

"Maybe. A lawsuit would invite discovery they may not want."

Caleb glanced at the civil-threat folder. "So the letter was the cheaper weapon."

Jack capped his pen. "That is often the point of a letter."

Jack called Ethan after the minute order arrived. He told him the court had restricted further legal demands to either parent concerning the sealed matter without court oversight. Ethan listened carefully and asked whether that meant Fairchild could not sue him. Jack said no. It meant they could not use threat letters inside the active custody environment without accountability. Ethan accepted the distinction more quickly than Jack expected.

"So I still make grilled cheese," Ethan said.

"You do."

"And maybe a short walk this weekend."

"Yes."

"She asked if trails remember people."

"I saw the guidance."

"I think I might say people remember trails."

"That is a safe answer."

Ethan went quiet. "Do you think I am doing better?"

Jack looked at the order on his desk. "Yes."

"I needed to ask somebody who would not say it just to be nice."

"You are doing better."

The call ended without more. Jack did not often think of his work as giving people permission to believe they had changed, but sometimes that was part of it. Ethan had been given accusations, restrictions, court dates, advice, and warnings. He had not been given many plain acknowledgments that he was becoming safer for his daughter. Jack had no objection to saying it when the record supported it.

At noon, Claire sent a note confirming Marissa had received the court's order regarding Fairchild communications and understood that no outside pressure should be discussed with Lily. She added that Marissa hoped Ethan was not too distressed by the letter. Jack read that sentence twice. It was cautious and probably sincere. It also asked for emotional information Marissa was not entitled to receive. He replied only that Ethan would continue following the parenting plan.

Mara came in while he was drafting the response. "Nice dodge."

"Necessary dodge."

"She is trying to see whether he is okay."

"She should ask that through her own therapist, not through me."

Mara sat down. "You think they ever get back to normal co-parenting?"

"No."

"That was fast."

"They may get to functional. Normal is usually gone after a case like this."

"Functional sounds bleak."

"Functional can raise a child."

Mara accepted that. The case had never promised to restore the family Ethan remembered or the family Marissa wanted to preserve. It promised a structure that could protect Lily from adult fear long enough for healthier patterns to grow. That was not romance. It was law doing one of the few things law could do well when people obeyed it.

The afternoon brought Amelia back with a new development. Fairchild had issued a public statement after the hearing, though it did not mention the hearing. The statement affirmed the foundation's commitment to privacy, responsible evaluation, and lawful protection against misinformation. It said Fairchild would not comment on matters involving minors. It also announced that the privacy working group would begin meeting the following month and would publish recommendations before year's end.

Amelia handed Jack the statement. "They are turning restraint into branding."

Jack read it. "Yes."

"Can I write that?"

"Not in those words if you mean this case."

"I mean the public statement."

"Then write from the public statement."

She sat across from him. "They know they can outlast individual families."

"Yes."

"Unless a public record makes the structure visible."

"Yes."

Jack's agreement surprised her. He could see it. He had spent weeks telling her no, wait, not yet, after Lily. None of that had meant the public work was unimportant. It meant the public work had to avoid making Lily pay for everyone else's clarity.

"You are closer to being able to write the larger piece," Jack said.

Amelia was quiet for once. "How close?"

"After the next compliance review. After we know Fairchild and Civic Bridge are not going to use Lily again. After the school rumors stay quiet."

"That is three afters."

"It is a child."

She nodded slowly. "All right."

By three, Caleb had prepared the ninety-day compliance calendar. It tracked therapy, exchanges, school communication, parent-guidance sessions, third-party no-use certification, media inquiry logging, and the next court review. Jack approved it with only minor edits. The order was becoming administration. Administration was boring until it saved someone.

Nora brought in a call slip from Dr. Patel's office. Not an emergency. Jack called back through Angela because the therapeutic channel had to remain clean. The general update was simple: Lily wanted to resume art club after school. Dr. Patel and Angela believed it could be beneficial if both parents agreed and the school could ensure ordinary participation without special attention. Jack forwarded the request through counsel. Ethan agreed first. Marissa agreed thirteen minutes later.

Jack sat with that longer than the issue seemed to require. Art club had become the next test of ordinary. The school that had mishandled her note would now host a room where Lily might draw again with other children. It felt risky because everything felt risky now. It also felt necessary. Protection could become another cage if adults mistook safety for removal from life.

Ethan called later to ask the question Jack knew was coming. "Should I be nervous about art club?"

"Yes."

"That is not helpful."

"It is honest. Nervous does not mean no."

"What if someone says something?"

"Then the school follows the plan. You do not preemptively make Lily afraid of the room."

He sighed. "So I say art club sounds fun."

"Yes."

"And I ask if she needs supplies."

"Yes."

"She likes charcoal pencils."

"Then ask about charcoal pencils."

Ethan paused. "This is parenting by court order."

"For now."

"I hate that too."

"I know."

The line softened. "She drew Pickle again. He has boots now."

"Good boots?"

"She said rain boots. For clouds."

Jack allowed himself a brief smile. "Then get the charcoal pencils."

After the call, Jack walked into the conference room and found Caleb reading through older pleadings. The younger lawyer looked up with a question already forming. Jack waited.

"Do we ever address what happened to Dana?" Caleb asked.

"Through the school process, maybe. Through this case, only if needed for Lily."

"She was central."

"Yes."

"And now she is just on leave."

"For now."

Caleb closed the binder. "That feels unfinished."

"It is unfinished."

"So are Fairchild, Civic Bridge, Tessa, Horizon."

"Yes."

Caleb looked frustrated. "How do you know when the case is allowed to end?"

Jack sat at the table across from him. "When the order protects the child well enough and further litigation helps adult accountability more than child stability."

"That seems hard to know."

"It is."

"What if accountability helps future children?"

"Then someone may need to pursue it. That someone may not be the custody court, and the vehicle may not be Lily's case."

Caleb nodded slowly. It was a hard lesson, and not one young lawyers liked. The courtroom where harm was discovered was not always the courtroom where every harm could be remedied. Jurisdiction mattered. Standing mattered. Procedure mattered. None of those limits made the harm less real. They only defined which tool could be used without cutting the wrong person.

Near six, Claire sent a brief note. Marissa had agreed to purchase a second set of art supplies for her home and would not ask Lily to explain her drawings. Ethan responded through counsel that he appreciated the coordination. Jack approved the message before it went out. It was the first polite exchange that did not feel forced. Not warm. Not repaired. Functional.

Amelia left early to meet her editor. Mara left with the compliance binder. Caleb left after scheduling the art club consent. Nora left last, after telling Jack she would file a motion with herself if he stayed past eight. He stayed until eight-twenty. Nora would not be surprised.

Before leaving, Jack stood before the whiteboard. Under stability, he added art club. Under accountability, he added civil threats restricted. Under Lily's protected space, he wrote

Pickle has boots. He knew it looked absurd. He also knew the absurdity was why it belonged there.

The case had spent weeks translating Lily into risk, outcome, language, stabilization, and court posture. A dog with wings and rain boots resisted all of that. It meant nothing to Fairchild, nothing to Civic Bridge, nothing to the legal theories forming in public. It meant Lily was imagining without permission from adults. Jack turned off the lights and left the drawing unseen by the court, which was exactly where it belonged.

42

Art club began on a Wednesday afternoon, and by nine that morning three adults had already tried to make it more complicated than it needed to be. Mercer wanted to assign a staff member near the art room without making Lily feel watched. Sonia Patel wanted the school to document the arrangement without creating a record that looked like Lily required special handling. Ethan wanted to know whether he should buy the charcoal pencils before or after she asked for them. Jack Sullivan answered each question the same way in different language. Let it be ordinary, and document only what the order requires.

The school sent both parents the standard art club permission form. Ethan signed within minutes. Marissa signed through the school portal later that morning and sent a brief message in the parenting app confirming she would pack Lily's art folder. No explanations. No apology. No reference to the case. Jack reviewed the exchange with Caleb and approved it without edits, which had become rare enough for Caleb to look briefly pleased.

Mara entered with the compliance binder and a fresh chart. "Art club is now on the calendar."

"Good."

"Mercer wants guidance on whether Mrs. Palmer should know anything beyond routine staff awareness."

Jack looked up. "Mrs. Palmer already knows more than routine."

"She does. Mercer is asking whether to tell her about the privacy order."

"Only what applies to her conduct. No discussion of the case, no special questioning, no comments on prior events, and report any concerning public inquiry through administration."

Mara wrote it down. "So ordinary with a paper trail."

"Yes."

Caleb smiled faintly. "That may be the title of family court."

Jack ignored him, which only encouraged Nora from the doorway. "I would buy that book."

At noon, Amelia arrived with an update on Fairchild's working group. The public announcement had drawn applicants from researchers, advocacy organizations, school administrators, and two parent groups, including the one connected to Elise Donnelly. Amelia suspected Fairchild would use the group to absorb criticism, define the vocabulary, and present reforms before anyone outside the sealed case knew what had prompted the change. Jack suspected the same. Suspicion remained outside the custody file unless it touched Lily.

"She will apply," Amelia said.

"Donnelly?"

"Yes."

"That may be useful publicly. It does not change the custody order."

"She helped spread the rumor."

"She is now bound by the no-disclosure order as to what she learned through Marissa."

"She will still talk generally."

"General talk is not prohibited."

Amelia sat back. "You ever get tired of saying what cannot be stopped?"

"Yes."

The answer softened the room more than he expected. Amelia had heard him say no so many times that she may have forgotten the no cost him something too. Jack was not defending Fairchild's public strategy. He was defending the line between public accountability and private harm. The line was thin, and everyone in the case kept stepping close to it for reasons that were partly noble and partly not.

At three-thirty, Lily attended art club. No one from Jack's office was there. No parent observed. No lawyer called the school. Mercer sent no update during the session because Jack had told him not to turn ordinary participation into surveillance. At five-sixteen, the school's automated attendance system emailed both parents that Lily had attended the club and checked out at the regular time. That was all. Jack considered it the best school record he had seen in the case.

Ethan called at six after his pickup. "She liked it."

"That is good."

"She said Mrs. Palmer acted normal."

"Also good."

"She drew Pickle with boots again. Now he has a backpack."

Jack leaned back. "Cloud travel?"

"That was my guess. I did not ask."

"What did you ask?"

"If he packed snacks."

"And?"

"Apparently he packed crackers and one emergency pickle."

"That sounds prudent."

Jack heard Ethan laugh, and the sound no longer felt like something pulled from him by force. It came easily, then settled. Ethan said Lily wanted spaghetti, and he had learned not to burn the garlic bread this time. Jack told him progress could appear in many forms. Ethan said he would not put garlic bread in a declaration.

The next morning, Claire sent a short note saying Marissa reported Lily seemed calmer after art club and asked whether the parties could agree to keep it on the schedule. Jack reviewed the message carefully, looking for hidden traps and finding none. Ethan approved continuation. The agreement was filed as a simple stipulation authorizing art club participation during either parent's custodial time unless Dr. Patel or Angela recommended a change. Judge Harrow signed it the same day.

The ease of that stipulation made Caleb suspicious. "That was too simple."

Jack looked at him. "Sometimes simple things are simple."

"In this case?"

"Rarely."

Mara entered before Caleb could answer. "Fairchild's civil firm sent another letter."

The room shifted. Nora appeared in the doorway, as if the building itself had alerted her to incoming irritation. The letter was addressed to Jack this time, not Ethan, and copied to Claire, Hale, and Amelia's editor. It stated that Fairchild respected the family court's order and would not communicate directly with either parent, but it reserved all rights regarding false public statements by any person acting with access to sealed proceedings. It did not accuse Jack of leaking. It did not accuse Amelia of using sealed material. It made sure both possibilities hovered near the paper.

Jack read it once and placed it in the civil-threat folder. "No response today."

Caleb looked surprised. "None?"

"None."

"They copied Amelia's editor."

"That is the point."

Amelia arrived twenty minutes later, already holding a copy from her editor. She looked angry in a controlled way, which was better than the alternative. Jack met her in the conference room with the sealed binders removed from the table. She placed the letter down and waited for him to speak.

"They are trying to chill your reporting without filing anything," Jack said.

"I know."

"Do not respond emotionally."

"I know."

"Your editor should have counsel respond, if anyone does."

"She does."

"Good."

Amelia sat down. "They think I got the story from sealed proceedings."

"They may think that, or they may want you to wonder whether they can make that argument expensive."

"I used public records."

"I know."

"Do you?"

Jack held her gaze. "Yes."

That mattered more than he intended it to. Amelia looked away first. She had spent weeks outside the sealed line, close enough to feel distrusted and disciplined enough not to cross it. Fairchild's letter touched the insult beneath that restraint. Jack could not protect her from every consequence of reporting. He could state clearly what he knew: she had not used Lily.

By afternoon, Amelia's editor's counsel sent a polite response stating the article relied exclusively on public records and protected opinion, made no allegation regarding any specific family or sealed case, and would not be retracted. Jack read it and nodded once. Strong enough. Brief enough. No invitation to fight the whole war in correspondence. Fairchild did not respond before the close of business.

The compliance review for the third-party no-use order occurred the next day. Judge Harrow reviewed certifications from Fairchild, Civic Bridge, Tessa, Horizon, and the school district. No new use of Lily's scenario had been identified. No additional dissemination had been reported. The court continued the order and required monthly certifications for ninety days. Hale objected to the ongoing burden. Judge Harrow overruled the objection because the burden was minimal compared to the risk of further use.

Jack did not argue much. He pointed to the certifications, the prior use, and the need for continuity while the custody order stabilized. Claire supported the continuation. Fray took no position beyond preserving Civic Bridge's objections. Hale made a record for Fairchild. The hearing ended in eighteen minutes, and the order did exactly what it needed to do. It kept Lily out of their presentations.

After the hearing, Judge Harrow asked counsel to remain a moment. Her tone changed enough that everyone sat straighter. She said the court would not keep the case open indefinitely as a platform for institutional oversight. At the next review, she expected the parties to identify what issues remained truly necessary for custody. If third-party compliance remained clean, the court would consider reducing institutional reporting while preserving the no-use injunction. The message was clear. Protect the child, then stop litigating around her.

Outside the courtroom, Caleb looked unsettled. "She is narrowing us."

"She should."

"What about Fairchild?"

"What about Lily?"

Caleb stopped, then nodded. He did not like the answer, but he understood it better than he would have a month earlier. The court had done more than most family courts would have done with nonparty institutions. It would not become a standing commission on grant ethics because Jack wanted more answers. The next steps would have to move elsewhere if they moved at all.

Back at the office, Amelia understood the significance before Jack finished summarizing. "She is closing the custody door."

"Eventually."

"And leaving the public door."

"Not her door."

"No. Mine."

Jack looked at her. "Only if you can keep Lily out of it."

"I can."

"Can you keep yourself out of needing this to be your victory?"

That landed hard. Amelia's mouth tightened. Mara looked at Jack from across the room, then looked down because the question was fair and personal. Amelia did not answer quickly.

"I am trying," she said.

"That is the honest answer."

"It is also the only one I have."

Jack nodded. "Then keep trying."

The exchange ended without apology. It did not need one. Amelia had pushed the public record forward, and Fairchild had begun reacting to it. That mattered. It also created the temptation to see every development as proof that her story was saving people. Maybe it was. Maybe it could. The danger was using Lily as the hidden engine while telling herself the child was absent from the page.

That evening, Ethan sent a parenting app message to Marissa about art club supplies. Lily had used up a charcoal pencil and needed a new set. Marissa replied that she would buy some for her house and asked whether Ethan wanted to split the cost for a larger set kept at school. Ethan sent the draft to Jack before replying. Jack approved it with one change, removing the word finally from Ethan's sentence. The final message said, That works. I can pay half.

Marissa replied, Thank you. I will order them.

Jack stared at the exchange and thought about how much litigation it had taken to produce two adults splitting the cost of pencils. It was absurd and sad and hopeful in equal parts. The law often arrived after common sense had already failed. Then it built scaffolding around the common sense until people could trust it again.

Before leaving, Jack updated the whiteboard. Under stability, he added art supplies shared. Under accountability, he added monthly certifications and public reporting pressure. Under Lily's protected space, he wrote crackers and emergency pickle. The board now looked less like a litigation map and more like a record of two competing worlds. One was built from orders, letters, hearings, and institutional statements. The other was built from pancakes, pencils, drawings, and a winged dog with boots.

Jack left both worlds there. The case was moving toward a place where the court would no longer need to supervise every adult sentence. That was good for Lily and unsettling for everyone who still wanted more answers. He turned off the lights and accepted, at least for that night, that a child's recovery might look less like truth being shouted from a courthouse and more like two parents agreeing on charcoal pencils without turning them into evidence.

43

THE CASE BEGAN TO shrink in the way healthy custody cases sometimes do when adults finally stop feeding them. Jack Sullivan noticed it first in the calendar. There were fewer urgent calls, fewer emergency conferences, fewer sealed notices filed after dinner. The remaining dates were ordinary ones: art club, therapy, school assembly, compliance certification, parenting review. A month earlier, those words would have sounded too small for the damage already done. Now they sounded like the only measure that mattered.

Ethan still sent messages for review, though less often. The drafts were shorter and usually needed no changes. Marissa's messages stayed careful but no longer read as if Claire had written each one. The app log had become boring enough that Caleb stopped bracing himself before opening it. Jack considered that one of the better developments in the case. Boring meant the parents were beginning to let the order do its work.

The next friction came from something no one could blame on Fairchild, Civic Bridge, or the court. Lily wanted to invite two girls from art club to Ethan's house for Saturday afternoon. Ethan sent the request through the app exactly as the order required. Marissa replied that she was not comfortable with playdates at either home until Dr. Patel approved social visits connected to school. Ethan sent the exchange to Jack with no added commentary, which itself showed restraint. Jack read it twice, then told Ethan not to respond until counsel spoke.

Claire called within an hour. She said Marissa was not trying to block Lily's friendships. She was worried that other parents might ask questions, that children might repeat rumors, and that Lily could be embarrassed in her own home. Jack understood the concern. He also understood that isolating Lily to avoid rumor could make the court order another kind of injury. The law had protected her privacy. It could not protect her by removing every doorway to ordinary life.

"Dr. Patel can weigh in generally," Jack said.

"I agree."

"No therapy content."

"Of course."

"And if she approves, we start with a public place or school-supervised activity before home visits."

"That may be easier for Marissa."

"It may be easier for Lily."

Claire paused. "That too."

Angela relayed the question to Dr. Patel, and the guidance came back that afternoon. Lily should be allowed age-appropriate social contact, beginning with low-pressure, structured settings where adults did not hover and no child was briefed on the case. Dr. Patel recommended a short art-club group activity at a public ceramics studio or school event before home playdates. The guidance was simple, cautious, and child-centered. Jack forwarded it to Ethan, who replied, I can do that.

Ethan still called later because compliance did not erase disappointment. "I wanted her to have friends over like before."

"I know."

"Everything has steps now."

"For now."

"Do you think she notices?"

"Yes."

"That hurts."

"Then make the steps feel less like steps."

He breathed out slowly. "Ceramics studio?"

"That sounds reasonable."

"She likes painting things."

"Then ask Marissa through the app if she agrees to a short ceramics outing with the art club friends, parent-to-parent coordination handled through the school directory, no case discussion."

Ethan was silent for a moment. "You just turned fun into a contract."

"I turned risk into a workable plan."

"That is worse and better."

The ceramics plan was approved by both parents the next morning. It required more adult coordination than any simple afternoon of paint and clay should have required, but it happened. Lily went with two girls from art club, painted a small bowl with uneven stars, and returned to Ethan's house tired in a normal way. No one asked about court. No one mentioned the blog posts. One mother asked Ethan whether he knew a good place for pizza nearby, and Ethan managed to answer like a father instead of a defendant.

He told Jack about it the next day, not as evidence, but as news. Jack listened and said less than he wanted to. He had learned, over years of practice, that clients sometimes needed one person to hear ordinary news as if ordinary news mattered. In family court, it did. The first normal outing after public pressure could be more significant than a favorable ruling.

On Monday, Fairchild filed its monthly certification. It stated no further use, dissemination, reporting, training, or presentation of Lily's scenario had occurred. Civic Bridge filed the same. Tessa filed through counsel. Horizon filed with a note that Dr. Warren was no longer serving as an advisor to Civic Bridge-related youth response programming pending internal review. That detail was new. Jack marked it but did not celebrate it. Internal review could mean reform, containment, or both.

Mara read the Horizon note and looked up. "Warren is stepping back."

"For now."

"Does that affect Lily?"

"No. Dr. Hannah Patel is neutral and separate."

"Does it matter for accountability?"

"Yes."

Caleb leaned forward. "Do we ask for the internal review?"

"Not in this custody case unless it touches Lily's records or future safety."

He looked disappointed, though not surprised. Jack understood. The evidence had trained the team to see institutional patterns everywhere. The court's narrowing order forced them to remember their case was still tethered to one child. That discipline felt like leaving doors unopened. Some doors did not belong in a custody hallway.

Amelia arrived after lunch with a different kind of news. Her article had been cited in a state legislative staff memo about youth privacy and nonprofit reporting, which was public and not tied to Lily. She placed the memo on Jack's desk with both pride and restraint. Jack read the paragraph referencing "recent reporting on court-facing youth program evaluation" and saw no reference to San Aurelio or any sealed facts. The public track was moving now under its own power. That was exactly what he had hoped and feared.

"This is good," Jack said.

Amelia's eyebrows rose. "That sounded almost wholehearted."

"Do not get used to it."

"It means the issue can move without Lily."

"Yes."

She sat across from him. "I keep thinking about that."

"You should."

"I am. More than I thought I would."

Jack believed her. Amelia had wanted the story when she first walked into his office. She still wanted it. The difference was that she no longer seemed willing to spend Lily to get it. That was not moral perfection. It was a professional adjustment with a child's face attached to it, and sometimes that was how people changed.

At three, Claire sent Marissa's latest compliance note. Marissa had attended parent guidance, agreed to the ceramics outing, and reported no public inquiries. She also asked, through Claire, whether Ethan would agree to a shared online calendar for school and activity items beyond the app. Jack brought the request to Ethan. He expected suspicion, and he got it for the first minute. Then Ethan surprised him.

"That might help," Ethan said.

"It might."

"Can it be read-only for appointments and activities, with messages still in the app?"

"Yes."

"I don't want side comments."

"We can set rules."

"Then yes."

Jack drafted the calendar protocol with Claire. It was almost painfully practical: shared school/activity calendar only, no comments except event details, no case references, no therapy content beyond date and time, no unilateral schedule changes without app confirmation. Judge Harrow did not need to sign it because the parties could implement it under the existing order. They did anyway through a written stipulation lodged for the file. Family cases had taught Jack that clarity today prevented accusations tomorrow.

The first entries appeared that evening. Art club. Ceramics pickup. Therapy. History project due. School assembly. Jack looked at the calendar and felt a strange satisfaction. It was not peace. It was infrastructure. For Lily, infrastructure meant fewer surprises and fewer adult conversations disguised as logistics. That was enough.

The week ended with no new Raines posts about the case. She wrote instead about the Fairchild working group and accused it of managing dissent. That was public debate, not Lily's problem unless someone dragged her back into it. Amelia covered the working group's formation in a short follow-up, naming only public entities and public records. Hale sent no letter. Jack noticed that too.

On Friday afternoon, Ethan sent Jack one more private note. Lily asked if she can give the star bowl to her mom. I said yes if she wants to. Was that okay? Jack read it and felt the small ache that came when a child moved naturally toward both parents while adults still carried files full of reasons to be cautious. He wrote back, Yes. Let it be her choice. No message attached unless she asks.

Ethan answered, Understood. She already wrapped it.

Jack did not forward that to anyone. It did not belong to Marissa's lawyer or the court or the compliance binder unless a fight later made it relevant. He hoped it never would. Some things were strongest when they remained unfiled.

Before leaving for the weekend, Jack stood at the whiteboard. The case had changed enough that he erased half the remaining arrows. Stability stayed. Compliance stayed. Accountability stayed, though it had drifted toward public systems and away from custody. Under Lily's protected space, he added star bowl. Then he looked at the phrase working order and underlined it once.

The order was working because people were following it, not because paper had power by itself. Ethan was learning not to turn every fear into action. Marissa was learning that apology meant behavior, not explanation. Amelia was learning that public truth could be written without exposing a child. Even Fairchild, whether from conscience or pressure, was learning to speak about safeguards it had once treated as optional. None of that repaired the beginning. It did make the next chapter of Lily's life less likely to be written by adults who needed her words more than she did.

44

The star bowl arrived at Marissa's house wrapped in tissue paper, carried in Lily's backpack between a math worksheet and a permission slip for a field trip. Jack Sullivan knew this only because the parenting app recorded the exchange in the plainest possible terms. Ethan wrote that Lily had packed a ceramics project she wanted to bring to Marissa's home. Marissa replied that she received it and would make sure it stayed on Lily's dresser. No one added meaning. No one thanked the other parent for allowing it. That restraint made the message stronger than warmth would have.

Claire forwarded the exchange with a note that said Marissa handled it well. Jack sent back a brief acknowledgment. He did not tell Ethan that Marissa had reported the bowl went on the dresser, because Ethan did not need to monitor how a gift lived in the other house. He did tell him the exchange was compliant and appropriate. Ethan replied, Good. Then, three minutes later, he sent another message: I wanted to ask if she liked it there. Jack told him not to ask.

The work of custody repair often happened in those small deleted questions. Parents learned to leave space around a child's experience, especially when that experience involved the other home. Ethan wanted to know whether Lily's gift was valued. Marissa probably wanted Ethan to know she valued it. Lily needed both of them not to turn the bowl into a referendum on trust. Jack had spent years arguing over grand issues of parental fitness, and sometimes the most important advice was to let a bowl sit on a dresser without cross-examination.

The next court date was still weeks away, so the office entered the slower rhythm of maintenance. Caleb reviewed the shared calendar twice a week. Mara tracked institutional certifications and public developments. Nora logged calls and grew suspicious when entire mornings passed without anyone threatening litigation. Amelia visited less often, which Jack regarded as progress for both of them. Her reporting had moved into public policy, and the case no longer required her to orbit the sealed record.

On Wednesday morning, Mara brought in the first real policy response. A state senator's office had announced an informational hearing on youth privacy in privately funded school and family-support programs. The announcement cited public reporting, grant records, and concerns raised by parents and educators. It did not reference Lily, San Aurelio, or Judge Harrow's orders. Amelia's name appeared as one of several invited witnesses. Fairchild was invited too.

Caleb looked at the announcement. "This is going beyond us."

"It was always beyond us," Jack said.

"Does this affect the case?"

"Only if someone tries to use Lily."

Mara placed the notice in the public-policy folder. "Fairchild will testify."

"Likely."

"Amelia will testify."

"Also likely."

Caleb looked toward Jack. "Will you?"

"No."

The answer surprised him. Jack could see it. Caleb had begun to see the larger system and wanted someone from the case to carry the record into public view. Jack understood the instinct. He also understood that testimony from Lily's lawyer, even if technically public-policy focused, would pull the sealed matter toward the hearing room. The case had fought too hard to separate Lily from the system that used her. Jack would not be the person who tied them together again.

Amelia called before lunch. "You saw the hearing announcement."

"Yes."

"I am going."

"I assumed."

"They asked me to testify about public records, not the case."

"Good."

"I want you to review my testimony."

"Send it."

She paused. "I knew you would say yes this time."

"I said send it. I did not say I would like it."

"That is the warmest support you offer."

"It is efficient."

Her testimony arrived two hours later. It was careful, more mature than her first article draft, and anchored in public materials. She described the rise of court-facing youth programs, foundation-funded evaluation models, and the danger of using unresolved family situations as evidence of program success. She did not mention Lily. She did not mention San Aurelio. She did not mention any sealed phrase Jack had marked before. He suggested two edits, both for precision rather than safety, and sent it back with the words: This stays outside the case.

Amelia replied, That is the point.

Jack let himself believe it, at least enough for the day.

The only active problem came from Dr. Warren. Horizon filed a certification that it had removed Dr. Warren from advisory roles related to youth response programming, but the certification also stated Horizon had completed an internal review and found no violation of its clinical policies. Jack read the sentence twice. The review had not been produced, and the custody court had not ordered it. Still, the conclusion bothered him because it suggested Horizon was ready to treat the nondisclosure of Lily's note as a documentation issue rather than a clinical failure. That distinction might matter later.

Caleb asked whether they should seek the review. Jack said no. Ethan's custody order did not need it, and Dr. Patel had replaced Warren's role entirely. The court had already made findings about the incomplete emergency record. Pulling Horizon's internal review into the case would satisfy curiosity more than protect Lily. Caleb accepted the answer with visible effort. He was learning that litigation discipline often felt like leaving bad facts unpunished.

Ethan called that evening about something unrelated to Horizon, Fairchild, or policy hearings. Lily wanted to take a short walk on a trail they used to hike before the case. Ethan had checked the schedule and sent Marissa the plan through the app. Marissa agreed and asked only that he keep the walk short because Lily had homework. Ethan wanted to know whether he should send a photo afterward.

"No," Jack said.

"Not even if Lily asks?"

"If Lily wants to send her mom a picture, let her decide and send it through the appropriate channel. Do not stage proof that the walk went well."

"I was not going to stage it."

"I know."

"I was going to send it because it might make Marissa feel better."

"That is not your job."

Ethan was quiet for a moment. "Right."

"Let the walk be a walk."

The walk happened Saturday morning. Ethan sent no photos. He sent the required app note that Lily returned on time and completed homework after lunch. That should have been the end of it. Later that night, he sent Jack a private message: She said the trail remembered us because the big rock was still there. I said I remembered it too. Jack read it twice and did not answer for several minutes. Then he wrote, That was good.

On Monday, the policy hearing drew public attention. Fairchild submitted written testimony emphasizing privacy, grantee independence, and responsible evaluation. Amelia submitted testimony emphasizing governance, consent, and the risk of unresolved private matters becoming program evidence. Civic Bridge did not testify, but it submitted a statement saying it supported youth voice and would review language-support protocols. The phrase youth voice appeared eight times in the combined materials. Jack counted them because he no longer trusted the phrase when adults used it too fluently.

Nora read the public hearing agenda over lunch. "Everyone supports youth voice."

"Yes."

"Except when the youth uses the wrong voice."

Jack looked at her. "That is too accurate."

"I have worked here a long time."

The custody case remained stable through all of it. Lily attended art club. She completed her history presentation. She moved the star bowl from her dresser to the window because, according to Marissa's app message, "it catches light there." Ethan did not respond with anything more than, Glad she found a place for it. Jack approved that reply and thought again about deleted questions. Ethan had not asked whether the window was safe, whether Marissa liked the bowl, or whether Lily had said why. He let the light be enough.

At the end of the week, Judge Harrow issued a routine minute order confirming the next review date and requesting short status statements only. No argument unless a party identified a concrete dispute. That was the court signaling it wanted the case to keep shrinking. Jack welcomed it. He also knew the file would never be as small as it should have been. Some cases leave residue even when the orders work.

Marissa's status statement came through Claire first. It reported compliance, continued parent guidance, no public discussions, and successful participation in art club and school activities. Ethan's statement said the same in different words. Jack removed a sentence Ethan wanted to include about the trail remembering them because it belonged to Lily, not the judge. Ethan accepted the edit without complaint. That may have been the clearest sign yet that he understood what the case was for.

Amelia testified at the policy hearing on Friday. Jack watched part of it from his office with the volume low. She spoke clearly, stayed inside public sources, and did not use the case as a hidden weapon. When a senator asked whether she knew of specific families harmed by these programs, she paused and answered with care. She said public records showed structural risks and that privacy laws rightly prevented turning individual families into examples without consent. Jack wrote down the answer because it was exactly the line the case had taught her.

Fairchild's representative testified later and announced voluntary reporting safeguards: no unresolved active matters in grant-impact examples without documented consent and review, clear separation between internal learning and renewal narratives, and expanded privacy screening. The safeguards were good. They were also reactive, though no one on the panel said so. Jack did not need them to. The public record had moved without Lily's name, and that was the only public victory he trusted.

That evening, Amelia called from the Capitol parking lot. Her voice sounded worn down and quiet. "I did it without her."

"Yes."

"You watched?"

"Part of it."

"Was it clean?"

"It was clean."

She exhaled. "I kept hearing myself wanting to say more."

"And?"

"I didn't."

"That matters."

She said nothing for a moment. "Do you think it will help?"

"Yes."

The answer was simpler than most he gave her, and she noticed. "That one sounded almost kind."

"Do not report it."

She laughed softly, then ended the call. Jack placed her testimony in the public-policy folder and closed it. It did not belong in Lily's custody binder. That separation felt important, almost ceremonial. The public system could change without making the child who revealed the problem carry the reform.

Before leaving, Jack stood before the whiteboard and erased exposure risk. He left accountability, but moved it away from the center. Under stability, he wrote status statements only. Under Lily's protected space, he added trail remembered. Then he stopped, marker still in hand. It was not legal language, and no one outside the office would understand it. That was why it mattered.

The case was nearing the point where the court would step back and the parents would have to live without daily supervision. Fairchild was reforming in public because pressure had made silence uncomfortable. Amelia had carried the story into policy without carrying Lily with it. Ethan and Marissa were learning to communicate in the narrow, useful language of schedules, supplies, homework, and light in a window. The truth had traveled far enough to change institutions, yet the best parts of Lily's truth were finally staying close to her. That was not perfect justice. It was the first version of peace the law had managed to make.

45

The next review hearing lasted less than fifteen minutes, which would have seemed impossible when Jack Sullivan first walked into Judge Harrow's courtroom with Ethan Cole beside him. The court received short status statements, confirmed compliance, and asked whether any party sought modification. Claire said Marissa did not. Jack said Ethan did not. Angela Morrissey reported that Lily continued to benefit from the current structure, regular activities, and protected therapeutic space. No one asked for testimony, no one raised their voice, and no one tried to make the hearing larger than the child.

Judge Harrow kept the parenting plan in place and reduced neutral exchanges in the way Dr. Patel and Angela had recommended. School-based exchanges would become the default during the school week, with neutral-site exchanges only when school was closed or the parents agreed in writing. The shared calendar would remain. The app would remain for parent communication. The no-public-discussion order and third-party no-use order would remain in place, though the court reduced institutional certifications from monthly to quarterly unless a violation occurred.

Ethan listened without leaning toward Jack for explanation. That was new. Marissa listened without looking like every sentence might turn against her. That was new too. Their lawyers still sat between them, and the case still had enough history to fill shelves, but the hearing itself belonged to the future rather than the emergency. Jack could feel the court letting the file become smaller.

Judge Harrow addressed both parents before ending the matter. "The court is encouraged by compliance. Compliance is not the same as trust, and the court does not expect trust to be rebuilt by order. It expects both parents to keep acting in ways that make trust less necessary for Lily's daily life."

That sentence landed quietly. Jack wrote it down because it was the best description of a working custody order he had heard in years. Trust was too fragile to build an entire child's week upon after a case like this. Structure could carry what trust could not. Over time, if the parents behaved well enough, Lily might stop noticing the structure. That was the goal.

Outside the courtroom, Ethan did not ask whether they had won. He looked at the minute order, then folded it into his folder. "School exchanges will help."

"Yes."

"She won't feel like we are passing her off."

"That is the idea."

Ethan looked toward the far end of the hall, where Claire was speaking with Marissa. "Do I say anything to her?"

"No."

He nodded. "I didn't think so."

"Later, maybe. Not today."

Ethan accepted that without resistance. He had learned that not every peaceful moment needed to be improved by talking. Sometimes adults ruined progress by naming it too soon. Jack had seen that mistake in courtrooms, churches, offices, and homes. Silence, when it was not punishment, could be a kind of respect.

Back at the office, Nora read the updated order and declared it "boring with benefits." Caleb filed it in the custody binder and updated the calendar. Mara moved the institutional certification deadlines to the quarterly review tab. The whiteboard looked emptier than it had in weeks. Jack resisted the urge to fill it. Empty space was not negligence. It was evidence that fewer things needed immediate control.

Amelia came by after lunch with a copy of the legislative committee's preliminary recommendations. The report proposed consent protocols for unresolved youth scenarios, separation of internal learning from grant reporting, and a prohibition on presenting court-adjacent matters as outcomes until independent review was complete. Fairchild's voluntary safeguards were quoted. Amelia's testimony was cited. Lily's case was nowhere in the document.

Jack read the recommendations while Amelia watched him. "This is clean."

She smiled faintly. "I was hoping for better than clean."

"Clean is high praise."

"I know. From you."

"It moved the public issue without touching the child."

"That was the point."

He set the report down. "Then it worked."

Amelia looked relieved in a way she tried to hide by reaching for her notebook. Jack let her have the dignity of pretending the answer had not mattered. She had spent months chasing institutions and weeks standing close to a child's sealed pain without using it. That kind of restraint deserved acknowledgment. He would not give her a speech. A sentence was enough.

The afternoon brought one final document from Horizon. Dr. Warren had resigned from Civic Bridge advisory work permanently and entered a continuing-education program on forensic documentation and child statements in family court matters. Horizon's letter remained protective of its internal review, but the practical change was clear. Warren would not be near Lily's care again, and her old network role was over. Jack placed the letter in the compliance file. It was not a confession. It was a correction.

Caleb read it and looked up. "Do we tell Ethan?"

"Yes, in limited terms. He should know she is no longer connected to any role affecting this case."

"Will that help him?"

"Maybe. It may also make him angry again."

"Then why tell him?"

"Because it affects his confidence in the safeguards."

Jack called Ethan before the end of the day. He explained that Dr. Warren was no longer involved in any advisory role connected to the programs that had affected the case and that Lily's care remained solely with Dr. Patel. Ethan was quiet, then said he was glad. He did not ask whether Warren admitted wrongdoing. Jack did not offer the answer. The old Ethan would have wanted a statement, a punishment, and a public correction. This Ethan let the safeguard be enough for the moment.

At home that evening, Lily asked Ethan whether school exchanges meant she could just go to class like before. Ethan used the guidance and told her the adults had made the schedule easier, and she could just go to class. He told Jack about it later, not as a panic call, but as a small report he seemed to know did not require legal action. Jack listened from his kitchen table and heard dishes in the background. Ordinary life had begun making noise again.

"She said good," Ethan said.

"That is enough."

"She did not ask anything else."

"Then do not add anything else."

"I didn't."

"Good."

Ethan paused. "I think she is tired of adults fixing things."

"Most children are."

"I am too."

"That is a healthy sign."

The call ended, and Jack sat for a while without moving. The case had asked too much of Lily and then built structures to ask less. That was progress, but it did not erase the asking. He knew there would be more reviews, more filings, more careful conversations. The difference was that the urgent fear had stopped being the center of every day.

The next week passed with school exchanges, art club, a ceramics pickup, and no new public posts about the sealed case. Raines turned her attention to the legislative recommendations and accused the committee of adopting half-measures.

Fairchild praised the recommendations as a constructive path forward. Amelia wrote a follow-up that described both reactions with unusual restraint. No one named Lily. No one hinted at San Aurelio. The public story had grown legs of its own and walked away from the child who had revealed its outline.

Marissa's messages in the app became less formal. Not casual, not warm, but less like prepared testimony. Ethan responded in the same register. They coordinated a school assembly, shared the cost of art supplies, and agreed that Lily could bring the star bowl back to the ceramics studio for glazing. The exchange about glazing required six messages and no lawyers. Ethan still sent Jack a screenshot afterward, mostly out of habit. Jack replied with one word: Good.

Nora saw the message on his desk and shook her head. "One-word legal advice now?"

"Efficient."

"I thought you hated one-line anything."

"This is not a paragraph."

She gave him a look. "Convenient doctrine."

Jack almost smiled. The office had changed too. It no longer held its breath every time the phone rang. Caleb had stopped looking surprised when parents behaved well. Mara had moved from crisis charts to closure checklists. Amelia visited only when there was a public development, and she left without trying to peek through the sealed wall. Even Nora's sarcasm had softened from defense to routine.

At the next internal case meeting, Jack laid out the remaining work. Maintain the parenting order. Monitor quarterly certifications. Prepare for a possible step-down of court supervision if compliance continued. Preserve the record in case future disputes reopened old facts. Keep Lily's therapy protected. None of it sounded like the case that had begun with a child mouthing help me across a courtroom. That was the point.

Caleb asked the question the room had avoided. "Do we close the third-party accountability track after the next certification?"

Jack looked at the board. "In family court, probably."

"And outside?"

"That depends on who has standing, what public agencies do, and whether the legislative process creates oversight."

"So not us."

"Not through Lily's custody case."

Mara nodded. "That is the right answer."

"It is not the satisfying one," Caleb said.

"No," Jack said. "It is the protective one."

The word protective had changed meaning over the course of the case. At first, everyone claimed it. Marissa used it. Civic Bridge used it. Horizon used it. Fairchild used it. Even Ethan used it in the desperate way parents do when fear takes over. Now the word meant fewer claims and more boundaries. It meant letting Lily's life continue without requiring her to stand as proof of anyone's virtue or anyone's wrongdoing.

That Friday, Ethan sent one final message for the week. Lily had glazed the star bowl. The art teacher said it would be ready after firing. Lily wanted one side blue and one side yellow because, according to Ethan, "different sides can still be one bowl." Jack read the line once and closed his phone. He did not reply immediately. The sentence was too easy to misuse, too tempting for a lawyer or writer or parent to turn into meaning.

After a few minutes, he wrote back: Let her keep that one.

Ethan answered: I will.

Jack stood before the whiteboard at the end of the day and erased almost everything. Stability stayed. Working order stayed. Under Lily's protected space, he left star bowl, trail remembered, Pickle has boots, and regular day. He added one final phrase: her own words. Then he capped the marker and looked at the board until the office lights dimmed.

The case was not fully over, but it had reached the place where the law should begin stepping back. The court had restored structure. The parents had begun to obey it without constant fear. The institutions had been stopped from using Lily and pushed, in public, toward safeguards that might protect children no one would ever meet. None of that made the beginning right. It made the next part possible.

Jack turned off the lights and left the office without taking a binder home. For once, the files could wait until Monday. Somewhere across town, Lily Cole had a bowl in a kiln, a dog with rain boots in a folder, a trail that remembered her, and two parents learning to answer fewer questions than they wanted to. That was not the end of truth. It was the return of custody to the person who should have had it all along.

46

THE QUARTERLY CERTIFICATION HEARING arrived in a courtroom that no longer felt like the center of Lily Cole's life. Jack Sullivan noticed that before anyone spoke. The benches were half-empty, the lawyers carried thinner folders, and the air lacked the strained attention that had filled the room during the emergency phase. Ethan sat beside Jack with a copy of the current order and no stack of printed grievances. Across the aisle, Marissa sat beside Claire with the same quiet restraint she had shown for weeks.

Judge Harrow reviewed the certifications first. Fairchild confirmed there had been no further use, dissemination, reporting, training, or presentation of Lily's circumstances. Civic Bridge certified the same and attached its revised youth-support protocol, which required consent review, exclusion of active court matters from grant-impact narratives, and documentation whenever language support intersected with legal proceedings. Horizon certified that Dr. Warren remained removed from all court-adjacent advisory work involving youth response programs. Tessa Laird certified through counsel that she had no contact with Lily, either parent, school personnel, or any organization about the Cole matter.

The certifications were not confessions. Jack had never expected them to be. They were boundaries made visible. Family court did not always need institutional remorse to protect a child. Sometimes it needed signatures, deadlines, and the threat of consequences if people who liked abstract language decided to get creative again.

Judge Harrow asked whether any party identified a violation of the no-use order. Claire said Marissa did not. Jack said Ethan did not. Angela confirmed she had received no report from Lily, the school, or Dr. Patel suggesting renewed outside contact or public use of the child's circumstances. The judge made a note, then looked at the institutional counsel appearing by video. Hale's face had settled into professional endurance, and Fray looked relieved that no one had subpoenaed another binder.

"The court will continue the no-use order," Judge Harrow said. "Quarterly certifications will continue for one additional cycle. If compliance remains clean, the court will consider terminating active reporting while preserving the injunction. This matter is not a forum for ongoing program oversight. It remains a custody matter, and the court's focus remains the child."

Jack wrote the language down even though he expected the minute order to match it. The judge had given them a road toward ending the court's direct involvement with the institutions. That was right, even if it left questions unresolved. Lily's case had opened a door that public policy might now walk through. Family court did not need to stand in that doorway forever.

After the hearing, Ethan asked to speak in the downstairs conference room. He waited until Caleb closed the door and then placed his copy of the order on the table. His face was calm, though Jack saw the effort beneath it. The old anger had not vanished. It had become something he carried more carefully.

"So Fairchild gets one more certification and then maybe they just go on," Ethan said.

"They remain bound by the injunction."

"You know what I mean."

"I do."

Ethan looked at the order. "I wanted someone to say they were wrong."

"They may never say that in court."

"I know."

"That does not mean the court did nothing."

Ethan nodded. "I know that too."

Jack let the silence sit. Ethan was not asking for a motion. He was making peace with limits, which was harder. A custody case had given him findings, safeguards, preserved authority, and a working plan for Lily. It had not given him the public reckoning he had imagined during the worst nights. The law rarely satisfies the person who has been falsely framed because clearing the emergency is not the same as healing the humiliation.

Ethan folded the order. "Lily asked if I could come to the school art show."

"That is good."

"Marissa will be there."

"Also good if both of you can behave."

"I can."

"Can you behave if she stands near you?"

Ethan breathed through a small smile. "That is a different question."

"It is the real one."

He looked toward the closed door. "I can stand near her and not make Lily manage us."

Jack nodded. "Then go."

The art show was the following Thursday in the school multipurpose room. Jack did not attend, and he told Ethan not to send updates during the event unless there was a problem. There was no problem. The next morning, Ethan sent a short message saying Lily had three pieces displayed, including Pickle with boots, a trail drawing with a large rock, and the star bowl under a small sign that read Mixed Glaze Study. Marissa had stood on the other side of Lily while parents moved through the room. They had both smiled for Lily without asking her to explain anything.

That was the report Ethan gave privately. In the app, he wrote only, Art show went well. Thank you for coordinating arrival time. Marissa replied, I agree. Lily seemed happy. No one added more. Jack read the exchange and felt the same quiet satisfaction he had felt when the school attendance email confirmed art club. The case had begun with adults fighting over what Lily meant. It had reached a place where both parents could stand in front of her art and not demand meaning from it.

Claire called later that afternoon. "Marissa said Ethan handled the art show well."

"I will tell him the event was successful."

"That is not exactly the same."

"It is what he needs."

Claire made a small sound of agreement. "She also said Lily introduced them both to a friend's mother without hesitation."

"That matters."

"It does."

Neither lawyer said more for a moment. They had spent weeks managing harm through orders and filings. Now they were quietly measuring repair through a child's willingness to introduce both parents in the same room. That kind of progress did not fit easily into pleadings, though it was the very thing pleadings were supposed to serve.

The public-policy track continued without needing Jack's hands. The legislative committee released a revised draft bill requiring privacy review and written consent before youth-serving programs used unresolved individual matters in grant reports, training materials, or public outcomes. It also required court-adjacent programs to maintain separation between support services and litigation-related documentation unless disclosed to all appropriate parties. The bill had a long road ahead, and Fairchild publicly supported "principles of transparency and responsible evaluation" without endorsing every provision. Amelia wrote about the bill from public records and did not call Jack before publishing. That independence felt like progress too.

Nora read the article over lunch and pointed at one paragraph. "She sounds less angry."

"She sounds more precise," Jack said.

"Same thing, after editing."

Mara took the paper. "No Lily."

"No Lily," Jack said.

Caleb leaned back in his chair. "So the case changed policy."

"The public record changed policy."

"Because the case exposed the problem."

"Because the problem existed before the case."

Caleb accepted the correction. Jack did not want Lily made into the origin story of reform, even inside his own office. She had revealed a structure because she was caught in it. She had not volunteered to become the reason adults improved themselves. That difference mattered to him more than it probably should have, which told him it mattered exactly enough.

At the next parent-guidance update, Dr. Patel recommended reducing the frequency of sessions unless new concerns emerged. Lily was engaging in school activities, tolerating transitions, and using ordinary language about both homes. The note said both parents should continue avoiding loaded words and allow Lily's feelings to remain unfinished when they were unfinished. Judge Harrow adopted the recommendation without hearing. Ethan accepted it. Marissa accepted it. No one asked for therapy content.

Ethan called after the order. "Less guidance feels good and scary."

"That is normal."

"You keep saying normal."

"It has become relevant again."

"She still has hard days."

"Normal includes hard days."

He was quiet for a moment. "That helps."

Jack looked out his office window at the parking lot below. "The goal was never to make every day easy."

"I know."

"It was to stop adults from making hard days worse."

Ethan exhaled. "We are getting there."

That evening, Jack found himself thinking about the first day in court, the crowded gallery, the emergency petition, Dr. Warren's declaration, and Lily's silent plea across the courtroom. The memory no longer felt like the opening of a fight. It felt like a warning about how quickly adult certainty can become a room a child cannot escape. The law had opened the door, slowly and imperfectly. Now Lily was walking through ordinary rooms again, and the adults were learning not to block the exits with explanations.

The next week brought a new school calendar entry: spring showcase rehearsal. Ethan approved transportation. Marissa confirmed costume details. The exchange took five messages and no lawyer review. Jack noticed because Ethan did not send it to him until afterward, with a note that said, I think we handled this one. Jack wrote back, You did. It was the first time he had given that answer without adding instructions.

Mara saw the message when she brought in the final quarterly tracking sheet. "They are outgrowing us."

"That is the idea."

"Clients rarely understand that."

"These might."

She sat across from him. "Are you ready to close this?"

"Not today."

"Soon?"

Jack looked at the binders. Custody. Third-party influence. Public-policy background. Civil-threat folder. Compliance certifications. Each one represented a stage of the case, and each one had become thinner through discipline or time. He had spent years learning not to mistake active files for importance. The best outcome in a custody case was sometimes to become unnecessary.

"Soon," he said.

At the final review before summer, Judge Harrow set the path. If the next ninety days remained stable, the parenting plan would continue by standing order, therapy would remain available as needed, active review would end, and the case would move to inactive monitoring unless a party filed a specific motion. The third-party injunction would remain for one year, with no further certifications absent reported violation. The institutions could stop filing paper, but they could not use Lily. That balance satisfied no one entirely. It protected her enough.

After the hearing, Ethan and Marissa stood in the hallway with their lawyers nearby. Lily was not there, and that made the moment possible. Marissa looked at Ethan and said, softly enough that reporters would never have cared, "The art show mattered to her." Ethan nodded. He did not forgive her in that hallway. He did not punish her either.

"It did," he said.

That was all. Jack watched Claire watch it, and for once neither lawyer intervened. The exchange ended naturally. Marissa left with Claire. Ethan stood still for a few seconds, then turned toward Jack.

"Was that okay?"

"Yes."

"It felt strange."

"Many good things do at first."

Ethan nodded and walked with him toward the elevators. He did not ask what came next. He knew. Follow the order. Let Lily be ordinary. Do less. Listen more. Keep the words hers.

Back at the office, Jack erased the litigation map from the whiteboard. He left only four headings: custody, privacy, compliance, closure. Under closure he wrote prepare final review. Then, after a moment, he added one phrase below it: no one owns her words. He stepped back and let the marker hang at his side. The sentence was not a filing. It was the reason for all of them.

The case would have one more chapter in court, maybe two if someone made a mistake. Jack hoped no one did. Hope was not strategy, but it had become less foolish than it was when Ethan first walked into his office. The orders were working, the parents were learning, the institutions were restrained, and the public story had found a path that did not require Lily's name. For once, every track of the case was moving in the same direction, away from possession and toward release.

47

The final review was set for the first Monday after school ended, which gave the case an ending that felt less like a ruling and more like a calendar turning. Jack Sullivan arrived at court with one slim binder, a proposed order, and no expectation that anyone would thank the process for taking so long to become simple. Ethan met him in the hallway wearing a gray suit and the same plain tie he had worn to the earlier reviews. He looked nervous, but not afraid. Jack had learned to separate those two things in clients the same way judges learned to separate anger from risk.

Marissa arrived with Claire a few minutes later. She held no folder, only a copy of the status statement Claire had filed the week before. Her posture was different now, less defensive, as if she had learned that every room did not need to be entered as an argument. Ethan saw her and gave a small nod. Marissa returned it. Neither tried to improve the moment, which made the moment work.

The courtroom was nearly empty. Angela Morrissey sat behind counsel table with a single page of notes. No institutional lawyers appeared because the third-party injunction was no longer under active review that morning. Hale had filed Fairchild's final certification the week before, Civic Bridge had done the same, and Judge Harrow had already indicated she would preserve the injunction without requiring more paperwork unless someone reported a violation. The absence of those lawyers made the room feel cleaner. Lily's custody hearing finally belonged to Lily's life.

Judge Harrow took the bench at nine-thirty and reviewed the status statements aloud only in summary. The parenting plan had functioned for ninety days. School exchanges had worked. The shared calendar had reduced conflict. Art club, the ceramics outing, the spring showcase, and therapy availability had continued without incident. Both parents had complied with privacy restrictions and no outside support channels had been introduced. The court had no report of public identification, renewed institutional use, or contact from prior third-party actors.

Claire spoke first. She asked that the existing parenting plan become the standing order, with annual review only if either parent filed a motion. She said Marissa accepted joint decision-making and the ongoing ban on undisclosed support resources. She said Marissa understood that apology, repair, and trust were matters of behavior over time, not issues the court could force into existence. Jack listened closely. The words sounded like they had cost Marissa something, which made them more credible.

When Jack stood, he did not repeat the history. The court knew it, the parties knew it, and Lily should not have to live under an order that read like a permanent indictment. He asked that the findings remain part of the record, the parenting plan remain in force, the privacy provisions continue, and the third-party no-use injunction remain for one year as previously indicated. He also asked that active court review end unless a specific dispute arose. It was strange to ask a court to step back after fighting so hard to make it look closely. It was also the right request.

Judge Harrow looked from Jack to Claire. "Any disagreement on the proposed standing order?"

Claire shook her head. "No, Your Honor."

Jack said, "No disagreement."

The judge turned to Angela. "Ms. Morrissey?"

Angela stood. "I support the order. Lily has benefited from predictability, reduced adult commentary, and protected therapeutic space. She should not remain under active court supervision simply because the adults around her once required it."

Jack wrote that sentence down because it captured the end better than anything he planned to say. The adults had required supervision. Lily had required protection. Those were not the same thing, though the case had forced them to travel together for a while. Now the protection could remain without the case living at the center of every week.

Judge Harrow signed the standing custody order from the bench. Joint legal custody continued. The parenting schedule, shared calendar, school-based exchanges, direct record access, and protected therapy provisions remained. Neither parent could involve undisclosed counselors, advocates, support lines, social-media groups, or third-party programs in Lily's life without written agreement or court order. Neither parent could use, authorize, describe, publish, or cooperate in public or anonymized use of Lily's circumstances. The institutional no-use injunction remained for one year, with continuing jurisdiction to enforce it.

Then the judge set the paper aside and looked directly at Ethan and Marissa. "This case began because the court was asked to act on a record that did not contain the child's full voice. The court has made findings about that. Those findings remain important. They are not a script for either parent to repeat to Lily."

Both parents nodded. Judge Harrow continued in the same even tone.

"Lily is not responsible for the fear, mistakes, programs, filings, or public conversations that surrounded her. She is not required to explain which adult was right. She is not required to use the same words forever. She is allowed to grow, change her mind, have ordinary preferences, and be a child in both homes. The court expects both of you to protect that freedom."

No one spoke for a moment after the judge finished. The silence was not awkward. It felt earned. Then Judge Harrow ended active review, set no further hearing, and told counsel to submit any necessary notice of compliance if the injunction was violated. The bailiff called the next matter before anyone had fully adjusted to the fact that the Cole case had moved from active battle to standing order.

In the hallway, Ethan stood with the signed order in his hand. Jack waited. He had learned that clients often needed a few seconds after a case ended because the body kept preparing for the next hit even after the court stopped swinging.

"So that's it?" Ethan asked.

"For active review, yes."

"If something happens, we can come back?"

"Yes. With a real issue, not fear alone."

He nodded slowly. "That is fair."

Claire approached with Marissa beside her. Jack expected a procedural comment, perhaps a question about copies or notice. Instead, Marissa looked at Ethan and spoke in a low voice.

"I will follow it," she said.

Ethan held the order at his side. "So will I."

There was more they could have said and more they were wise enough not to say. Marissa's eyes shifted briefly toward Jack, then back to Ethan. Ethan did not soften into forgiveness, and he did not harden into accusation. The hallway held the kind of peace that still needed structure beneath it. For now, structure was enough.

Back at the office, Nora took the signed order from Jack and scanned it before he had removed his jacket. "Standing order entered," she said. "Active review ended. No emergency, no sanctions motion, no one screaming in the lobby. I assume this is what victory looks like when lawyers remove all joy from it."

"It is what protection looks like."

"That too."

Caleb placed the final order into the custody binder. Mara updated the closure checklist, marking active review ended in neat block letters. The room did not erupt. No one clapped. The case had never been the kind that invited celebration. A child had been harmed by adults who believed too much in their own framing. The best outcome was a quieter future, and quieter futures rarely announce themselves.

Amelia arrived after lunch, already aware that the hearing had ended because court dockets were public and she watched them like weather reports. She did not ask for sealed details. She stood in Jack's doorway and waited until he looked up.

"It's over?" she asked.

"Active review is over. Standing order remains."

"And the no-use order?"

"One year, continuing enforcement."

She nodded. "Good."

Jack studied her. "That is all?"

"For now." She gave a small smile. "I am capable of growth."

"Nora will want documentation."

"She already said that."

Amelia sat across from him and placed a printed copy of the legislative bill on his desk. It had gained two coauthors. Fairchild had issued a statement supporting the intent while proposing technical amendments. Civic Bridge had announced a pause in its youth language-support pathway pending protocol review. None of it mentioned Lily. None of it needed to.

"She changed something," Amelia said.

Jack looked at her. "The public record changed something."

Amelia shook her head slightly. "No. A child telling the truth changed something. We just learned not to steal it."

Jack did not answer immediately. The sentence was true enough to hurt and careful enough to keep. Amelia had arrived in the case chasing an institution. She was leaving this stage of it with a better understanding of ownership. Truth could have public consequences without becoming public property. That was the lesson too many adults in the case had learned too late.

That evening, Ethan called from his car outside Lily's school. He had arrived early for pickup because he did not know what else to do with the first day after active review ended. Jack answered while standing near the office window.

"She has the showcase tonight," Ethan said.

"I remember."

"Marissa will be there."

"Yes."

"I'm fine."

"I believe you."

"That was fast."

"You have given me reasons."

Ethan was quiet, then said, "She asked if both of us could sit where she can see us."

"And?"

"I said yes. I told Marissa through the app. She said yes too."

"Good."

"I didn't ask Lily why."

"Better."

Ethan laughed softly. "I know."

The showcase took place in the school auditorium under bad lighting and an unreliable sound system. Jack knew that only from Ethan's later report, which came the next morning and contained no legal emergency. Lily had stood with her class, read two lines from a poem, and looked toward both parents before sitting down. Ethan and Marissa sat on the same row with three empty seats between them. They did not speak much. They did not need to. Lily saw them both.

When Ethan told Jack, his voice carried something close to peace. "She looked for us."

"And you were there."

"Both of us."

"That matters."

"It does."

Jack let that be enough. He did not ask whether Marissa cried, whether Lily seemed anxious, whether anyone from school stared, or whether other parents whispered. The point was that Lily looked and found what she needed. A child should not have to scan a room for safety. That night, at least, the room gave it back to her.

Over the next week, the office closed the active file in stages. Caleb prepared the final index. Mara archived the third-party production under the protective order. Nora sent the closing letter with enough formality to satisfy procedure and enough plain English for Ethan to understand what remained enforceable. Jack reviewed every page before signing. He had learned not to trust endings that arrived too neatly, but this one had earned its simplicity.

Ethan came in to pick up the closing packet. He stood in Jack's office holding it with both hands, as if it were heavier than the paper justified. Then he looked at the wall behind Jack's desk, where no family photographs or diplomas competed for attention. Jack kept the office sparse because clients brought enough memory with them.

"I don't know how to thank you," Ethan said.

"Follow the order."

"I will."

"Let her be ordinary."

"I'm trying."

"That is enough for now."

Ethan nodded, then looked down at the packet. "You believed me when the record didn't."

Jack did not answer quickly. Lawyers liked to say they believed evidence, not people. It was safer and often true. In Ethan's case, belief had started as a professional instinct and become something the record later justified.

"I believed the record was incomplete," Jack said.

Ethan smiled faintly. "That is the most you answer I could get."

"It is also true."

He held out his hand. Jack shook it. The handshake was firm, brief, and free of performance. Ethan left through the front door, past Nora's desk, carrying the order that would govern the next stretch of Lily's childhood. It was not the life he had imagined. It was a life that could work.

After the office emptied, Jack stood before the whiteboard one last time. Most of it had already been erased. Only a few phrases remained: working order, her own words, star bowl, trail remembered, Pickle has boots, no one owns her words. He looked at them for a while, then erased everything except the last one. The marker squeaked against the board, leaving a faint ghost of the phrases beneath the clean surface.

No one owns her words.

He left that sentence there overnight.

The next morning, Nora would erase it because the conference room was booked for another client, another family, another set of facts that would arrive broken and ask the law to make something livable. Jack knew that. He also knew the sentence had done what it needed to do. It had reminded him what the case was really about before it disappeared into memory.

Lily Cole would never know every filing, every objection, every letter, every careful refusal that had kept her name out of the public fight. That was right. Children should not have to understand the machinery built to protect them. They should be free to draw impossible dogs, argue about pencil colors, glaze bowls badly, hike short trails, and decide what words fit today without owing anyone consistency forever.

Jack turned off the conference room lights and left the sentence in the dark. The custody of truth had returned, imperfectly but truly, to the only person who could carry it without turning it into a weapon.

48

Three months after active review ended, Jack Sullivan found Lily Cole's case again in a place he did not expect: a legislative committee packet, page forty-seven, footnote twelve. The footnote cited no names, no court numbers, and no family details. It referenced "recent family-court privacy concerns involving court-adjacent youth programming" and then pointed to public testimony, grant records, and policy submissions. Amelia had kept her promise. The public record had moved without Lily.

Jack read the packet at his desk before the morning calendar call. Nora had placed it there with a sticky note that said, Your favorite thing: policy written by committee. He had no affection for committee language, but he respected what the packet represented. The proposed bill had been narrowed, softened, and amended into something that might actually pass. It would not fix everything. Laws that try to fix everything usually fix less.

The bill required youth-serving programs receiving foundation or public-school partnership funds to adopt written consent policies before using active or unresolved individual matters in training, grant reporting, or impact narratives. It required disclosure protocols when support services intersected with court-related proceedings. It required outcome examples to exclude active cases unless reviewed for consent, privacy, and procedural fairness. It did not mention Fairchild. It did not mention Civic Bridge. It did not mention Lily.

Caleb came in with coffee and a filing stack from another case. "Is that the bill?"

"Yes."

"Does it have teeth?"

"Some."

"That means not enough."

"It means enough to survive."

Mara entered behind him and looked over Jack's shoulder. "That may be the most depressing definition of lawmaking I have heard this week."

"It is only Tuesday."

Nora called from the hallway. "Give him time."

The office had returned to normal, which meant everyone carried too many cases, too many deadlines, and too little patience for people who mistook emergency for strategy. Lily's file sat closed in the cabinet, still protected by orders that would outlast the office's daily memory of the crisis. Ethan checked in only when a real issue arose. Marissa did the same through Claire. That was the way a custody case should end, not with affection forced by court order, but with reduced need for lawyers.

At ten, Ethan emailed a question about the school field trip. Lily wanted both parents to sign the volunteer availability form, though only one would be selected. Ethan did not object to Marissa volunteering if the school chose her, and Marissa had written the same about him in the app. Jack reviewed the exchange and sent a short answer: Both may submit forms. School selects volunteers under routine policy. No case discussion. Ethan replied, Understood. Routine policy sounded like a miracle in bureaucratic clothing.

Claire called after lunch about the same field trip. She sounded amused, which Jack had rarely heard. Marissa had asked whether submitting the form would look like she was trying to compete with Ethan. Claire had told her no, not if the school selected normally and both parents respected the outcome. Jack agreed. They spent four minutes resolving an issue that once might have become an emergency motion. Neither mentioned Fairchild, Civic Bridge, Dana, or the blog posts. That omission was progress.

After the call, Jack looked at the closed file cabinet. He knew the peace was not pure. Ethan and Marissa still carried hurt, shame, suspicion, and private interpretations of the past. Lily still had therapy available if needed. The orders still held hard boundaries because soft promises had failed her once. A working custody order did not require healed adults. It required adults who could behave while healing remained unfinished.

Amelia arrived late afternoon with a copy of her prepared testimony for the bill's final committee hearing. She no longer came to the office like someone entering a war room. She came like a professional bringing work to a colleague who had earned the right to mark it up. Jack read the testimony while she waited near the window. It was shorter than her first draft months earlier and far better.

She wrote about public records, consent gaps, and the danger of turning active family matters into success metrics before neutral review. She described how privacy can protect children and also conceal institutional failure, and why policy has to distinguish between the two. She did not mention Lily. She did not borrow Lily's phrases. She did not build the speech around any invisible child.

Jack circled one line and handed it back. "Change this."

Amelia looked at it. "Too close?"

"No. Too broad. You say 'court-facing programs routinely shape child language.' The record supports risk, not routine practice."

She read it again and nodded. "Fair."

"Use 'can create incentives to shape language.'"

"That is less sharp."

"It is more accurate."

She smiled faintly. "You always think those are the same."

"They should be."

She made the edit in pencil. "Anything else?"

"No."

"That is it?"

"That is it."

Amelia looked down at the page, then back at him. "You know this started because I wanted a story."

"Yes."

"I still want stories."

"I know."

"I think I understand better now which ones belong to me."

Jack leaned back in his chair. "That is probably the only way to keep doing your job without becoming part of the harm."

She accepted the sentence without arguing. Months earlier, she would have told him harm also comes from silence. She still believed that. He did too. The difference was that both of them had learned silence and exposure were tools, not virtues by themselves. Used badly, either one could injure a child.

The final committee hearing drew more attention than expected. Fairchild supported the bill with technical amendments. Civic Bridge supported it in principle and described its revised protocols. Parent groups argued it did not go far enough. Program providers warned it could discourage youth from seeking help. Amelia testified between a school privacy attorney and a child psychologist. Jack watched from his office, volume low, with Mara and Caleb pretending to work beside him.

Amelia stayed inside the public record. When asked whether she knew of individual families harmed by failures in program evaluation, she answered the way they had practiced. "I know that individual family matters are often private by law and should remain private unless the family chooses otherwise. My testimony is based on public records showing that structural safeguards were not always clear. The point of this bill is to reduce the need for families to become public examples before systems improve."

Mara looked at Jack. "That was good."

"Yes."

Caleb nodded. "Clean."

Nora appeared at the doorway. "You all sound like proud parents and it is unsettling."

Fairchild's representative spoke after Amelia and used the words responsible evaluation seven times. Jack counted because habits were hard to break. The representative endorsed consent review, privacy screening, and clearer separation between internal learning and public impact claims. He also emphasized that foundations do not direct case-level decisions. That statement remained carefully true in the way institutions prefer. The bill did not require proof that a foundation directed anything. It required safeguards before anyone could benefit from unresolved private suffering.

The bill moved out of committee by one vote. Amelia called from the hallway afterward, and Jack could hear voices behind her, reporters asking questions, advocates giving quotes, staffers moving people along. She did not sound triumphant. She sounded tired and steady.

"It passed committee," she said.

"I saw."

"One vote."

"Enough."

"You are going to say enough is enough."

"I do not need to. You did."

She laughed softly. "I hate that you are right."

"Then the day is consistent."

She paused. "I did not say her name."

"No."

"I did not need to."

"No."

After the call, Jack closed the livestream and opened Ethan's latest app exchange. The school had selected Marissa as a field trip volunteer because Ethan's work schedule conflicted with the departure time. Ethan wrote, Thank you for volunteering. Please let me know if the return time changes. Marissa replied,

I will. Lily is excited about the museum. Jack stared at the messages for a moment, then saved the log. A custody case, in the end, should look more like that than anything said in a committee hearing.

That evening, Ethan called from home. He had seen a headline about the bill, though he had not read the article. He wanted to know whether it had anything to do with Lily. Jack answered carefully. The public policy issue was related to the kind of problems the case revealed, but Lily had not been named or used. Ethan took that in quietly. Then he asked the question Jack had expected.

"Should I tell her someday?"

"Not now."

"When she is older?"

"Maybe. In a way that belongs to her, not to your anger."

"I'm less angry."

"I know."

"Not all the way."

"That is also allowed."

Ethan was quiet for a while. "She asked if the museum has paintings with dogs."

"Does it?"

"I have no idea."

"Then say you will find out."

"That one I knew."

The call ended without legal instruction. Jack placed the phone down and looked at the old whiteboard through the glass wall. Nora had erased the sentence months ago, as expected. The faint shadow of marker remained when the afternoon light hit the board from the side. Jack could not read the words anymore, but he knew where they had been.

The bill passed the full Senate two weeks later. It still needed the Assembly, the governor, and a thousand compromises that could weaken it or kill it. Amelia covered the vote. Fairchild issued another statement. Raines claimed victory for parent activists. Civic Bridge announced a formal review panel. None of those things required Lily. That was the part Jack trusted most.

The day after the vote, a small envelope arrived at Jack's office addressed in careful handwriting to Mr. Sullivan. Nora brought it in with unusual silence. There was no return address, only a school sticker on the back. Jack opened it at his desk. Inside was a folded piece of paper with a drawing of a dog with wings, rain boots, a backpack, and what appeared to be a pickle in one side pocket.

Beneath the drawing were three words: Pickle says thanks.

Jack sat with the page in his hand for a long time. It should not have come directly, and he would make sure no boundary was blurred because of it. He would tell Ethan through the proper channel that future communications should go through the parents. He would place the drawing in a protected correspondence folder, not the evidentiary file. He would do all the correct things.

For a few seconds, he did none of them.

Nora appeared at the doorway and saw enough to stop. "Good mail?"

Jack looked at the drawing. "Yes."

"Need me to log it?"

"In a minute."

She nodded and left him alone.

Jack studied the rain boots, the crooked wings, the emergency pickle, and the uneven letters. The drawing did not prove the system worked. It did not erase the fear, the note, the phone, the adults, the filings, or the institutional machinery that had tried to turn Lily into language it could use. It proved only that a child who had once mouthed help me had found enough room to draw something no adult could translate into a program outcome without looking foolish.

He placed the drawing in a folder marked Protected Correspondence and wrote one note for the file: Received unsolicited child artwork; no response to child; counsel to notify parent regarding boundaries. Then he emailed Ethan and Claire together, keeping the tone practical. Lily sent a drawing to my office. I will not respond directly. Please route any future communication through parents, and please tell her, in ordinary terms, that I received it and appreciated it.

Ethan replied first. Understood. Thank you for handling it correctly.

Claire replied ten minutes later. Marissa agrees. We will keep boundaries clear.

Jack leaned back and let the moment settle. Boundaries clear. Appreciation ordinary. No evidence. No argument. No adult need placed on the child. The case had taught everyone something, even if they would forget parts of it later and need the order to remind them.

Before leaving, Jack took the protected correspondence folder to the file room. He placed it in the cabinet beside the closed custody binder and locked the drawer. Then he returned to the conference room and looked at the blank whiteboard. He considered writing the old sentence again. He did not. Some truths did not need to stay on display after they had done their work.

He turned off the lights and left the room empty for the next case.

49

The Assembly hearing came two months later, and Jack Sullivan watched only the first twenty minutes before turning the livestream off. The bill had survived amendments, opposition letters, supportive editorials, and the slow erosion that comes when public urgency enters legislative procedure. It no longer carried every safeguard Amelia wanted. It no longer carried every exception Fairchild wanted. That probably meant it had a chance. Lawmaking, like settlement, often produced documents everyone could tolerate and no one could love.

Amelia testified again, this time with less fire and more command of the record. She spoke about consent, unresolved family matters, and the danger of program narratives moving faster than factual review. She cited public reports, committee materials, and the plain need for boundaries when youth-serving programs touched court-adjacent systems. She did not mention Lily. By then Jack did not watch to make sure. He trusted her enough to stop supervising every sentence.

Nora noticed the livestream had gone silent from the hallway. "You done watching government happen?"

"Yes."

"Did it improve your mood?"

"No."

"Then it was government."

Jack returned to a deposition outline for another case, one with a father who insisted his ex-wife was poisoning the children against him and a mother who insisted every missed homework assignment proved emotional abuse. The facts were different. The temptation was familiar. Adults wanted courts to turn pain into certainty. Children needed courts to slow certainty down long enough to hear them.

At noon, Ethan sent a routine update through email, not because anything was wrong, but because the standing order required him to notify counsel of any major schedule question and he had learned to ask early. Lily wanted to attend a summer art program hosted by the city library. Marissa supported it. The program had no counseling component, no advocacy language, and no outside support track. It was paint, clay, sketching, and snacks. Jack reviewed the flyer and gave the answer any sane adult would have given without needing a lawyer.

Approved as routine enrichment under the existing order.

Ethan replied, Thank you. She wants to know if dogs can be abstract.

Jack wrote back, That is outside my jurisdiction.

The answer was a mistake only in the sense that it made Ethan respond with a laughing emoji and the words, I'll tell her to ask Mrs. Palmer. Jack sat with that for a moment and let himself be glad. Not triumphant. Not sentimental. Glad.

Claire sent a separate confirmation that Marissa agreed to the summer program and would handle registration if Ethan handled supplies. There was no sarcasm in the exchange, no hidden accusation, no attempt to attach moral meaning to markers and glue. Jack approved the arrangement. The order had become less visible because the parents had begun doing what it required before the paper forced them to. That was how structure became practice.

Later that week, the Assembly committee passed the bill with additional amendments. Fairchild released a statement saying the foundation was proud to support reasonable safeguards that preserved both youth privacy and program innovation. Amelia wrote a restrained analysis pointing out which provisions had been strengthened and which had been weakened. Raines posted that the bill was a watered-down victory and blamed insiders for protecting foundations. Each of them claimed some part of the outcome. None of them named the child whose case had helped reveal the gap. That was the only part Jack cared about.

Mara brought the final version of the bill into Jack's office. "It is not enough."

"No."

"It is something."

"Yes."

"Do you ever let yourself enjoy something being something?"

"Rarely."

She sat across from him. "The bill would have stopped Lily's scenario from being used."

"If followed, yes."

"That matters."

"It does."

Mara nodded as if she had gotten the admission she wanted. Then she left him with the pages.

Jack read the bill again after she left. It required consent review before active matters could become impact narratives. It required grantees to separate internal learning from external reporting. It required court-adjacent programs to document when support language might intersect with legal proceedings. It included enforcement mechanisms through grant conditions, not private lawsuits. The remedies were administrative, modest, and real. The law would not save every child. It might make the next adult pause before calling a child's fear an outcome.

The final custody review never happened because no one requested it. The standing order remained in place, and the case moved into the kind of legal quiet that depends on people continuing to behave when no judge is looking. Ethan stopped sending Jack every app exchange. Claire stopped copying Jack on every minor adjustment. Angela remained available but no longer active in daily coordination. Dr. Patel's role became as-needed, and Lily did not need it every week.

One afternoon, months after Pickle's drawing arrived, Jack received a final closure letter from Claire. Marissa had completed parent-guidance work and would continue private counseling. She did not request any change. She did not ask for communication with Ethan outside the order. She did not frame herself as victim or hero. The letter was plain, almost dry. Jack respected it for that reason.

He forwarded the relevant portion to Ethan and asked whether he had concerns. Ethan called instead of emailing. His voice had changed over the months. It still carried caution, but not constant readiness.

"I don't have concerns," Ethan said.

"That is good."

"I still don't trust her like before."

"You are not required to."

"I trust the structure."

"That may be enough."

"For now."

"For many people, for a long time."

Ethan was quiet. "Lily seems lighter."

Jack did not ask him to define it. He knew what parents meant when they said lighter. Fewer pauses before answering. Fewer glances to see how words landed. More interest in snacks, drawings, friends, weather, and whether abstract dogs needed noses. Those changes did not fit neatly in a court order, but they were the point of every paragraph.

"She still has moments," Ethan said.

"She will."

"I do too."

"You will."

"I used to think the goal was proving I was right."

Jack waited.

"Now I think the goal is making sure she does not have to keep proving anything."

Jack looked toward the closed file cabinet. "That is exactly right."

The governor signed the bill in early fall. Amelia called from the Capitol steps, surrounded by noise, cameras, advocates, and people claiming credit. She did not sound triumphant. She sounded steady.

"It's signed," she said.

"I saw the alert."

"Your enthusiasm is overwhelming."

"It will be tested in implementation."

"That is the most you sentence ever spoken."

"It is true."

She laughed softly. "It is also signed."

"Yes."

That was enough. She did not say Lily's name. Jack did not say it either. They let the silence hold the person who had been protected from becoming the face of the law that now, in some small way, protected others.

Fairchild adapted quickly. It announced a statewide youth privacy initiative and placed Malcolm Reese on the advisory board for implementation. Civic Bridge relaunched its support program with new disclaimers and clearer referral boundaries. Horizon issued training materials on preserving original child statements in court-related matters. Publicly, every institution became part of the solution. Privately, Jack knew that was how many reforms survived. Institutions rarely confessed their way into better practice. They branded their way there and hoped no one remembered why the branding became necessary.

Amelia wrote the definitive public piece after the bill was signed. It traced the public record from foundation grants to school partnerships to legislative safeguards. It quoted experts, parents, advocates, and Fairchild's own statements. It did not mention a sealed custody case. It did not need a hidden key to work. Jack read it twice, found nothing that touched Lily, and sent Amelia one line.

This is yours.

She replied five minutes later. Not just mine. But I understand what you mean.

He accepted that answer. It was better than claiming pure ownership over a story built from public effort and private restraint. Amelia had learned the line. She had also learned that the line did not diminish her work. It strengthened it.

The office moved on because offices always do. Another emergency order came in. Another parent cried in the conference room. Another school produced records late. Another expert used too much certainty with too little foundation. Jack handled those cases with the same precision and fatigue he brought to all of them, but Lily's case stayed with him differently. Not as a wound. As a standard.

Nora found him one evening looking at the closed file index. "You planning to reread it?"

"No."

"Then why stare at it?"

"Making sure it stays closed."

"That is not how cabinets work."

"It is how lawyers work."

She leaned against the doorframe. "You did good on that one."

Jack looked up. "The order worked."

"That is not what I said."

He did not answer. Nora did not need him to. She had worked for enough lawyers to know when silence was gratitude.

On the anniversary of the first emergency hearing, Ethan sent one final note. Not a legal question, not a compliance issue, not a request for review. Just a message that said Lily had entered one of her drawings in the library art show. The title was Dog for Weather That Changes. Pickle had wings, boots, a backpack, and a long scarf that looked like it had been added at the last minute. Ethan wrote that both parents attended. They stood together long enough for Lily to take a picture of them with the drawing.

Jack read the message at the end of a long day. He did not save it to the evidentiary file. He placed it in the protected correspondence folder with Pickle's first drawing. Then he wrote back.

That is good news.

Ethan replied, It is.

The exchange ended there. No legal advice. No warning. No next step. Jack set the phone down and sat in the quiet office until the hallway lights clicked off.

Before leaving, he went to the conference room. The whiteboard held notes from another case now, names and dates and a custody evaluator's schedule. No trace of Lily's case remained except what Jack carried. He did not write anything on the board. He did not need to. The sentence had already done its work.

No one owns her words.

He turned off the lights, locked the office, and left the file closed.

50

The new law took effect on the first day of January, announced by a state agency bulletin that used the careful language of government and none of the pain that had made the language necessary. Jack Sullivan read it before court while standing at the window of his office, coffee cooling in his hand and traffic moving below him in slow morning lines. The bulletin described consent review, court-adjacent safeguards, active-matter exclusions, and grant-reporting boundaries. It did not mention Lily Cole. It did not mention the courtroom where a child once mouthed help me to a father who could not reach her.

That was the way it should have been. Jack had spent months making sure the public record could change without making Lily the public reason for it. The law was imperfect, narrowed by negotiation and softened by amendments, but it stood where nothing had stood before. Programs that wanted to use unresolved family situations as proof of success now had to slow down, document consent, and separate support from legal influence. It would not stop every misuse. It would make the next misuse harder to call a misunderstanding.

Nora came into his office with a file for another hearing and saw the bulletin on his desk. "Is that the law?"

"Yes."

"Does it do what it is supposed to do?"

"Some of it."

"That sounds like a yes with bruises."

"It is."

She picked up the bulletin and read the first paragraph. "No names."

"No names."

"Good."

Jack nodded, and Nora placed it back where she found it. She knew enough not to turn the moment into a speech. The office had learned to treat Lily's case with the same restraint the court had demanded from everyone else. Even in memory, the child did not need adults leaning too heavily over her story.

Ethan emailed later that morning, though not about the law. Lily had been accepted into a citywide youth art exhibit at the library, and both parents had agreed to attend during the public reception. The drawing selected was Dog for Weather That Changes. Ethan attached no image, which told Jack more than any attachment would have. He wrote only that Lily was excited and that Marissa had offered to bring cookies for the reception table if the library allowed it. The message was ordinary enough to make Jack sit down before answering.

He replied that the event sounded appropriate under the standing order and reminded Ethan to keep the focus on Lily's participation, not the history behind it. Ethan answered with one sentence. We will let it be art. Jack read the sentence twice.

It may have been the best legal compliance report he had ever received, and it would never appear in a court file.

Claire sent a parallel note an hour later. Marissa agreed that neither parent would discuss the case at the reception, respond to any public questions beyond normal parent conversation, or use the event for social media without Lily's comfort and both parents' agreement. Jack approved the language. It was the kind of agreement that would have seemed impossible at the beginning and overly formal in any normal family. In this family, it was care translated into workable boundaries.

The library reception took place on a Thursday evening. Jack did not attend because he had no role there, and his absence mattered. Lily did not need her lawyer in the room where her drawing hung on a temporary wall beside watercolor birds, clay animals, pencil portraits, and paintings of sunsets that looked more hopeful than accurate. Ethan and Marissa attended. They stood close enough for Lily to find them and far enough apart to let the space between them remain peaceful.

Ethan sent Jack a message the next morning, not from panic and not for approval. It was a short report, almost a courtesy. Lily showed both of them the drawing, introduced them to Mrs. Palmer, and told a librarian that Pickle was prepared for weather because weather changes without asking first. Ethan said he almost made that mean something and then decided not to. Jack smiled when he read it. The restraint had become instinct, and instinct was better than instruction.

He called Ethan after lunch because the case had been quiet long enough for a conversation not built around crisis. Ethan answered from his truck, parked somewhere with wind tapping lightly against the phone. Jack could hear the sound of traffic in the distance.

"She did well?" Jack asked.

"She did. She looked happy."

"And you?"

"I did okay."

"That is good."

Ethan was quiet for a moment. "Marissa brought the cookies. They were terrible."

Jack waited.

"I did not say that."

"Excellent judgment."

"She asked if Lily could take some to art club. I said yes. That was it."

Jack leaned back in his chair. "That is what functioning sounds like."

"It feels strange."

"It will for a while."

Ethan's voice softened. "She stood between us for one picture. Lily did. Not Marissa. The librarian offered, and Lily looked at us first. We both said yes."

Jack said nothing because he heard what Ethan was really telling him. Lily had asked permission without words, and both parents had given it without making her choose. That was not reconciliation. It was not erasure. It was a room where the child could stand between two adults without holding them together.

"That was good," Jack said.

"It was."

The call ended there. No legal advice followed. No warning was needed. The order still existed, and so did the hurt beneath it, but the family had begun to operate without bringing every feeling back to Jack's desk. That was the point of the work, and one of the reasons the work could feel so lonely when it succeeded.

A week later, Amelia visited the office with the first printed copy of a long-form feature that would run in a legal policy journal. The title was not dramatic: When Youth Support Becomes Court-Facing. It traced the new law, the public records, the funding structures, and the safeguards now required. It mentioned no sealed case, no child, no parent, no school, and no courtroom scene. The article had force because it did not borrow force from Lily.

Jack read the first page while Amelia stood by the window. She had learned not to hover over him while he reviewed her work. The piece was accurate, unsentimental, and careful about what the public record proved. It did not accuse Fairchild of directing case-level conduct. It did show how incentives, language frameworks, and reporting structures could reward premature certainty. That was harder to dismiss.

"This is good," Jack said.

Amelia looked over. "Good like clean?"

"Good like good."

She smiled a little. "That took fifty chapters."

Jack looked at her.

"Sorry," she said. "Writer's habit."

He closed the article and placed it on his desk. "You did it without her."

"I know."

"That matters."

"It matters more than I thought it would."

Jack believed her. Amelia had not become less ambitious. She had become more exacting, which was better. She still wanted institutions held to account, and he still believed institutions needed people willing to keep asking questions after the court file closed. The difference was that she no longer treated a private child as the shortest path to a public truth.

Before she left, Amelia paused at the door. "Do you ever think about what would have happened if Mrs. Palmer had not copied the note?"

"Yes."

"Me too."

"She did what adults are supposed to do. She preserved the child's words without owning them."

Amelia nodded. "That may be the whole story."

"No," Jack said. "It is the part that saved the story from becoming something else."

Amelia accepted that and left with the article under her arm. Jack watched her pass Nora's desk, where Nora gave her a pastry wrapped in a napkin and said something that made Amelia laugh. The office had absorbed Amelia too, in its own guarded way. She had arrived as a complication and left as someone who understood why some doors stayed closed.

In the spring, the court's one-year injunction approached its final review. No violations had been reported. Fairchild filed its certification early. Civic Bridge filed with revised protocols attached. Horizon filed nothing beyond compliance because the court had not asked for more. Tessa Laird's counsel confirmed continued no contact and no use. Judge Harrow reviewed the filings and issued an order preserving the permanent privacy provisions attached to the custody order while allowing active third-party reporting to terminate.

The order was brief. It stated that the child's circumstances could not be used, disseminated, published, trained from, or included in program materials without further court order or later lawful consent when Lily reached an age and posture allowing meaningful decision-making. It ended the reporting obligation because compliance had remained clean. It retained jurisdiction for enforcement. That was legal closure without pretending memory had closed.

Jack sent the order to Ethan and Claire. Ethan replied first. Thank you. I understand. Claire replied that Marissa understood and would continue following the standing order. No one asked for a hearing. No one asked for clarification. No one turned the ending into an argument.

That afternoon, Jack took the Cole binders from the file cabinet and prepared the long-term archive. Custody order. Findings. Privacy order. Third-party injunction. Compliance certifications. Protected correspondence. He did not reread everything. He knew where each document belonged. When he reached the folder with Pickle's drawing, he opened it once and looked at the crooked wings, the boots, the backpack, and the emergency pickle tucked into the pocket.

Nora appeared at the door. "Still good mail?"

"Yes."

"You keeping it?"

"In the protected correspondence file."

"Sounds very lawyerly."

"It is a legal file."

"It is also a kid's drawing."

Jack looked at the page. "That is why it stays protected."

Nora nodded, and this time she did not joke. She understood the difference between sentiment and custody. Sentiment would put the drawing on a wall. Custody kept it safe from becoming evidence, publicity, or proof of a lawyer's virtue. Jack placed it back in the folder and closed the flap.

The last time Ethan came to the office, he came without panic, without a court date, and without a folder. He brought a final payment check and a simple update. Lily was doing well. She still had therapy available, but she was not using it regularly. She had joined the library art program for the summer and was considering drawing something without animals, which Ethan described as a major development with a seriousness that made Jack almost smile.

They sat in Jack's office with the door open. Nora moved around outside, pretending not to listen and listening anyway. Ethan looked at the file cabinet, then back at Jack.

"I used to think if the truth came out, everything would feel fixed," Ethan said.

"It rarely does."

"It helped."

"Yes."

"But it didn't fix everything."

"No."

Ethan nodded. "Maybe that's okay."

"It can be."

"She has her words back. Not all at once. Not perfectly. But more."

"That is what matters."

Ethan looked down at his hands. "I still get angry when I think about it."

"You probably will for a long time."

"I don't let her carry it."

Jack studied him for a moment. "That is the work."

Ethan nodded again, then stood. There was no dramatic goodbye. He shook Jack's hand, thanked Nora on the way out, and walked into a day that did not require a court filing. Jack watched him leave through the glass door and felt the muted satisfaction of a case that had done what it could and stopped before becoming another burden.

The office closed late that evening. Caleb left first, then Mara, then Nora after reminding Jack that a man could not bill time to staring at old files. Jack stayed long enough to place the archive box on the shelf marked closed protected matters. The label read Cole, Ethan and Marissa — Custody / Sealed. It was plain and correct. It gave away nothing that did not belong to the file.

Before turning out the lights, Jack returned to the conference room. The whiteboard held notes for another case now, one involving school refusal and dueling evaluations. He erased a corner of old marker dust with his thumb. For a moment, in the angle of the light, he thought he could still see the faint ghost of the sentence he had once left there overnight.

No one owns her words.

He did not write it again. He did not need to. The case had taught it to everyone who was willing to learn.

Jack turned off the lights and stood in the doorway as the room darkened. Courts could make orders, lawyers could expose records, reporters could shape public debate, and lawmakers could write safeguards that might help the next child. None of them owned the truth they touched. At their best, they held it long enough to return it to the person who had been forced to surrender it.

Somewhere beyond the office, Lily Cole was growing older under a standing order that had become part of the background of her life. She would remember some things and forget others. She might one day read parts of the record, or she might decide not to. She might keep drawing Pickle, or let him disappear into older folders and new interests. Whatever she chose, the choice would be hers.

That was the ending the law could give her. Not perfect justice, not erased harm, not a world without adults who mistook control for care. A door back to her own voice. A life where different sides could still be one bowl. A truth no longer held in custody by people who needed it more than she did.